In The Presence of Greatness

Unleash Your True Power & Shine

Marguerita Vorobioff

In The Presence of Greatness: Unleash Your True Power & Shine

© Marguerita Vorobioff 2018

Cover Image
Artist: Tracie Eaton
Photographer: Quanita Photography
Illustrator: Jess Burton

www.PitBullMindset.com

The moral rights of Marguerita Vorobioff to be identified as the author of this work have been asserted in accordance with the Copyright Act 1968.

First published in Australia 2018 by Pitbull Mindset

ISBN 978-0-9805848-1-3

Any opinions expressed in this work are exclusively those of the author and are not necessarily the views held or endorsed by Pitbull Mindset.

All rights reserved. No part of this publication may be reproduced or transmitted by any means, be it electronic, photocopying or otherwise, without prior written permission of the author.

Disclaimer

All the information, techniques, skills and concepts contained within this publication are of the nature of general comment only, and are not in any way recommended as individual advice. The intent is to offer a variety of information to provide a wider range of choices now and in the future, recognising that we all have widely diverse circumstances and viewpoints.

The information given in this book is not intended as a substitute for professional medical or financial advice. Always consult a medical practitioner or qualified financial advisor prior to coming to conclusions or making major decisions about your physical, mental and financial health and wellbeing.

The techniques offered in this book have not been scientifically validated as effective and as such, are considered experimental. Whilst many report positive experiences and outcomes from their use, this may not apply to you or to your particular problem or issue.

Should any reader choose to make use of the information herein, this is their decision. The author and publisher/s do not assume any responsibilities whatsoever under any conditions or circumstances. The author does not take responsibility for the business, financial, personal or other success, results or fulfilment upon the readers' decision to use this information. It is recommended that the reader obtain their own independent advice.

With immense gratitude, I dedicate this book to my wonderful, ever patient and tolerant husband, Laurie, who always believed in me even when I didn't believe in myself. He is my rock, my soul mate, my teacher, my lover and my best friend. Thank you for lending me your strength when I needed it the most, and for loving me through the darkest parts of this journey to discovering myself.

I also wish to thank my loving family who have never shunned, judged or rejected me, no matter how strange things got. Thank you for your unconditional acceptance, support, encouragement and love.

Divine Mission Statement

I have come to be a beacon of light
I have come to restore faith and trust into the deepest parts of humanity.
I am here to bring light, truth and to eliminate the darkness that lives within the hearts of humanity.
I am here to light the fire of faith, hope and truth within each and every human being.
I have come to reconnect people with spirit, with truth and with their power.
I have come to reignite the flame of love, peace, and freedom that exists within each and every human being.
I am here to restore balance, reignite passion and restore wholeness.
I have come to open up the pathway to the infinite power we all come from and that lives within each and every living being.
I have come to eliminate division and separation.
I own my reason for being.
I own my power.
I own the light that lives inside me and I unleash it to bring light and love to the world."

Table of Contents

1. A Consciousness Revolution 5
2. Conversations With Wayne 21
3. Everything Is A Story 29
4. You Are Not Broken..41
5. Life Is Happening For You, Not To You 51
6. Have You Had Enough Yet?...59
7. What Have You Decided? 73
8. The Power Of Surrender 97
9. What Is Seeking To Emerge?...113
10. Ten Things I Learnt From Millionaires In 10 Days.........127
11. Eight Steps To Being Unstoppable..................................157
12. The 9 Environments of Success 169
13. Congruence..189
14. Emotional Freedom Technique 211
15. Build Your Wealth Muscle..221
16. What Is Abundance?...249
17. The Seven States of Wealth...265
18. Stack The Odds In Your Favour 293
The Final Word...363

Introduction

The world is waiting for you to show up in all your glory. Its future, and yours, depends on it.

You have untapped power and potential that is beyond anything you could possibly imagine. The dreams you have are but a trifle of what you're actually capable of achieving.

For the longest time, my heart yearned to make a bigger difference, but I was in an unwinnable battle with my subconscious belief systems and paradigms that had kept me shackled to a life of mediocrity, frustration and disappointment. I was disappointed in my results and myself. I was in a long cycle of self-sabotage, desperately wanting to shine brightly for all the world to see on one side, and terrified of what 'unseen monsters' lurked beyond my comfortable anonymity on the other.

Of course, the 'unseen monsters' were merely a creation of my subconscious mind. Those fears, doubts and worthiness issues were created by my unconscious predominantly as a result of early childhood experiences that caused stories and limiting decisions to be formed which determined my behaviour and my results. I lived my life by these limiting decisions for far too long.

The journey of personal development to finally breakthrough to the other side of these limitations was challenging and way too long; particularly for someone as impatient as me!

My intention with this book is to help you navigate and release the blocks and limiting decisions, fears and doubts as quickly as possible so you can achieve the dreams for which your heart yearns. They are calling you; you just need to get out of your own way.

This manuscript is about helping you unleash your wisdom, your greatness and your ability to be exceptional, so you can be, do and have more than you ever imagined possible.

It's a bridge between two worlds: the spiritual 'woo-woo' world, and the world of business, success and achievement.

Commit to following along and implementing the techniques and strategies in the book to help you reconnect with who you truly are so you can realise your infinite power and potential, as well as your extraordinary capacity to achieve literally anything you put your mind to. It is a book about achievement through mindset and spirituality.

Many extraordinary visionaries and spiritual masters, whom I have adopted as my personal mentors over the last 20 years, have contributed to helping me become the person I am today. Leaders such as Dr. Joseph Murphy, Dr. Wayne Dyer, Byron Katie, Jack Canfield, John Assaraf, Dr. Bruce Lipton, Gregg Braden, Eckhart Tolle, Marianne Williamson, Dr. John Demartini, Marci Shimoff, Kurek Ashley and many more have helped me evolve spiritually, emotionally and mentally.

Introduction

A variety of private coaches and mentors have also contributed along the way. It is their collective wisdom, interpreted through me so I could deliver it to you, that resides within the pages of this book.

Success doesn't have to be as hard as you're making it. In fact, it can be relatively easy when you reconnect and collaborate with spirit. Beyond the stories and limiting decisions lies a path of ease and grace that will surprise and delight you as it carries you along to the realisation of your heartfelt intentions and your grandest dreams for yourself and this world.

Together, we can change the world. We just need to remember where we came from, commit to where we are going and collaborate with the Universe, which is conspiring in our favour every minute of every day.

In the wise words of Buzz Light Year: "To infinity and beyond!"

1. A Consciousness Revolution

"A problem cannot be solved at the same level of consciousness with which it was created."

Einstein

Like Lemmings marching relentlessly toward a cliff with seemingly no will or desire to halt their procession, the human race appears unyielding as it continues to stride toward what is fast becoming our inevitable demise. The warning signs are everywhere, and have been for decades, but year in and year out, we have continued to ignore the deafening alarms bells, instead maintaining our determined stampede toward self-destruction.

Is it because individually, we feel powerless to do anything about it? Is it because we're waiting on our leaders to take the helm, turn this ship around and steer us toward salvation? The same leaders whom we will crucify and dethrone if they dare to make any decision which may impact our quality of life or cause inconvenience? Is it because it's just not convenient to change the way we live and dedicate some of our spare time and energy to creating change that will save the human race and the planet? Is it because we are so busy just trying to navigate and survive our increasingly complex financial and social environments that we don't have the impetus to turn our attention to the greater good and survival of the human race?

Whatever the reason, apathy and indifference are not a luxury we can afford.

There is a clear and growing disparity between the haves and the have nots. The rich continue to get richer and the low to middle tier income earners are increasingly squeezed into survival mode, whilst the poorest among us seem to be completely abandoned and forgotten altogether. This is a recipe for the self-destruction of the collective human race, as millions of people don't have the capacity to think beyond themselves and how they're going to get through today, let alone tomorrow.

This is not a criticism, but an intrinsic part of the human condition inherent in each and every one of us: the survival instinct.

No matter how well off an abundant our society may be in real terms, the vast majority of people are still struggling to make their resources stretch to ever increasing demands.

Even though our western society is comparatively a lot wealthier now than it has been at any other time in its history, life has become increasingly more complicated and difficult to navigate. Life used to be a lot simpler. There were no mobile devices, vast arrays of electronic gadgets, mechanical vehicles to facilitate us travelling further faster,

1. A Consciousness Revolution

food that disrupts our cognitive function and causes a litany of diseases, entertainment devices to turn us into zombies and disconnect us from life and from each other and disrupt our creative natures, and the list goes on and on.

But just because it was simpler, doesn't mean it was easier. The irony is that, as our wealth status has multiplied, demands on our resources have multiplied much faster. This has created a situation where, more often than not, we are left with less, not more, than we had before all these thousands of choices were available to us.

As wealth has increased, so has the greed of corporations that have expanded their wealth exponentially by becoming multi-national monopolies and taking over the global market place. They will do virtually anything not only to protect their very large slice of the pie, but also to continue to increase it. Crushing their competition as they go, seemingly oblivious and uncaring about the personal and environmental destruction they leave in their wake.

The machine has become a veracious monster munching every resource it can find with an insatiable appetite and no conscience nor concern for others or even the very planet we rely on to sustain us.

So how did we get here? Are we beyond the point of no return? What do we need to do to turn this around?

The truth is there has been a war waged on consciousness by the wealthiest and most powerful members of our society. The psychopaths are in control and we've been deliberately and systematically disempowered, distracted and dumbed down through chemicals in our food and water supplies, in our medicines, by external authorities we've appointed, and in the images that fill our minds and strike fear into our hearts through mainstream media.

The assault on our senses has been designed to distract us and keep us disconnected from our consciousness, from who we truly are, our divinity and our true power. This disconnection has created a vast landscape of destruction of our planet and of ourselves. It is as if we have hit the self-destruct button and no one can, or is willing to, engage the abort procedure.

We've allowed our minds to be conditioned by the entities we have appointed as the ultimate authorities in our lives to the extent that we have given away our power to them almost completely. We look to these entities to determine whom we must be, how we must behave, what we are allowed to do and how much we are allowed to achieve.

Instead of being self-determining individuals who trust in our own infinite power as the ultimate creator we are, we submit and defer to authorities such as the government, media, the medical professionals, law enforcement agencies and even our family and friends to tell us who and what we're supposed to be.

The evidence is clear: we currently have a global crisis on our hands on many levels. At the moment we're moving way too slowly to rectify the situation before we reach the point of no return. We are running out of time.

The only feasible answer to this insanity is a shift in consciousness. The answer to every problem that has ever been or ever will be, personally or globally, lies in a shift in

1. A Consciousness Revolution

our consciousness. What we must do is liberate and mobilise an army of efficient and effective consciousness leaders to transform the hearts and minds of people, and alter the course of humanity.

It's time for humanity to reconnect with who we truly are and take our power back.

If we move collectively now and stop waiting for somebody else to fix the problems we've created, we have a chance.

Whilst empathy and compassion are essential for healing the minds, hearts and souls of humanity, we must be prepared to take a stance, make tough decisions and take strong, definitive action to make crucial changes and fix the problems we have all collectively caused. Love will heal us. Powerful, collective action will save us.

We need to unleash the greatness that lies within each and every one of us to turn the ship around.

With powerful systems established and deliberately contrived to dis-empower and enslave the vast majority of the human race, is it any wonder we have fallen into a trance of apathy and apparent indifference? We cry out for change, but feel powerless to do anything because we've become separated from our Communities and each other. Working independently in silos with a focus on competition, getting ahead individually, and out-performing our peers and colleagues. This is driven by the conditioned fear that 'there is not enough' and we feel compelled to grab as much as we can while we can.

These systems provoke, play on and exacerbate our human fears and keep us pitted against each other in a 'survival of the fittest' kind of mentality. At least, this is my observation.

Those who implemented these systems knew that, as long as we were focused on individual survival, we would never consider coming together as a community to rise up collectively and overcome these powerful entities in order to thrive as a whole, instead of just individually.

This ongoing contest that has been going on for decades has no legitimate basis for continuing. Once we move beyond our perceived limitations and realise just how magnificent and powerful each of us truly is, and come together to rise up as a collective community, anything really is possible.

In a recent compelling and controversial TEDx talk titled 'The War On Consciousness' by Graham Hancock, which not surprisingly was banned, Hancock talks about ancient plant medicines, such as ayahuasca, which have been made illegal in western society. These plant medicines have been used to facilitate the expansion of human consciousness over millennia, but we are now unable to access these legally in Western culture.

These plant medicines have been substituted for other less potent and highly damaging forms of mind-altering drugs and stimulants, such as alcohol, caffeine and chemically enhanced tobacco because they don't interfere with what Hancock refers to as the 'alert problem solving state of consciousness' deemed acceptable by our society.

He goes on to talk of our current level of consciousness:

"It's good for the more mundane aspects of science. It's good for the prosecution of warfare. It's good for commerce.

1. A Consciousness Revolution

It's good for politics, but I think everybody realises that the promise of a society over-monopolistically based upon this state of consciousness has proved hollow, and that this model is no longer working. That it's broken in every possible sense that a model can be broken.

And urgently, we need to find something to replace it. The vast problems of global pollution that have resulted from the single-minded pursuit of profit. The horrors of nuclear proliferation. The spectre of hunger that millions every night go to bed starving. That we can't even solve this problem despite our alert problem-solving state of consciousness.

And look what's happening in the Amazon, this precious home of biodiversity. The old growth forest being cut down and replaced with soy bean farms to feed cattle so that we can all eat hamburgers. Only a truly insane global state of consciousness could allow such an abomination to occur."

By his calculations, a mere six months expenditure on the Iraq war would have solved the problem of the Amazon forever and compensated the peoples of the Amazon so that no single tree would have ever had to be cut down again. In his words, we spend countless billions on warfare, hatred, fear and suspicion and division, but we are unable to get together a collective effort to save the lungs of our planet. It's a truly frightening prospect when you think about it in those terms.

I entirely agree with Graham Hancock that we have disconnected from Spirit, and if we fail to reconnect with it, and do so soon, we are going to bring the whole house of cards tumbling down on all our heads. Unless we do something now – not tomorrow or next week, but now – we may not have any chance of saving the current state of our planet or species. That's if we're not already too late.

This is why I'm on a mission to help humanity take our power back through other forms of consciousness altering techniques other than plant medicines. It will take years to have such bans lifted, and not everyone can get to those places where these plant medicines are still legally available and used in safe, controlled environments, so we must use other means.

Through this book, I will share with you information, techniques and strategies to assist you in unleashing your own greatness and become unshackled from the lies you have been told that have kept you from realising your infinite power and potential. A powerful meditation CD accompanies the book to help you to access new states of conscious awareness safely through the healing power of sound.

I trained as an opera singer for many years during my late teens into my early thirties. Like many artistic pursuits, it is often just as brutal as a career choice, as it is enormously rewarding personally.

Throughout my pursuit of this career, I worked hard both at my day job in corporate, which helped to pay the mortgage and the bills, whilst training to be an opera singer. I eventually transitioned from corporate to being a personal trainer, as I had always loved fitness and helping others, and found the jobs I had quite soul destroying. I felt as if they were eroding me physically, emotionally and mentally every passing day. I had a deep calling inside of me causing a great deal of personal internal conflict and, whilst they

1. A Consciousness Revolution

paid well, those jobs where directly affecting my quality of life emotionally.

I loved the personal training and helping others to overcome health and fitness challenges and it was very rewarding to see their lives transform in other ways as they took control of their physical health. It didn't take long for me to realise the actual physical training wasn't the key to transforming their lives permanently, but the mindset they had. This was about the same time as the movies 'What The Bleep Do We Know' and 'The Secret' came out and this started my obsession with the power of the mind, personal development and transformation. I wanted to know why some people succeeded and others didn't and how to help people who wanted more to access their true genius and achieve their dreams. This obsession eventually led me to become a global influencer and mindset mentor.

Meanwhile, as all this was going on, I tried multiple options with my singing, including funding my own little opera group, which was engaged to do a few small corporate functions, and we put on little concerts. Sadly, over several years, it drained me emotionally and financially until finally I felt beaten and broken and, for the sake of my mental and emotional wellbeing, I had to walk away from the industry and the profession I loved so much. I just didn't have the stamina, emotional fortitude, or resources required to pursue a career in the arts.

I walked away with my dreams in tatters, but still clinging to a strong inner knowing that I had been given this voice for a reason. What that was, I had no idea.

There is a saying that the Universe abhors a vacuum, and as soon as I relinquished my strangle hold on the relentless pursuit of my one true passion, to sing, a whole other world opened up to me that I'd had no idea existed.

My husband and I had moved from the big city lifestyle of Sydney, which didn't really suit us as we were both born in relatively small communities and loved the country life. We relocated to the Central Coast of New South Wales where I struck up friendships with a whole new group of extraordinary people who were on a spiritual path.

This was not something I had consciously asked for, but it was exactly what I needed. While I was intrigued and interested in being a passive bystander in their spiritual journey, all the while I was thinking, "This isn't my path". I had no idea the Universe had plans for me that contradicted mine.

I enjoyed the entertainment of watching my friends feeling the vibrational energy of trees and participating in spiritual journeys all the while secretly questioning their sanity and loving their quirky weirdness. As far as I was concerned, it wasn't for me.

Now, just to back track a little, regularly when we awoke in the morning, my husband would inform me I had been speaking a strange foreign language in my sleep. Apart from a short and not very successful attempt to learn some French at school, I was not aware of any multi-lingual skills at all. My father on the other hand, whose heritage was Russian, had learnt to speak seven languages as a boy and I had often heard him speak French, Russian and Mandarin to friends and relatives growing up. So, I dismissed this 'foreign language' I was speaking as merely my parroting

1. A Consciousness Revolution

what I had heard my father speak when I was a child. The mind is pretty amazing after all. Nothing to see here; move on.

Little did I know what was about to open up for me when I attended a spiritual gathering on Kincumba Mountain on the Central Coast of New South Wales many years ago.

It was the opening of a Mystery School. I didn't even know what this meant, and to be perfectly honest, I still don't. My spiritual friends were going, so I went and dragged my husband along with me.

There were three speakers that night, and while I was becoming more and more tired as the night went on, I felt compelled to stay until the very end, even though I kept asking myself why I was really there. Then, the last speaker nervously got up to speak in front of us. She was very tall and slender with beautiful red hair. I later learned she is Pleiadian. The Pleiadians are among us to help raise the frequency of humanity.

When Mayanya, as she is professionally known, got up to speak, she started to speak in another language. A channelled language called Light Language. This was something I had never knowingly encountered before, but my body certainly seemed to recognise the language on a very deep level. I felt all of my cells started to vibrate and it felt like my body was about to take off. I had no idea what was going on, but I found it quite disconcerting. My cells seemed to be rejoicing at the sound of this language. Meanwhile, my husband had suddenly come to life and was digging me in the ribs saying, "That's the language. That's what you speak in your sleep."

You could have knocked me over with a feather. I was tempted to pinch myself to wake up and say "Beam me up Scotty". For a Catholic girl who considered she had her feet firmly planted on the ground, this was not something I had anticipated and certainly not something I initially welcomed.

The fact is, far from being in a dream, I was starting to wake up from the dream. The dream of being plugged into a 'reality' that was keeping me from my true self. The journey of awakening is continuing today as I explore the truth about who I am and what I am here to contribute to humanity and the planet.

From that moment a very strange, and at times hazy, series of experiences ensued, more like something out of the Twilight Zone compared to the life I had known. No, I can honestly say I was not taking drugs. I have never in my life taken a mind-altering drug, apart from small amounts of alcohol, which I stopped drinking entirely two years ago because it never agreed with me. So this experience was happening to me entirely drug and alcohol free.

I realise you may be currently questioning my sanity, depending on where you are at with your spiritual journey, what you've experienced yourself and how open minded you are. If this is way too 'out there' for you at this point in time, I get it. That's exactly how I felt when I was going through it myself.

If that's you, I encourage you to take this part of the story with a grain of salt, and take whatever you came to this book for. Having picked it up, you've been drawn to it for a reason and it holds value for you, and your future. Take what resonates and leave the rest behind. Just because my truth

1. A Consciousness Revolution

in this realm is not your truth, don't dismiss the rest of the content out of hand as you might miss the one thing that could change your entire life.

So, not long after this encounter, and working with Mayanya, I discovered my own ability to speak and sing Light Language consciously. If you've heard of speaking in tongues, this is what I do. Light Language is an ancient healing language that dates back to the Mayans and the Incas and unlocks a code of consciousness in each and every one it touches.

I'm not going to go into a deep explanation of Light Language here, as this is not primarily what this book is about. You're welcome to research the topic for yourself if you are curious. This short account is simply so you know a little about me, and where I come from, to give you some context for my intention in writing this book.

This all happened in 2005 and at about the same time I discovered the magical powers of Emotional Freedom Technique. It was a very big year for me emotionally and spiritually. These new developments changed me dramatically. It didn't really change my focus immediately, however, as I was reluctant to embrace this new age mumbo jumbo with gusto. It challenged my identity and I would actually spend years running away from who I truly was chasing a variety of more traditional business opportunities, most of which failed miserably. Funny that.

From here, I began in some ways a long, and in other ways accelerated, journey into consciousness, that has, at times, been quite scary for me. It was particularly scary in the beginning, as I had no understanding of what was going on.

As a self-proclaimed control freak, surrendering to this gift that works through me was probably the most challenging part of my journey. I'm pleased to say my more experienced and very supportive friends helped to coax me through this to the point where I now relish this gift and love giving it wholeheartedly and without fear or question.

I have now been in business for 13 years with varying degrees of success. I have pursued many opportunities and learned a great deal about what does and doesn't work in success principles and strategies, marketing and balancing spirituality with the world of business. Most of all, I've learnt about the mindset it takes to be truly successful. I also learnt that, when you're not aligned emotionally and mentally with your purpose, and your mindset isn't primed for success, nothing works.

It was only when I truly surrendered to my purpose and started to leverage my God-given gifts and talents in the way they were intended to be used to serve others, that the world of success began to open up for me. My greatest asset is my ability to help others to expand their consciousness and adopt a success mindset through a variety of techniques and strategies, some of which I will share with you in the following pages.

I encourage you to enjoy the benefits of my gift of sound healing via the MP3 that is available for you to download. Listen to it during meditation and allow it to transport you to other states of consciousness that will transform how you see and live in the world.

It's time to fuel the uprising of humanity and accelerate the consciousness revolution.

1. A Consciousness Revolution

To download the free MP3 Sound Healing Meditation for creating a profound shift in your consciousness and unleashing your greatness, go to www.pitbullmindset.com/sound-healing-greatness/.

~ *Key Reflections* ~

1. Our model of the world is broken in every possible. In spite of all the warnings, we are marching relentlessly toward our own destruction. At the heart of this is international corporations insatiable desire for profit at all cost.

2. The answer to all our problems is a profound shift in collective consciousness. Each and every person, starting with you, needs to reconnect with their infinite power, unleash their greatness, and come together to demand a dramatic shift in the way we live, work and play.

3. We cannot wait for our leaders to fix what we have broken. You are the answer you have been looking for. It's time for you to decide to participate in the uprising of humanity and the consciousness revolution.

2. Conversations With Wayne

Recently, whilst driving home from a night out with friends on the Gold Coast, I was listening to a wonderful collaboration with Dr. Wayne Dyer and Eckhart Tolle called *The Importance of Being Extraordinary*. It is a two hour interview between these heavy weights in the personal development world and it is well worth listening to.

Dr. Wayne Dyer had recently passed away in August, 2015 and it was the third time I had listened to this particular recording. As I was driving along I had the thought, "I wish I had the privilege of meeting and speaking with Wayne before he passed away." Well, no sooner had the phrase formed in my head than a voice came in and said, "I'm here now".

I almost lost control of the car. I've experienced and facilitated, some pretty extraordinary things, but this was a brand new one for me. Obviously, as I listened to the recording I had tuned in to Dr. Wayne's frequency and his presence from the other realm was now in my field. After all, Wayne hasn't really died, he's just been liberated to another plane and we actually have greater access to his wisdom now than we did before he passed.

This was a watershed moment for me, and suddenly I was lost for words, which is a very rare occurrence. I wasn't prepared for this encounter at all.

I kind of stuttered in my head, "No way! Is that really you?" The reply came; "Yes, of course", as if this was a perfectly normal thing to happen.

So, as I had been feeling somewhat challenged during the last six months, fumbling my way through a major transition in my business in a quest to make a bigger impact, I asked Wayne his advice about what I should do.

He told me that firstly I needed to drop my agenda. I wasn't quite sure what he was referring to, so I asked him what he meant.

Wayne told me to drop my agenda of having to save the world. That in fact, this focus of mine, which seemed all noble and altruistic, was not about the world at all, but more about my grand standing and wanting to be somebody. It was about me wanting to be noticed and feel significant by doing something grand.

Ouch! He was right.

What he said was that I needed to focus on being of service in every moment. "Just serve", he said. "Be present to each moment and ask the question, how can I best serve in this moment?" It was so simple yet so profound. I've always been fairly aware of the needs of others and providing help where I felt I could. But this took it to a whole new level.

2. Conversations With Wayne

So in the coming couple of days I woke up thinking, "How can I best be of service today?" As these days unfolded, my interactions with people changed and the way I approached life changed. By being present, just doing what I'm inspired to do and intending to serve in whatever way I'm called in each moment, I'm doing what I came here to do. If I make a big difference to a lot of lives, great. If I don't, that's fine too. It's not actually up to me to 'save the world', and maybe the world doesn't need saving. Maybe the only one I'm meant to save is me, and if I have a positive influence on people along the way, all the better.

This was actually a huge relief for me as it took an enormous burden and weight off my shoulders.

I do intend to help others and give my gifts to those who want to receive them. I love to collaborate with others to make a difference, and maybe, collectively, we will be able to bring about a shift in consciousness that is big enough to create Heaven on Earth for everyone, not just a select few of us.

So, now I'm off the hook and can just focus on doing what I love. Yay! As I was unprepared for this conversation with Dr. Wayne Dyer, I respectfully asked him if we could continue it at some other time when I actually knew what I wanted to ask him. To my delight, Wayne said, "Yes. Any time." Wow! How blessed am I?

However, in true Marguerita style, this initial encounter quickly became forgotten. (I know right? Some of us take a little longer to get the message. Cut me a little slack.) After a couple of days, I go right back to doing all the things I think I have to be doing with marketing, lead funnels, website stuff, blah, blah, blah, and all the stuff that really doesn't give me joy, and in fact, I find a great pain! This is what I had been doing my head in before and I really had not got the message.

So, a couple of weeks later, I go through another mini melt down. These are coming thick and fast at this time as we all encounter 'the shift' in our own way. As the world is transitioning, so are we. I'm feeling lost, confused, frustrated, disappointed, unmotivated and over it! I know where I want to go, what I want to create, my mission and my passion, but every time I sit at my computer to do all the things I think I'm supposed to be doing, mentally and emotionally I just want to throw up!

Sure, sometimes in business we have to do things we don't like so we can do the things we do like. We have to do the things other people won't do so we can have the life others will never have. But at that time all I seemed to be doing was the stuff I don't like! Yuck!

So, during this little mini breakdown, I remembered Wayne's response that we could continue our conversation anytime. Whilst I'm not really prepared this time either, I say "OK, Wayne. What am I supposed to do? I'm feeling so unmotivated and I just can't force myself to do what I need to do. Tell me what I'm supposed to do."

Wayne simply says, "Write your book."

The book Wayne is referring to is the one I've been stalling on for three years. I had written bits and pieces but I had not really made any great effort to write it. It's been calling to me all this time, and I had been doing my best to ignore it. So I respond with, "But what about all the marketing and things I'm supposed to do to expand my client base and make my business more profitable and make a bigger difference in the world?" (Yep. Still with the agenda!)

Wayne says, "Write your book."

I say, "But what about …"

Wayne, "Just write the book."

Ok. Finally, I stop arguing with Dr. Wayne Dyer and commit to writing the book. Or should I say, allow the book to be written. I can't tell you how difficult it has been to give myself permission to do this. I actually love to write, but my perception is that this process is unproductive and indulgent, because I actually enjoy it. This points to a belief I have that I need to do stuff I don't like in order to succeed at my goals. A belief which is actually quite common, and I'm well aware of. How can I have this belief, considering I'm the one who always teaches creating a business and a life doing what you love?

It just is. We all have beliefs and conditioning which don't serve us and we are all a work in progress, including me. So surrendering to writing this book is a daily lesson in giving myself permission to just do what I want to do and am called to do and trust the rest will sort itself out.

So, I finally commit to writing the book. As you're reading it, I've actually written and published the book now.

I'm hoping Dr. Wayne Dyer's advice was sound and you find value in the following pages. Writing it has been a liberating experience and I'm grateful for having completed it. It's certainly been a journey of extraordinary growth for me and I've already received great value from it, regardless of the level of impact it has on anyone else.

For that, I am extremely thankful to my inspiration and co-conspirator who insisted I write it, Wayne.

2. Conversations With Wayne

~ *Key Reflections* ~

1. Focus every day on how you can best be of service to others. Being of service is the best way to live your passion, make a difference and create wealth.

2. Do what you love, and drop the belief that you have to work hard at something you don't like in order to create the life of your dreams.

3. Everything Is A Story

Throughout your whole life, from the date of your birth, and even before, as you were developing in the womb, your subconscious mind has been observing your surroundings and processing your many different experiences. Your observations are run through your perception filters, and your subconscious mind then creates a series of stories, which either support the successful realisation of your vision or sabotages your efforts.

These stories are beliefs and judgements made in an effort to keep you safe and affect all aspects of your thoughts and behaviours and, ultimately, your results. They determine your state of health, relationships, careers, spirituality, finances, business outcomes, and every area of your life. Once you begin to pay attention and recognise the stories that don't serve you and are causing you to think and behave in ways keeping you from the life you desire, you will be able to change the stories and transform your life.

Awareness is the key. If you are not aware of the stories that are dictating your results, you will unable to do anything about them. But once you see them, then you have the power to change them.

This is not easy initially. If you can recognise and distinguish your true self from your ego, then this becomes a lot easier. The voice that is chattering away in your head 24/7 is your ego. Your fears, doubts, and anything that prevents you from believing in yourself is also your ego.

The ego is what is keeping you distracted from who you truly are, just to make sure you don't do anything that might jeopardise your safety and put you at risk. Something stupid, like stepping into your greatness, realising your infinite power and sharing your brilliance with the world. That is a mighty risky behaviour for the subconscious mind.

Interestingly, most of the thoughts and beliefs that are running your life aren't even yours. You've adopted them from people and influences in your environment as you've journeyed through life. So if they're not yours, and you've just adopted them without question, are they true? What if you were to stop and start questioning those thoughts and beliefs by asking "Is that true?", "Whose thought is that?" and "Where did I learn that?" Simple questions that will impact your life in profound ways as you realise your entire life has been shaped predominantly by lies you've adopted without any critical analysis or reasoning, just because that's what was demonstrated to you in your earliest, most impressionable years.

Your true self lies quiet and steadfast behind the ego. It's the essence of who you truly are. Meditation is a great way to connect with your true self by quieting what is often quaintly referred to in spiritual circles as the 'monkey

3. Everything Is A Story

mind' or by simply watching the ego run its programs as you observe without judgement.

Think about your constant stream of thoughts like the scrolling ticker running across the bottom of the television screen during the news broadcast, providing you with headlines and updates. Practice separating your emotions and your identity from the 'ticker' and be a conscious observer to the stories it's running. Only connect mentally and emotionally to the thoughts that are supportive of your journey, and will help you to become all you can be.

If you remove the emotional connection and charge from a set of thoughts and beliefs, they no longer have any control over your life and behaviour. This is why I'm such a huge fan of tools like Emotional Freedom Technique, Sound Healing, Peace Process and Byron Katie's *The Work*, as they remove the emotional charge and give you back control of your life.

As you practice this more and more, your life will no longer be run by the limiting beliefs and stories because you're able to recognise them as soon as they surface, and replace them with ones that come from your true power and essence. Imagine if, when you created your goals and made your decisions, they came from a place of confidence, power and love, instead of from a place of fear, powerlessness and lack and any negative beliefs you have stored in your subconscious mind.

Any thoughts of "I'm not good enough", "I don't deserve it", "I'll be rejected if I'm successful and wealthy", "I'm not strong enough", "I'm a failure", and so on are just stories your subconscious mind has constructed based on judgements about what it has experienced and what others have demonstrated to you. All your decisions and actions are a result of these thoughts, whether you know it or not.

Most people mistakenly believe they're consciously deciding their outcomes when, in reality, their subconscious beliefs are in control of the results in all areas of their lives. By working directly with the subconscious you can truly become a conscious and deliberate creator of your life.

Positive thoughts are stories as well because every thought or belief is a story. The negative stories keeping you from realising your full potential and achieving your goals and dreams are based on lies. In contrast, supportive beliefs like you're strong and smart enough, and you have the ability to achieve everything you put your mind to, are based on the true essence of who you are as infinitely powerful being capable of extraordinary things.

There is a very easy way to tell the difference between a story that is a lie and one that is the truth. Start by saying the thought or belief out loud. For instance, say the statement "I'm not smart enough." Notice how you feel when you make that statement. Is the feeling heavy or light? It feels heavy, doesn't it? That means it's a lie. Now say, "I have all the intelligence I need to achieve my vision" and notice how that feels. It feels light, which means the statement is true.

The heavy feeling, or contraction, is the energy of resistance and the light feeling, or expansion, is the feeling of alignment. Whatever feeling you're experiencing is an energetic response, and energy is the force of creation. Whatever

3. Everything Is A Story

energetic state you're in is a powerful creative force and the more intense the energy, the greater the force.

Whatever story you put your focus and attention on is the one you will see manifest into your reality. The subconscious mind has no judgement or preference about what your belief systems are. Its only concern is to support what it believes will keep you safe and aligns with its paradigms.

For instance, if you look in the mirror and you have the thought "I'm fat", the subconscious mind simply takes on that statement, without judgement, and continues to guide you to display behaviour that reinforces the statement and perpetuates the experience of being 'fat'.

The underlying reason you may have become overweight in the first place comes from your subconscious mind believing you're safer being overweight. There are a plethora of reasons and any of these could be the case: such as protection from sexual abuse, fear of conflict, avoiding unwanted attention, constant criticism, need for acceptance by your family and friends, fear of loss, lack of self-worth, etc. The resulting self-fulfilling prophecy becomes the consistent observation "I'm fat."

A way to break this pattern would be to offer a contrasting observation in place of "I'm fat", such as, "I'm beautiful" and "I'm safe." If you were to consciously replace the critical judgement with this supportive statement consistently and often, your behaviour would change to fit that belief and recreate your experience.

This is just one example of the power of becoming aware of the stories you're telling yourself and taking positive steps to change those stories. Whilst this is effective, it's also the slow way to affect change. When you add transformation tools and techniques such as Emotional Freedom Technique, Sound Healing, and reframing to the equation, changing the thought patterns determining your results happens a lot more quickly.

I read about a story of a woman who had gained weight and just could not lose it no matter what she tried. Over a series of sessions working through a variety of potential causes for the stubborn weight gain, the woman revealed it had begun not long after she lost her young son. Interestingly the amount of weight she had gained was exactly the amount her son weighed when he died. When she allowed herself to let go of her son, she was then able to lose the weight. Her weight gain was a result of the story around the death of her son.

The fact that the intensity of an emotional response affects how quickly something will manifest also means the energy of fear is one of the most powerful creative forces there is because fear is such a fierce and sometimes all-consuming emotion. It hijacks all our senses, thoughts, overwhelms us emotionally, blocks our creativity and inspiration, and sends strong waves of creative impulse out to the Universe. For this reason, the things you fear are likely to show up in your experience if you allow those fears to fester over a prolonged period of time.

This realisation can sometimes cause people to panic and multiply their fear because now they're afraid of being afraid.

The good news is there is no reason to panic. Due to the nature of our existence, there is a grace period between

3. Everything Is A Story

our thoughts and feelings, and what we manifest. So, on the one hand, it means when we concentrate positive thoughts and feelings on something, it takes a certain period of time for them to manifest into our reality. It's also a safety mechanism that allows you to adjust and correct the thoughts causing fear and anxiety before they show up in your life.

Fortunately, you have a built-in system that tells you when you are in the flow of truth and light and on the right path, and it never fails. Your feelings are your emotional guidance system, constantly sending you signals about whether or not you are moving in the right direction and focusing on the right things. So when you feel joy and happiness this is a sure sign you're in alignment and on track to achieving your goals and dreams. Feelings that make you feel uncomfortable, such as anger, fear or frustration, are a sign that your focus is not in alignment with who you truly are, or what you want to achieve, and you need to re-align your focus and your vibration.

So, if you remember that the thoughts and stories causing you fear are lies, and those that make you feel good are truth you are in a much more powerful position to change the stories that aren't serving you.

The vast majority of us live most of our life and achieve almost all of our results based on lies of lack and limitation. These lies are designed to keep us safe, but in the process, also keep most of us locked into a life of mediocrity and quiet desperation because we dare not risk our perceived consequences of stepping outside of our comfort zone and sharing our brilliance with the world.

Dr. Wayne Dyer speaks of the six stories of the ego and the control they have over our outcomes and our happiness. The first is our belief 'We are what we have'. Our attachment to our possessions becomes something that defines us, and we embrace them as a part of who we are. When you take those possessions away, we feel a sense of loss and emptiness because of our attachment and identification with them.

The second is the belief that "We are what we do". Our activities, jobs, relationships, behaviour, the roles we play, the causes we stand for, come to define us, and if you take all of those things away, we feel as if we've lost our identity. This is the ego at play because, in truth, nothing can ever define us, contain or limit us unless we allow it to.

The third belief is that "we are what other people think of us". This plays a huge role in how we think and act as many of us put on masks in a desperate attempt to fit in and have people like and accept us. It stops us from expressing our individuality for fear of being judged and criticised because they make us feel ashamed, wrong or unworthy. This damaging belief and yearning to be accepted and trying to fit in are preventing billions of humans all over the world from being all they can be.

The final three stories are the stories of separation. We are separate from each other, we are separate from what we want and we are separate from God or the Universe. These are the greatest lies of all because they are denying us our essence and power, and keeping us locked in a world of mediocrity and suffering.

Imagine for a moment we embraced that we are all One and whatever you do to one person, you do to yourself. If we were to just embrace this one truth the human race would be kind, considerate, compassionate, understanding, accepting, loving. Wars would end, there would be no judgement, criticism, division or greed, and there would be peace.

At the time of our birth, we're fully aware that we are an extension of the source from which we came. We know we're connected to 'All That Is' and there is no sense of separation. As we navigate the initial days, weeks and months of our life, our experience flies in the face of this innate knowing, as we are immersed in this new 'reality' and all our senses are tuned into learning how to survive this world. We are gradually programmed out of this ancient wisdom into the belief that we are separate to everything around us. We develop an identity distinguishing us from our surroundings, and the line of separation is established.

We spend most of our lives wanting something different to what we have. We feel like something is missing, and instead of realising it's our connection with our true self and All That Is, we mistakenly believe it's because we don't have the elusive possession or achievement that will supposedly bring us the fulfilment and satisfaction we crave. There is a sense that our happiness is dependent on acquiring this thing we don't yet have.

This has caused the human race to relentlessly pursue this fruitless quest to gather more and more possessions. Possessions that provide just a fleeting feeling of satisfaction, until we slip back into that seemingly unquenchable need to fill the void in our hearts. We see something else we don't have that is supposedly denying our happiness and we latch onto it as our new obsession to acquire.

Imagine for a moment you're emotionally detached from all your possessions and achievements and you choose to be satisfied and happy with your life exactly as it is. Nothing to achieve. Nothing to acquire. Nothing to prove. No one to be. Just recognising everything is perfect and there is nothing for you to be, do or have. Imagine you could be happy with everything just as it is right now. Nothing is wrong. Everything is perfect. You may have to stretch yourself for this exercise, but I encourage you to drop into your heart space and exercise your creative powers to entertain the possibility for just a moment.

It's peaceful, isn't it? In this place, there's a sense of contentment and calm. Now you are able to reconnect with who you truly are and access all your power to create whatever life you would like to experience, not from a sense of need or desperation for fulfilment or happiness, but just for the sheer fun of what it would be like to have that in your current experience on this amazing, beautiful planet we call home.

The third line of separation is that we are separate from God. Many would think it blasphemous that I suggest we are One with God or even that we ARE God. I believe it's blasphemous not to embrace this belief. When we truly embrace that we are the creator, the destroyer, the Almighty, the alpha and the omega, everything starts to make sense.

Some believe it is this kind of belief in our true power that corrupts, but that is not the case. It is fear that corrupts, not true power. Acknowledgement of ourselves as the ultimate power brings incredible humility, compassion, understanding and love. We see ourselves differently and we see others differently. It isn't just you that is God, but every person, creature and entity on this planet. Everything is a different expression of the one God or Universe: Everything coming from the one Source, no separation, just one living organism having an experience of itself.

Separation in any form is an illusion reinforced by the human condition. Drop the illusion. Drop the yearning. Drop the wanting. As long as you acknowledge that all things, including you, are Source, God, the Universe, whatever you want to call it, you will be at peace. When you reach this understanding you will step into your greatness and, by your example, you will give others permission to step into theirs.

~ Key Reflections ~

1. You are a master creator and have the power to create anything you want in your life. What stops us from living the life we truly desire is the stories, belief systems and paradigms that our subconscious has created from our environment and our experiences. These beliefs are designed to keep us safe. However, many of them just keep us from living life in our truth and power and stop us from being all we can be. These stories and belief systems are determining all of your results in life.

2. You have an inbuilt guidance system that tells you when you are on the right track. Your emotions are constantly guiding you to live your truth and your passion. When you're feeling the lighter emotions such as joy, fulfilment and peace, you are on the right track. When you're feeling frustration, anger, overwhelm, etc., you've strayed from your path and from the truth of who you truly are.

3. The illusion of separation is the only belief we need to correct in order to be free and create everything our heart desires. Embrace the truth of Oneness with everything, and you are on the path to unimaginable riches in every part of your life.

4. You Are Not Broken

There's a fallacy that has unwittingly been fostered by our own minds and by popular culture: the fallacy that you are broken and need to be fixed. The truth is you could never be broken and there is nothing about you that needs to be fixed.

You are whole, perfect and complete in every way. You always have been and you always will be. There is nothing missing. If you are feeling like there's something wrong with you, it's because you've misunderstood the nature of your existence and who you truly are.

If you feel less than whole or less than perfect, then you're ascribing to the stories you've created or adopted from your experiences and your emotional attachment to events of the past. Once you let go of the stories and emotional attachment you will see yourself through the eyes of the creator, and you will see the perfection that is YOU.

When you accept the truth of your perfection and the perfection of 'all that is' by dropping your stories, judgements and perceptions, you suddenly see how there can never be anything wrong with you or your situation.

Think about a tree that's been growing for decades or even hundreds of years. Over those years it has endured numerous storms with gale force winds, lashing rain, possibly lightning strikes as well as broken limbs, insect infestations, droughts, fires, floods, etc. These events in the life of the tree cause it to twist, bend and grow in a unique way as it adapts to changing conditions. The tree didn't shout at the wind for breaking it or causing it to bend. It didn't scream at the insects for daring to infest it, or fight against conditions that caused it to grow crooked or have knots in its bark, or drop enormous limbs. Instead, it absorbed whatever Mother Nature threw at it and adapted its growth path accordingly.

When we look at this tree, we don't see imperfections. Instead, we marvel at its unique beauty and the way it has masterfully managed to grow into such a glorious specimen of a tree in spite, or because of the hardships it has faced along the way. We are in awe of its magnificence and the scars it bears from the adversity it's endured. We see the tree's beauty, character and majesty.

We know the tree hasn't struggled to grow, fought against or resisted the many and various challenges it faced. Instead, it continued to focus purely on its single-minded purpose to grow toward the light, become the most amazing expression of a tree it could possibly be and contribute to the collective field of nature. It's focused purely on playing its role of service in the grand scheme with Mother Nature. Its growth has provided refuge for many thousands of animals and insects. Its fallen foliage provides essential nourishment for the soil. Its leaves provide essential oxygen for the animals of the planet. Its canopy provides shade and comfort for animals in the heat of the day. Without doing anything apart from processing the nourishment the planet provides, turning it into gradual, steady growth, the tree makes a valuable contribution to the planet which gives and sustains its life.

If we don't see the gnarled, twisted, misshapen tree as imperfect, why do we see or judge ourselves as anything other than perfect?

Our souls and our spirit can never be damaged. The deepest and most powerful version of who we are remains perfectly intact, solid, exquisitely beautiful and perfect. What we experience shapes us as the unique, multi-faceted individual we become.

Tragically, we have been taunted by impossible representations of what we should look like, how we should behave, what we should achieve and who we should be to prove our worth on this planet. This means we are doomed to fail in pretty much every area of our lives when we compare ourselves with these depictions and try to live up to these unrealistic expectations.

Photoshopped images on billboards, glossy magazines and street advertising, as well as beautiful people in movies, television shows and ads, music video clips with young, lithe, slim dancer's bodies tell us this is what we should be striving for. We compare ourselves and our achievements with the super successful and those who are revered, reinforcing common beliefs that we're not good enough.

This unrealistic portrayal of 'perfection' is flaunted in our faces from thousands of different sources every day. Is it any wonder we have a tendency to give up and not even try when society's portrayal of success seems virtually unattainable for the person on the street. What these images and stories don't tell you is the story of where these people started from, how many times they've failed, their own doubts and insecurities, how they gradually built their own success and the adversities they faced along the way.

Only YOU have faced the many and varied combination of challenges that you have. Only YOU have processed them and overcome those challenges in the unique way that you have. Only YOU have made the unconscious decisions and come to the conclusions about life and how to navigate it that you have. YOU have become the unique person you are today as a direct result of those experiences and adversities. Only YOU have the ability to impart the unique body of wisdom and knowledge you've developed as a result of these trials to those who need them. Only YOU have developed the skills that, when combined with your unique talents, gifts and experiences can make the rare and distinctive contribution to the lives of others that you are here to make.

There is a story about two clay water carriers. Every day a young woman would take these two clay water pots down to the river to collect water in them and bring them back to her village for drinking, cooking and cleaning. One of the pots had a small crack in its side, and by the time the young woman had returned to the village, half of the water she had collected would have leaked out onto the road. One day the cracked pot spoke to the young woman and said it was ashamed about the crack that caused it to lose half the water that she had to walk so far to collect.

4. You Are Not Broken

The young woman smiled and said to the pot, "As I return from the river, I always carry you on my right side. Have a look at the right side of the path and you will see it's covered in beautiful little flowers that have sprung up due to the steady trickle of water you drop every day. There are no flowers on the left side of the path. I treasure these flowers for they make my walk more beautiful and enjoyable every day. I would not have you any other way and you are perfect just as you are with your crack, as you give life which would not otherwise be there."

Your cracks, chips and scars are what make you uniquely, beautifully, perfectly you and give you the ability to make the contribution you are here to make.

I recently had the privilege of meeting an extraordinary woman named Turia Pitt. Her courage, strength and dogged determination in the face of some of the most extreme challenges are truly inspirational and a testament to the resilience and strength of the human spirit in the face of incredible adversity.

In 2011, mining engineer, part-time model and athlete, Turia Pitt, set out on a gruelling ultra-marathon event in the Australian Kimberley called 'Racing The Planet'. This 100-kilometre run across rugged terrain and in searing heat would be enough to test any athlete, but it was a challenge Turia was accustomed to and one she welcomed. Yet, few have survived the challenges she was about to face. Turia not only survived against the odds, she has somehow managed to thrive.

In spite of warnings and calls to cancel the event because of the pending danger, organisers went ahead with it.

Completely unaware of the danger that lay in front of them, at the head of the pack, Turia and several other runners ran headlong into an out-of-control fire which, before they knew it, was upon them with no way out. Several runners were severely burned with Turia being the worst of them. Burned beyond recognition with more than 60% of her body affected, some of the burns almost to the bone, Turia was flown to Sydney's Prince Alfred burns unit for treatment. The medical team had to fly in skin from the U.S. as they didn't have enough stocks to treat her deep wounds. She was put into a coma for two weeks and her doctors held little hope for her survival. In fact, her doctor said he had never had a burns victim survive with such deep wounds before.

Turia's story is harrowing as she tells of lying in her bed terrified and unable to sleep at night in anticipation of having her bandages changed in the morning. Listening intently each day, knowing how close the nurses were to her room by how loud the cries of agony were from other patients. She had to wear a compression mask on her head and face, as well as full body compression bandages for two years to help her body heal. Turia had to learn to walk again and do so many of the simple things we take for granted. She has now had over 100 surgeries on her body and continues to undergo procedures to improve her look and body function.

One day, as part of her therapy and learning to walk again, she took an agonising and shaky climb up one flight of stairs at the back of the hospital. She was so proud of herself. When she told her doctor with great glee about her achievement, she expected to be rewarded with high praise. Obviously, her doctor knew her better.

4. You Are Not Broken

His response would have seemed cruel to the majority of people. He said something like, "So what? When you've managed all twelve flights, let me know." Turia was initially guttered and defensive, but the very next day she went to the bottom of the steps and somehow managed to climb all twelve flights! Her doctor obviously knew she was a super high achiever and gave her the incentive she needed to really push her limits.

How someone endures that kind of unimaginable agony is beyond comprehension. And yet, seeing her now, you cannot help but be in awe of this incredibly strong, resilient, courageous young woman who has endured so much. In fact, 4 ½ years on, Turia has just completed an Iron Man event 40 minutes ahead of the time she anticipated. This required her to swim 3.8km, cycle 180.2km and run 42.2km which she did all in 13 hours 24 minutes.

When you see Turia for the first time, the mind naturally and automatically responds with shock and a sense of pity. Her physical scars are quite confronting. Remarkably, when you hear her speak and see her incredible achievements post the accident, the scars fade away. You see beyond the outward façade to an incredibly beautiful, inspiring, courageous, generous, present, strong, spirited, powerful, formidable force who invokes a sense of awe from those who meet her. The package and vehicle Turia uses to traverse this planet may be scarred, but her spirit, her beauty and her life force are stronger than ever.

Instead of allowing this event to define her, Turia has used this tragedy in her life to turn her into someone with an incredibly strong sense of purpose. Rather than diminish her, the fire that once ravaged her now fuels her. She works tirelessly raising funds and awareness for Interplast, an organisation that provides free reconstructive surgery for people who desperately need it in developing countries. She has also just started a group called Turia's Champions, which I am proud to be a part of, where she helps inspire, encourage and coach those who want to be more, do more and achieve more in their lives. She shares how she has overcome the many challenges she has faced and how we can use the same methodology to do the same in our own lives.

Your experiences have all been perfect and designed to create the person you are today. There is no imperfection in life, or in you. It's up to you to turn the experiences of your life into the gifts you give to others, and the contribution you make to this world. This will give meaning to your trials and tribulations and instead of wasting energy lamenting them, you'll create something positive from them.

Drop the misconception that you or anything you have experienced is less than perfect. When you view your life as a rich tapestry orchestrated specifically for you to develop into the person who is destined to make a wonderful contribution to the world, you begin to work with the system the way it was designed. The way YOU designed it. You have the potential to make a valuable contribution no one but you can make, one the world is crying out for. This awareness will help you to put everything in your life into perspective and take your power back so you can use it to help change the world.

Whether you directly impact one person, or a thousand people, or a million people, you will change the world, as

4. You Are Not Broken

the ripple effect flows out to many, many others. Mahatma Gandhi's mother did nothing, except giving birth to Mahatma Gandhi. Imagine if she had never existed?

T. Harv Eker put the T in front of his name to signify 'The' which reminds him that he is the only person who has ever has been or ever will be like him on the planet. No person will ever replicate him in full, and the same goes for you too. Not a single person on the planet now, or in the past, or who will come in the future will ever be the same as you. You're it! You're the only one.

Think about that. You are THAT unique and special. One of a kind, never to be repeated. Don't you deserve to share that with everyone you meet and leave a positive impact on them? Start to see everyone you meet from this perspective and you will be better able to see the incredible uniqueness in yourself.

It's time to stop judging your life or yourself as wrong, damaged, incomplete, broken, or in need of fixing. Acknowledge the perfection of your entire life, and use your experiences to contribute to the world in the way no one else can. This will ensure you live the most extraordinary, rewarding and fulfilling life you possibly can and give meaning to the trials and tribulations you have endured and triumphed over. This is the gift of life and all its many challenges. They cannot define you, but they will determine the secret sauce of your success when you let them.

~ Key Reflections ~

1. You are whole, perfect and complete in every way. You always have been and you always will be. There is nothing missing. If you're feeling like there's something wrong with you, it's because you've misunderstood the nature of your existence and who you truly are.

2. Nothing can define you. No experience, no matter how painful or traumatic can determine who you become. Only you can do that. You get to choose the meaning of your past, and who you become because of it. Embrace your infinite power and rise above every experience that you see as less than perfect.

3. The human spirit, your spirit, is much stronger than you can imagine. Everything you have experienced and survived has made you who you are today. You can allow those experiences to break you, or make you. Your biggest breakthroughs will potentially come from your darkest moments. And the truth is, you are not broken, and do not need to be fixed. Embrace every experience as an opportunity.

5. Life Is Happening For You, Not To You

Life is a labyrinth of challenges, emotions, experiences, realisations and rewards. Some of the experiences are great, and some are pretty crap. That's the way life is. It doesn't matter if you're a master co-creator or someone who's only just starting to learn about the power of co-creation, sometimes things happen in a way which we would not have consciously chosen, and appear less than ideal for our state of happiness and wellbeing.

Challenges are the Universe's way of getting us to step into our true greatness, step by step, one challenge at a time. The bottom line is: Shit happens! Deal with it!

The vast majority of people spend a significant portion of their time complaining about how bad things are and how other people are to blame for their own struggles, society's struggles and global struggles. They're in victim mode. We are facing multiple crises in the world today and instead of taking responsibility for them, we're demanding someone else to take action!

In fact, we are where we are, personally and globally, because of our collective consciousness and the action, or inaction, we are guilty of as a collective global community.

We've created the ultimate challenge for ourselves. If we take the stance that life is actually happening FOR us, not TO us, we take back our power and the ability to create great change, without having to rely on the actions of others.

When someone decides to pursue their dreams what often happens is they have the bizarre notion that, all they need to do is point themselves in the general direction and everything will work out. Those afraid of failure are the first wave of people to fall by the wayside. They get as far as the idea of pursuing the dream, but not much further. They're waiting for everything to be perfect before they take action and there's always something not quite right. To these people I say, "just get started". Circumstances are never going to be perfect and there will always be a variety of perfectly legitimate reasons for you not to take action. There will always be a lack of time, money or resources, so deal with it, figure a way around it and take action.

For the rest of the population intent on doing something about their circumstances, they start out well and very soon they come up against their first challenge. For many, this is where the story ends. Suddenly it all seems too hard and their doubts and fears get the better of them. They wave the white flag and surrender justifying their lack of persistence saying, they tried and it didn't work. These people slide back into a life of mediocrity secured in their own minds that they gave it a shot, but the odds were stacked against them and they couldn't have succeeded.

A small percentage of people manage to overcome their first challenge and maybe even their fourth and fifth, but, just as in a video game where the nature and intensity of the challenges increase with each level, so it is with life. As you prove yourself with each challenge and master a level, the challenges become more difficult and complex at the next stage. Some people don't understand that this is the nature of success and the way the Universe works. Instead of embracing each challenge as it comes and cherishing their growth in the face of adversity, they crumble under the pressure and think it's just all too hard.

The people who are left are a very small percentage of rare, persistent, committed, tenacious individuals who are willing to accept and embrace the challenges that arise and rise to the challenges. These people are not particularly special in any way other than the way they think and their ability to remain steadfast and persevere in the face of adversity. They don't think the Universe is out to get them, they understand the rules of the game they have chosen to play and know they're always going to be faced with trials at every step of the way. At their core, they believe in themselves that, no matter what, they're bigger than any challenge they face. They choose to navigate those challenges by stretching themselves, getting out of their comfort zone, using and improving their skills, talents and knowledge to master the game. They have a strong sense of purpose and a big 'why'.

Do you think people like Richard Branson, Steve Jobs, Bill Gates, Oprah Winfrey, and all the high wealthy individuals and high achievers in the world don't have challenges? Do you think they had an extraordinary amount of luck that has helped them to get to where they are? The truth is, these super-achievers face far greater challenges each day in their businesses and pursuits than we could currently ever hope to overcome with our level of business and life mastery. Having navigated the lower and middle levels of the game, they're into the advanced stages and their skills, knowledge and abilities are such that they're able to negotiate the much more complex challenges they face and solve them. The key is they're willing to continue learning every step of the way. It's what fuels them, not defeats them.

These people create their own luck by focusing on their vision and where they're going. Consequently, they nearly always seem to be in the right place at the right time, meeting the right people, leveraging the opportunities placed before them and growing their network, team, knowledge, skills and abilities every step of the way. They have a 'can do' attitude where no challenge is too great or set back too disastrous to stop them from achieving their ultimate goal. They see challenges as the spice of life.

When the going gets tough, as it inevitably will, the tough get going. They don't waste precious time and energy on regrets, beating themselves up, blaming others, and generally being a victim. They choose to access the greatness within them, their determination, their will to succeed and they take whatever action they know to turn adversity to their advantage.

Take the video game analogy. Why do you think they're so addictive? One of the reasons is because each level is

5. Life Is Happening For You, Not To You

designed to test our current skill level and develop our mind. As we practice and master one level, our mind yearns for the next. Progressing to the next stage gives us a feeling of fulfilment, satisfaction and achievement. The beauty of a video game is the consequences of losing aren't quite as daunting as when you're playing the game of life.

Imagine if you took the same attitude as you did with a video game and you applied it to life. Let me tell you what would happen. You would become addicted, just as so many people do with a video game. That feeling of achievement and satisfaction of accomplishing and mastering something new is so rewarding, even more so than in a virtual world where the stakes aren't as high.

When you leverage your specific skills, gifts and talents and apply them to your life, intent upon mastering this game and being the best you can be, the rewards are incomparable.

Apathy has spread throughout the world like a sickness. This disease serves to repress the human race and stop us from realising our full potential. If it has a hold on you, it's like an invisible force infiltrating your being and working to keep you playing small and feeling powerless and unimportant.

It's time to shake this apathy free because deep inside you is a tsunami of power waiting to be unleashed. It's been lying dormant for decades, waiting for you to reach out for it and wield it with courage and conviction. When you entered the world, you knew this power intimately. It is the essence of who you are. But in order to fit in and conform, you turned your back on this power and your subconscious chose to forget it.

Now it's calling you. The call resonates so loudly within you that you're not able to ignore it for long. Choose to reconnect with that calling now. Close your eyes, feel the power building deep within you crying out to be unleashed and to make the positive impact you want to make in the world. Take just 60 seconds to do this. I dare you!

When you reconnect with it and bring it to bear, the tide will turn for you and for those you serve, and those you touch will feel your impact like a tidal wave.

The challenges you've already faced and overcome in your life, and those that are yet to come, are all designed to serve you, build your belief in yourself and your strength. All the adversity that has occurred in your life that, you asked for, subconsciously, because you knew you needed those challenges in order to become the person you are and have the impact you are destined to make.

Own it! Be it! Declare it! Your time has come!

5. Life Is Happening For You, Not To You

~ *Key Reflections* ~

1. Your challenges, failures and set backs are an essential and inescapable part of your journey toward success. These are invitations to step up and be the best version of you, and develop the skills and knowledge you will need to become who you need to be to achieve your vision.

2. Super successful people believe in themselves and know they are bigger than any problem they will ever face. Work on building your self-belief and self-confidence, and know that there is no problem or challenge that you are not capable of solving.

3. Bring a solution focused, can do, "I've got this" attitude to your business and your life, and you'll surprise yourself just what you're capable of when you decide to step up and knock it out of the park!

6. Have You Had Enough Yet?

There's a question that has stuck with me ever since I read it in Neale Donald Walsch's first book, *Conversations With God*. This is a series that impacted on me many years ago at the beginning of my journey into deepening my spirituality and my relationship with who I truly am.

In the beginning of the book, Neale explores his slide into the depths of despair following a series of events including a car accident, which resulted in a serious neck injury, relationship collapse, unemployment, depression and ultimately, homelessness. Just as he was seemingly getting back on his feet, he was dealt another blow and he was desperate for answers. So he started asking questions.

He wrote down on a piece of paper some questions for God, not really expecting an answer. Then fell asleep on the couch. In the middle of the night, he was woken by a voice speaking to him. It was saying, "Have you had enough yet?"

The significance of this question is enormous when you reach this point where you've finally had enough. You're ready to make the definitive decision to do whatever it takes to achieve your goals and dreams; make the impact you want to make; live the life you came here to live; to be all you can be, and so much more. It's the point where you're finally willing to do whatever it takes, without question, without compromise.

I reached this point in my life in the middle of 2015. I was stuck, floundering and fed up. I'd hit a wall. Nothing I did seemed to be working and suddenly it felt like I splintered into a thousand pieces mentally and emotionally. I just wanted to walk away from everything I had built over several years. I had had enough!

With the help of my friends, colleagues and my coach, I pieced myself back together. It was at this point that I went, "Enough." I was done with playing small and I made the biggest financial investment I've ever made in myself. From there, I made a series of strategic decisions to launch myself onto the world stage and I will never look back. I made some of the gutsiest decisions I've ever made in my life in the past 12 months, and I've become a different person: a person who is no longer willing to compromise and do things by halves. It is everything, or nothing at all.

Success is never convenient, and whilst you're waiting for the circumstances and conditions in your life to be conducive to taking action to your success, you're wasting valuable time, and time is a precious gift you can never get back.

The truth is, there will always be a variety of reasons and excuses that appear valid for not taking action toward creating a new future. This justification for your lack of action is stealing

6. Have You Had Enough Yet?

your dreams from you and you're using them to deny yourself the realisation of a life beyond your wildest dreams.

When you've decided you've had enough, all of these reasons and excuses will disappear and all you'll be left with is a blank canvas ready for you to start creating your new future.

So, have you had enough yet?

Have you had enough of living a life of mediocrity and settling for less than what you truly want?

Have you had enough of the struggle?

Have you had enough of living in quiet desperation, knowing you're capable of so much more, but not sure how to unlock it?

Have you had enough of battling through the endless stream of unsatisfying challenges and disappointments?

Have you had enough of playing small?

Have you had enough of feeling powerless?

Have you had enough of not living up to your full potential?

Have you had enough of the uncertainty?

Have you had enough of the fear, sadness and frustration?

Once you are ready to declare that you've had enough and that you're willing to do whatever it takes to achieve the results you want, EVERYTHING changes.

When you finally reach that point that you've had enough, you're willing to do whatever it takes to achieve the dreams you've been harbouring for so long. After taking two steps forward and three steps backwards for years or even decades, this moment is the tipping point.

Up until now, you've been dabbling with your success, hedging your bets, playing it safe, just in case it didn't work out, which means you've less chance of losing face and being a laughing stock. But suddenly all of this pales into insignificance compared to the price you've been paying for not committing fully to your dreams.

Coming to this point and knowing in your heart that there's no backing out now, is a scary moment. You'll have all sorts of doubts, fears and loud, obnoxious internal voices laughing at you and telling you that you're not capable of doing it. Saying it won't last and predicting you'll sink back into 'dabbling' with your future and 'trying' to succeed for years and years until the day you die. Internal voices telling you that you don't have what it takes, that you don't know how, that people will laugh at you. Internal voices asking sceptical questions like, "But what if it doesn't work? It hasn't worked before, so what's different now? What if you fail?" These voices are loud, almost to the point of deafening, demanding your attention and trying to derail you.

The thing is, you've been listening to those voices and seeds of doubt for far too long. You've allowed them to steal your dreams and terrorise you into submission. They've been your constant companions and saboteurs for as long as you can remember. They're reliable, familiar and they seem to make a few good arguments. Or at least they did, until now.

Now, you're hearing those voices and you've realised the only power they have is the power you give them. You've suddenly come to understand the truth that they've been deliberately holding you back for years. Okay, maybe they

6. Have You Had Enough Yet?

had a good motivation. They were trying to keep you safe, which is what our subconscious belief systems and paradigms are designed to do.

Now, you've finally come to the point where 'safe' is overrated and the pain of regret, discontent, frustration and underachievement is far more of a threat than the fears, doubts and belief systems that have kept you stuck in mediocrity. What if those voices were wrong all along?

You're ready to stare down those demons and stop them from ruling your life.

You're done stuffing around and playing it small. You have so much more to give, be, do, achieve! This is your future you're talking about. There is a difference you want to make in the world. Suddenly you're uncompromising and unyielding. Those voices can just get ... STUFFED! Enough is enough.

This is the moment you've arrived. As soon as you decide you're going to move heaven and earth to achieve your vision, suddenly and somewhat perversely, heaven and earth start to move for you. When you send out this booming message that you're going to do whatever it takes no matter what and begin to take definitive, uncompromising action toward your goals like never before, it's like the Universe says, "Right. Now you're serious, let's do this."

If you want radical success or radically different results, you've got to do something radically different.

The Universe will be your most faithful collaborator in all of this. It's always been there for you, but it won't show up until you do. You will feel tested at times, but this is all a part of your journey to success.

Everything that happens is the Universe colluding with you and for you. The events that occur, though they feel like they're trying to stop you, are in fact happening to encourage you to step up, evolve into someone greater than you were before, be the best you can be, develop more skills, be more resourceful, learn more about yourself, increase your faith in yourself, and be more creative. Sometimes those challenges are telling you there's a better way, or you're going the wrong way- go back.

Your ability to decipher the messages the Universe is sending you will develop over time and you'll get better at understanding what it's trying to say or encourage you to do.

In the face of adversity, there is a strategy I love to use that was taught to me by a colleague: instead of getting upset, disappointed, frustrated and thinking the Universe is conspiring against you, choose to stay curious. Accept that this event, person or situation has happened to help you to be more, do more, create more, and stay curious. Ask the questions, "How is this for my highest good?" "How can I turn it into a blessing?" "What can I learn from this situation that will help me to achieve my goals?" The more you stay curious about what has happened and seek to understand its purpose, the more open you will be to creating a good outcome regardless of the circumstance you're presented with. The more difficult the situation, the bigger the opportunity for you to grow, step up and evolve into the person you need to be to succeed.

The reason you haven't achieved your goals and dreams yet is that you haven't evolved into the person you need to be to achieve those goals and dreams. Your challenges are sent to you for you to become that person. The greater your dreams, goals and visions, the greater the challenges will be.

Everyone experiences challenges, setbacks, disappointments and roadblocks when working toward their vision. Everyone! How you respond to those challenges will either make them a satisfying experience that you resolve with ease and grace, or a frustrating one that's a lot harder if you react and offer resistance.

When you lean into the situation, stay curious and ask good quality questions, you'll discover more resources available to find a solution. The more quickly you will be able to find a way around, under, over or through what has presented itself.

What most people do in the face of adversity is throw their hands up in the air and react to the situation automatically. This is when we act out of fear, frustration, anger, sadness or disappointment, and from this place, you will never be able to find the best solution.

Unless you're highly emotionally evolved, these emotions are going to arise many times on your journey toward your goals and dreams. It's all a part of the process. What's important is you don't stay in these emotions or allow them to be the driving force behind the action you take. Breathe, acknowledge those emotions and do what you can to release them, knowing you are safe and bigger than any problem or challenge you will ever face.

There's a story I heard from Mary Morrissey that Nelson Mandela shared with her during an interview she was conducting with him.

In The Presence of Greatness

When Nelson Mandela was imprisoned for trying to end apartheid, he was understandably angry, but most of all he was feeling despair. For the first couple of years, he thought, "It's never going to happen now. It's never going to happen now. It's never going to happen now." The feeling of failure weighed on him heavily and he thought his dream of freeing his people from slavery and oppression would never be realised. What could he do from prison?

Then one day, a new thought cut through his despair and negative thinking like a ray of sunshine cuts through the clouds and shines a light into the middle of an open field. The new thought was, "What if this is what it looks like while it's happening?"

This thought filled him with a sense of hope. He took that thin and tenuous hold on hope and explored it. He started to think about what he could do from prison to realise his dream. Then the idea came to him to write letters to world leaders and get them to take action for the cause. It was a slow, arduous process, but you don't end the oppression of a people overnight, and eventually, it worked. His action from the confinement of his prison cell was the catalyst that started the process that eventually ended apartheid.

We have this preconceived idea of what our success and the road to it should look like. We anticipate the path to be clear, lined with gold and strewn with rose petals. In direct contrast, the reality is that the path is more often indistinct, even almost impossible to make out sometimes, and rocky with thorny bushes growing over it and much of it is uphill.

Release any idea of what success looks like because the likelihood is it will not look anything like the concepts you've

6. Have You Had Enough Yet?

constructed in your mind. You hold onto those fanciful ideas at your peril, because when it doesn't look the way you expect it to, you think you're doing something wrong, or it's not working, or you're not meant to succeed.

Remember the saying "It's darkest before the dawn." This is often the case with realising your vision. Sometimes it feels like the Universe is throwing obstacles and challenges at you left, right and centre, testing your metal.

This is not a journey for wimps. I'm not trying to discourage you, just letting you know that this is the reality of the journey. Nothing great was ever achieved easily, and to expect it to be handed to you on a platter is setting yourself up for failure. It's important to expect good things to happen, just don't expect all those good things to come wrapped in pink wrapping paper with a gold bow and a card that says 'Just because'.

All things that happen are neither good nor bad. They just are. If you're expecting something bad, you're going to make any result that looks contrary to your preconceived ideas wrong, which sets up resistance, and resistance is what makes the journey hard.

When you stop resisting and start allowing, the struggle disappears. The challenges are still there, but suddenly they're just mountains to climb, not scary monsters trying to destroy your happiness. You will see them for what they are: Which is, opportunities to grow and evolve into the successful person you need to become in order to realise your vision.

For some, this realisation may be very liberating, because you've been judging your journey and yourself harshly and thinking surely it doesn't have to be this hard. No, it doesn't have to be 'hard' at all. It's just your judgement and perception that makes it hard.

If the road to success was super easy, everyone would be travelling it. Interestingly, something you may not have considered is that it would be bloody boring too. Imagine if there were no challenges in life ever! Nothing to aspire to. Nothing to achieve. No mountains to climb or fjords to cross. Everything was simple, easy and given to you without any fuss or prerequisite or contribution.

Depending on where you're at right now, you may be thinking "Man, that would be really nice." Think again. Really think about what a world like that would look like. Seriously, you would be bored and you would deliberately create challenges just to spice things up a bit and make things interesting. You kind of already are! (Wink, wink, nudge, nudge.)

I believe you came here to experience life in this time and space reality and express who you truly are and make a worthwhile contribution to the experience for yourself and others. This requires effort, growth and commitment.

You also have the choice not to grow, strive, or set goals, and just sit on your couch, eat Tim Tam's or Oreos and watch movies all day. But I would suggest that if you're reading this book, that would not satisfy your soul and it would bore the daylights out of you very quickly.

I also hold firmly to a belief that challenges are an inevitable part of life whether you like it or not, and if you don't choose your challenges, they will choose you. If you do allow your

6. Have You Had Enough Yet?

challenges to choose you, the quality of the challenges and subsequent outcomes will be much lower and will be far less satisfying than if you decide to choose your own challenges. This is like allowing life to happen to you instead of being an active participant in your results.

So the next time you face a challenge or problem, and you feel frustrated, angry or a sense of despair because it doesn't seem to be happening, or at least not the way you think it should, ask yourself, "What if this is what it looks like while it's happening?". You cannot see the bigger picture and how all the pieces of the puzzle for your vision will fit together. Trust the Universe knows what it's doing because it can see the whole picture, where you only have access to a very tiny part of it.

You cannot possibly know, from your human viewpoint, each component of your vision, how it will play out and how it will come together. To you, it may feel like a tangled mess of random happenings that fall together when really the Universe is carefully orchestrating your vision for you.

It's a divine collaboration that, when you decide to trust in the process, becomes a magical flow where small miracles occur on a regular basis and sometimes even big ones. Synchronicity becomes commonplace. When you choose to lean into the process and follow your inspiration, it's remarkable how people, events and situations will occur to help bring it all together.

This kind of attitude of acceptance and allowance prevents you from offering resistance to the situation and gives you an opportunity to see the perfection. This is something one of my favourite authors and teachers, Neale Donald Walsch, states is the first step to freedom: To "see the perfection" in every situation in your life.

The saying "resistance is futile" comes to my mind when thinking of this subject. Resistance just causes more pain and struggle. Acceptance allows you to direct your energy and your response from a place of evolved awareness. It gives you the opportunity to create the perfect solution from a place of inspiration, which will bring incredible rewards.

So, have you had enough yet? Are you ready to make an unequivocal decision to do whatever it takes and be unstoppable? If you are, then you're on an exciting precipice of realising your greatness and the journey of a lifetime that is beyond comparison. Strap yourself in, because things are about to get very interesting.

6. Have You Had Enough Yet?

~ Key Reflections ~

1. Hitting the end of your rope is often an important turning point. That defining moment when you've had enough of the cycle of struggle, disappointment, and frustration and you're prepared to do whatever it takes. This is when you bring your 'A' game. This is when the Universe starts to collaborate with you, creating opportunities and providing you with what you need, including the necessary challenges, to bring your big dreams and vision to life.

2. If you want radical success or radically different results, you've got to do something radically different. Get out of your comfort zone. Be a rebel and decide not to follow the crowd. Conforming has gotten you to where you are. Now it's time to do what others won't, so you can have what others never will.

3. Challenges, setbacks, disappointments and roadblocks are all a necessary part of the journey. Your response to them is what defines them and will either make them a satisfying experience through which your success comes, or a frustrating one that stops you in your tracks. When you lean into the situation, stay curious and ask good quality questions, you'll discover more resources available to find a solution. The more quickly you will be able to find a way around, under, over or through what has presented itself.

7. What Have You Decided?

Every result in life is preceded by a decision, either conscious or unconscious. These decisions can be made and altered at any time in your life. Your decisions shape your destiny.

Many of the unconscious decisions were made when you were a toddler through the experiences and observations you made watching the most influential people in your life. They were your authorities when you were born and your primary caregivers. Most often they are your parents, as well as grandparents, relatives, teachers, carers, other significant figures and, sadly, the media.

The kind of behaviour you witnessed when you were a child, particularly from the ages of 0 to 7, have shaped your subconscious mind, your belief systems, your thoughts, your behaviours and your results.

Fortunately, because of what we now know about the plasticity of the brain, regardless of what decisions you made when you were a child, you can change those decisions, beliefs, behaviours and results at any time, starting right now.

When you listen to elite athletes speak of their success, often they'll attribute it to hard work and dedication. But many of us work hard and are dedicated, only to achieve mediocre results. So what's the difference between a super achiever and the majority of the population?

When you get right down to it, those who achieve great things decide they are going to go for their dreams and make them happen. They may be talented at what they do, but so are you. They're no different to you except choosing to make a decision, stick to it, and take deliberate, progressive steps each and every day until they reach their goal.

This may sound boring, but it's the reality of any great achievement. There's no quick fix or replacement for the mundane reality of having to take specific, strategic action toward your vision every day. If a magic pill or quick fix is what you're waiting for, then come back in five years' time and let me know how you get on, because I can almost guarantee you'll be in exactly in the same place you are now.

Super achievers have no question in their mind they're going to give it everything they have until they reach the goals and vision they have for themselves. They still have doubts, fears and limiting beliefs, but they don't allow those things to dictate the ultimate results they get. If they come up against a block, they find a way around, over, under, through, beyond the results they're getting.

Usually, this requires hiring a coach or mentor because someone on the outside is better able to see the problem when often we can't because we're too close to it. An

7. What Have You Decided?

outsider, particularly a professional, has the benefit of not being emotionally attached to what's going on in the story.

If you want to be a champion at what you do, the first step is to make the decision to be a champion. Not, "I'll give it a shot and see how it turns out." Once you've made that decision, everything beyond it is academic. You will be challenged, but because you've made the decision, you will be unstoppable in your quest.

Does it always work out the way we expect or want? Rarely. Whilst a selected few make it to the very top, others will make it a certain distance and not quite reach the pinnacle of their profession, but they will none the less be champions of their lives and their chosen field. The critical thing to remember is that it's not possible to make it to the top, or even part way, unless you make the decision that that's where you're going.

It's important to remember, there is never a problem without a solution, and you're never given a problem or a challenge you're not able to solve. That's the way the Universe works. Achievers intuitively know and understand this concept, which is why, when they come up against a challenge, they stay primarily focused on finding the solution they know exists. Most people stay stuck in the problem and that's all they can see. They fail to see beyond their own limitations and use the power of their subconscious mind and the knowledge and wisdom they have to seek and apply a solution.

The actor Will Smith, gives a great analogy. He says he isn't where he is today because of extraordinary talent, but because of an insane work ethic. If someone challenges him to run on a treadmill longer than he does, he's going to run on the treadmill longer, or die trying. Once he's committed to the task he's not giving up and he is going to give it absolutely everything he has without question.

Personally, I don't think Will gives himself enough credit for his natural ability and talent. It's obvious he's very talented at his craft. But the point is, talent will only take you so far. Commitment, hard work and dedication are essential to get you the rest of the way. What has taken Will, and so many other super achievers, to the top of their profession is a combination of both talent and an uncompromising commitment to their vision.

Mostly what stops us from making the decision to reach for the stars is our limiting decisions and conditioning that it's not safe, we're not good enough, or we don't deserve it. Fortunately, in recent decades we have been engineering ways to release the limiting beliefs that cause us to self-sabotage and slow down or stop our progress. There are many different personal development tools and programs available to change the subconscious mind effectively and quickly, eliminating limiting beliefs and installing new ones, sometimes within a matter of minutes.

One of my favourite techniques for doing this is Emotional Freedom Technique or EFT Tapping. Tapping stimulates the acupressure points of the body releasing the attachment and charge around emotional trauma, limiting beliefs, negative feelings, painful memories, etc. EFT has changed the lives of hundreds of thousands of people all around the world and is fast becoming recognised as one of the most powerful transformational tools of our age.

7. What Have You Decided?

So, when you make the definitive decision, there is no excuse for anyone not to be able to achieve anything to which they put their mind.

I've worked with many clients over the years and I've seen all manner of belief systems acquired from things that were told, experiences people have had, or the way they were treated, that caused them to behave in a way that stopped them achieving the results they desired.

Once these beliefs are identified, it's a simple case of applying Emotional Freedom Technique to those limiting beliefs to clear the blocks. It's so gratifying to hear and see peoples' results change from that point forward. Solutions present themselves seemingly from out of nowhere for situations that were previously difficult, or seemingly impossible. Everything is resolved and suddenly the path is clear to move forward and results change.

Your job, once you've made the decision to succeed in any area of your life, is to then take whatever action needs to be uncovered and release the belief systems standing in the way of your progress so you can move forward faster and with confidence.

Here are the seven most common overarching blocks to success. There are many subtle distinctions and variations on these themes, but one or several of these are at the base of pretty much any block someone encounters. Fear is nearly always involved at some level.

1. Fear of Change

Everyone fears change to some extent, and some more than others. It's a natural tendency of the primitive brain. Men, in particular, are prone to a fear of change. The subconscious mind likes familiar territory, even when it's uncomfortable, as when it enters unfamiliar territory it doesn't have any benchmark as to how to respond to a situation, and the unknown is met with suspicion and trepidation. The subconscious craves a feeling of safety and certainty, and, even when your circumstances seem less than desirable, the unknown is still a scarier prospect. For all the subconscious knows, it could even be worse than the familiar uncomfortable territory it's used to navigating.

This will remain the status quo until you overcome the fear of change through sheer will and taking action in spite of the fear, a major event happening where suddenly the current situation is less safe than the prospect of change, or you use processes and techniques, such as EFT to release the fear of change and embrace the prospect of new experiences, new challenges and new horizons.

2. Fear of failure

This is a well-recognised fear that makes perfect sense to all of us. What doesn't make sense is how we came to have this fear when failure is an essential part of achievement and progress. When we were toddlers, we didn't fear failure. We all failed hundreds of times to walk, and probably hurt ourselves in the process sometimes, but not once did we make a conscious decision to give up and crawl through life.

7. What Have You Decided?

There was no judgement or shame about falling over. We just fell over, got up and tried again. We didn't ask, "What's wrong with me? Why haven't I mastered this yet? Why am I such a loser?"

We had dozens of role models who were walking and expected us to walk and believed we could walk. So they encouraged us, picked us up when we fell over and hurt ourselves, and championed us every step of the way. Failing our way to walking was recognised as the only way to learn how to walk.

So what happened? How did we go from being a legend at failing our way to success to having this perception that failure defines who we are and somehow makes us unworthy?

Our environment happened. Whilst embracing failure being accepted as part of the normal process in learning to walk, the influential people in our lives were brought up being taught that generally, failure is a bad thing. It is a statement about who we are and there is all this shame and judgement around failure. So they passed this onto us. Because they perceive failure to be painful, they want to save us from that painful experience, so they discourage us from even trying.

Then, there are the experiences we have when we fail. Like when other children at school, who have been taught that failure is a bad thing, make the experience painful. Instead of recognising the importance of failing your way forward, children and even adults become critical and judgemental and make fun of people who stuff up and get things wrong.

So, instead of embracing failure as an essential part of success, we hide ourselves away and don't dare to attempt anything where we don't know whether we can achieve it, because of our fear of failure.

This is a sure recipe for living a life of mediocrity and disappointment.

Decide to let go of your fear of failure and embrace it as an essential part of realising your dreams. You will fail many more times than you will succeed, and failure is just feedback as you learn how to succeed in whatever discipline or area you have chosen as part of your dreams.

Never allow others to discourage you. Don't share your dreams with those who will make your failed attempts wrong, or tell you that you can't do what you want to do. Hang out with people who know temporary failure is inevitable when someone steps up to go for their goals. People who will champion you, encourage you, believe in you, support you, pick you up when you're down, brainstorm solutions with you, collaborate with you to succeed and celebrate your successes.

3. Fear of success

This one is not spoken of or understood as much as fear of failure, although it has become better recognised recently as it is surprisingly common. Where a typical trait of fear of failure shows up as a reluctance to start a project, fear of success often shows up as being unable to finish a project.

In Australia, there is a well-recognised and common phenomena called the Tall Poppy Syndrome. This is where

7. What Have You Decided?

we love to tear down high achievers at the first opportunity. The public is often exceptionally critical without any consideration for personal circumstances or requiring the full facts before lynching someone.

The media is well-known for sparking a feeding frenzy for the sake of ratings with little regard for the full facts. Selective editing makes this a simple task and this makes it difficult for those in the public eye to blink without a potential judgement on their actions. There are a number of reasons for this pattern.

One is that people who are high achievers make us look bad. Or at least we think so. We see what they're doing and because some people can't possibly imagine themselves achieving the same heights, they feel bad about themselves. Instead of feeling inspired by their achievements, they want to bring them back down to their level so they can feel good about themselves again. For these people, there's a feeling of shame around the beliefs of their own inadequacies. They have fears and shame around their own success, or lack of, so they'd rather pull someone back down than attempt to succeed and risk failure.

There could also be a feeling of resentment or jealousy: "Why should they succeed when I haven't?"

Some people may even feel threatened by their achievements or be super competitive themselves and will attack them to upset them psychologically so they can outperform them, rather than focus on lifting their own game. This is a well-known tactic in many professional sports, to 'psyche the other player out'. Personally, I don't think it's a fair way to play, but it's generally accepted as part of the game, which is why it's important that sports people are mentally tough to endure the mental and emotional rigours of their sport as well as the physical.

People who feel threatened by others achievements tend to be critical of them and will deliberately seek to take advantage of a person's mental or emotional weakness to undermine them psychologically.

This happened to me as a child in primary school. I was naturally a high achiever and always top of the class the first couple of years, attaining 98% and 99% in class with little effort. My teacher, Mrs. Cox, who was English, took my mother aside and told her that in the UK, I would have been put into a special class to cater for my intellect, but they didn't have that option in Australia. I'm not saying this to blow my trumpet, it's just the way it was and I'm proud of that.

I was in a private school and the other children in my class were very competitive. Even though we were just 7 years old, they didn't like the fact that I outperformed them.

I was a soft and sensitive child. The other children started to bully me psychologically and it continued for about 18 months until my mother removed me from the school and put me in a small public school close by our home. Emotionally and mentally, I crumbled during the year and a half of torment. The teachers knew it was happening but seemed unable to put a stop to it. I rapidly went from the top of the class to developing hearing problems that required surgery – no doubt from trying to shut out their taunts – and quickly dropped to being an average student. My grades never recovered throughout the whole of my school years.

7. What Have You Decided?

Being a high achiever was just too painful. As soon as I realised this was affecting me several years ago, I went to work to release my emotional connection to that period in my life and spent several years releasing all the threads that had attached themselves to it. Because it happened so early in my life, it's been a highly charged emotional event with lots of neural pathways making it tricky to release. I'm not sure even now that I won't still come up against some emotional attachment to that period of my life. Fortunately, I have the awareness to recognise them, and the tools to be able to release them and move on.

This fear of success affected my ability to achieve my goals and dreams greatly. It was only when I recognised it as an issue and began to work on it continuously that I was able to start changing it.

So, as you can see, fear of success can be a very real and difficult issue. I'm not the first and certainly won't be the last to go through this kind of painful experience. What's important is you're able to recognise these kinds of issues and go to work to release them so they don't hold you back.

4. Fear of loss

We're all conditioned to hang on to what we've got as if our existence depends on it. We become emotionally attached to our possessions, friends, family, identities, status, labels, appearance, significant relationships, belief systems, circumstances, results, everything we believe makes up who we are. This takes a great deal of emotional energy, particularly when we're seeking to change our level of achievement as it means that inevitably we'll have to give up some of the things we've become attached to.

Maybe we were punished as children for losing something. Somewhere we picked up the idea that loss is a bad thing. In truth, unless you are willing to give up some of the things in your life, empty your cup a little, there is no room for anything else to come in. There is no room for expansion.

Imagine if you could give up your attachment to everything in your life. Many great spiritual teachers refer to this as becoming 'unclutched'. It's a very liberating practice for all areas of life.

We have this belief that the things we have in our life define who we are when, in truth, nothing can ever define who we are because we are infinite beings with infinite power and potential. To allow anything to define you, whether it's your possessions, your relationships, your job, your health, your past, your future, anything at all, is to put serious limitations on yourself. What a shame when you are limitless!

Who would you be if you could let go of your emotional attachment to all of those things? What would you be able to achieve? How would you approach life differently?

This does not mean you become an emotionless robot. To the contrary, releasing your attachment to 'what is' results in ultimate freedom, joy and the richness you truly deserve. You will love more deeply and unconditionally because you will not be dependent on the status of your relationships for your happiness. You will appreciate the things in your life more fully because you'll realise everything in life is only temporary and you'll be ok with that.

7. What Have You Decided?

Ultimately, when you step up and decide to go for your dreams, some relationships will fall away as new ones develop, your identity will change, your lifestyle will change, who you are will change, what you value will change. All of this is inevitable and beautiful, and once you embrace this and let go of your attachment to everything in your life, so much more will be possible.

This is not necessarily easy. Many spiritual masters have taken years to achieve a detached state, but once you make the decision to let go and release your attachment to the things in your life, you will start to feel a deep sense of relief and liberation.

5. Fear of Rejection

We've all been there and felt the painful sting of rejection. It often hits us right in the heart or the stomach. That moment when someone tells you 'no' or lets you know they don't like you or something you do. I can feel it right now just writing about it.

None of us like rejection because we all want to be liked and appreciated for who we are. This is why we wander around wearing masks pretending to be someone we're not, often not even aware we're doing it, in an attempt to be what we think others want and need us to be to avoid judgement, criticism and rejection.

To be authentic and true to ourselves means risking being vulnerable, and when we're vulnerable the sting of rejection can be even more painful. At least if someone rejects you when you're hiding behind a persona that's not truly you, it's a little easier to brush off.

This is because our self-worth is often tied up in what others think about us. As Wayne Dyer pointed out in one of the 6 false beliefs he outlined, we adopt the belief that we are what other people think of us.

Sometimes people end up with the 'disease to please' in an attempt to avoid rejection and have others like and accept them. This is exhausting and doomed to failure because you will never be able to please all of the people all of the time, no matter how hard you try. It also stops you from being all of you and stepping into your greatness. How can you when you're expending so much energy hiding your true self from the world?

This is largely why sales can be such a difficult skill for people to master because when someone says "No", we take it as a personal rejection like it's a statement about our self-worth. We also don't want to seem pushy, salesy, sleazy, deceptive or manipulative, which are common perceptions of salespeople. A fear of sales is a fear of judgement and rejection.

Sure, we've all experienced that type of salesperson who will say anything and would be willing to betray their own grandmother to close a sale, but fortunately, they are actually the minority. When you sell from the heart, you are being of service, and by adopting this attitude when speaking with a potential new client, it changes the equation for you and for them.

Do you believe in the service or product you provide? Do you believe you can help them? If you don't help them, how will they get their problem solved? If you allow them to walk away without a solution, which you are capable of providing, are you serving them to the best of your ability? Authentic selling is present, actively listening and then demonstrating how you have what they need to solve their problem.

There was a study conducted in the US by the Wharton Business School which revealed the number one reason people bought a product or service from a provider wasn't the state of the economy, the person's credentials, or the price on offer. It was the clarity and confidence with which the provider stated the benefits and price of the service.

Any rejection of what you have to offer is not a statement about you, but about the other person. Understanding this will empower you to be free to be yourself, serve more people and achieve your goals with no attachment to what others think about you or fear of rejection.

You are perfect, whole, complete and beautiful just the way you are. Anyone who suggests or tells you otherwise is just projecting their own feelings of inadequacy and self-judgement onto you. Remember this, and the rejection of others will be water off a duck's back.

6. Fear of not being good enough

This is another fear that affects all of us to some extent in a variety of ways. We all have doubts about our abilities and whether or not we deserve to achieve our goals and dreams.

Limiting beliefs like these are common:

    I'm not smart enough

    I'm not pretty / good looking enough,

    I'm not educated enough

I'm not focused enough,

I'm not tough enough,

I'm not tall enough

I'm not healthy enough,

I'm not creative enough,

I'm not strong enough

I don't know enough

I'm not qualified enough,

I'm not hard enough

I'm not enough

All of these beliefs come back to thinking that you're not good enough and that's a load of rubbish.

History has shown it's not the smartest, most creative, best looking, most educated, hardest working people in our society who are the most successful. In fact, if you study the super achievers in this world you will discover this is far from the case. What they are brilliant at doing is committing to their vision and leveraging their strengths to find a way, under, around, over or through their weaknesses, limitations and challenges. They work efficiently and stay focused to get the most done to move toward their goals in the shortest period of time.

In researching for this book, I found a very candid interview with the late, great Kerry Packer who is recognised as one of Australia's highest achievers in the country's history and has helped to shape where we are today. He is considered an enigma in Australia and whatever anyone's judgements might be about him, he really was a great man in business who achieved extraordinary things.

7. What Have You Decided?

In this interview, he states he was not very smart at school and was left way behind in his academic work. For this reason, he put a great deal of energy into playing a variety of sports and being the best he could be at those sports. He also said he wasn't necessarily the best sports person either, but he did have a certain amount of ability and what he lacked in that, he made up for by working hard.

Achievers will tell you that talent will only get you so far. The greatest portion of achievement comes from commitment, dedication and hard work. Do talent and natural ability play a role? Definitely. Should you do what you love and what you're good at in pursuit of your goals? Well, it's a damn sight more enjoyable than trying to do something you're not good at or don't like. Leveraging your natural talents is definitely a key factor, but without putting in the work, you're never going to achieve your goals.

Even the high achievers admit they have doubts, and days where they feel like a fraud. Yes, that's right. I've interviewed and listened to interviews of high achievers whom you would think would never have any self-doubt, and appear to be super confident. Surprisingly, they sometimes have serious questions about whether or not they're capable of living up to their goals and if they're worthy. The difference is they don't allow those feelings to dictate their results and stop them from moving forward.

It doesn't matter where you learnt to doubt yourself, it's a rare individual who believes 100% in their ability to achieve their grandest vision for themselves. In fact, I doubt very much that anyone has 100% belief in themselves.

People like Richard Branson and Steve Jobs grew up in supportive environments where they were told they could achieve anything they put their mind to and to never give up. Their level of belief in their ability is obviously a great deal higher than the average person. But I would bet they still had moments of doubt.

The truth is you are worthy and capable of achieving anything you put your mind to. I will continue to reiterate this throughout the book because it is the ultimate and only truth, and as you believe this more and more fully you will grow to be absolutely unstoppable.

You were born worthy and deserving and that has never changed. The only thing that did change was your limiting beliefs and misconceptions about this truth. Decide now to let them go and stop allowing them to shape your future and results and prevent you from putting all your heart and soul into your goals and dreams.

7. Negative emotions such as anger, resentment, shame, guilt, sadness, grief, frustration, hopelessness, etc.

Any emotion that causes discomfort is born from fear. Love and fear are the only two real emotions. I've highlighted other negative emotions here because we gradually accumulate and store negative energy in the form of these emotions in our energy systems and our bodies. They have a very powerful effect on our ability to achieve what we want as they become trapped within our energy systems and stop us from unleashing our greatness, shining our brilliance and being our truly powerful selves.

7. What Have You Decided?

Let's take anger as an example. Anger is an emotion that has a number of effects on our lives when it gets trapped in our energy system. One effect is it potentially blocks wealth and prevents you from ever achieving the results you desire.

Have you ever wondered why we have road rage, shopping rage, sport rage, and even surf rage? It's because from the day we are born we're told anger is not an acceptable emotion, and prevented from expressing it. We aren't taught how to process anger in a healthy manner and as most people are uncomfortable with anger as an emotion, we're made to think there's something wrong with us if we feel angry. So, instead of dealing with it intelligently, we internalise it. This is the same for all the other negative emotions.

If we were taught emotional intelligence, in other words, to process our emotions when they arise in a healthy and appropriate way, we wouldn't have all the emotional and mental illness that people are suffering from in epidemic proportions today.

When I refer to processing and expressing these emotions, I don't mean that when you're angry you go around punching walls, yelling at people or acting out your anger. I mean you learn how to process your emotions and let them flow through you without negatively impacting other people, yourself, or your environment.

We are human, and a wonderful part of being human is we get to feel the exquisiteness of a huge range of emotions. They are also what Abraham Hicks calls our 'emotional guidance scale'. Our emotions are a critical piece to knowing when we're on track and moving in the right direction.

Without our emotions, we would be lost, confused and unable to point ourselves in the right direction.

Think about this and the fact that more than 50% of our population is medicated to not feel their emotions. How can we successfully navigate life when our navigation system has been shut down and medicated away?

All our emotions are there for a reason, and when processed effectively, they're all wonderful. When not processed properly, they don't actually go away. Instead, they get stuck in our energy system and in our bodies causing disruption and eventually we become sick because these trapped negative emotions are toxic to our bodies.

Scientific studies have shown that the most toxic of all emotions are shame and guilt. Taking a sample of people's sweat as they felt particular emotions led to the discovery of this fact. Under controlled conditions, testing was done to measure the corresponding level of acidity within the body in response to a triggered emotion. The more toxic the emotion, the greater the level of acidity in the body secreted through the sweat glands.

When you think about this it makes perfect sense that trapped negative emotions cause illness because the acidity is literally eating away at your cells.

These emotions also affect your behaviour, actions and the level of success you achieve in your life.

If you want to be truly successful and be the best you can be, you must learn to be emotionally intelligent, releasing and processing your emotions as they arise, allowing them to flow through you without interference.

7. What Have You Decided?

- Awareness is the first step in this process.
- Learning the tools to do this is the second vital step.
- Using them consistently and effectively is the final piece of the puzzle.

Now you know the seven most common blocks to success and wealth, what are you going to do with this information?

There are so many powerful tools that we have access to which help to overcome and release our fears, doubts, limiting beliefs and negative emotions so they don't stop us from living our lives to the fullest.

I've done dozens of videos using Emotional Freedom Technique, and I've use it with all of my clients consistently as one of my primary techniques to create positive change. I encourage you to use tapping on a daily basis in your life on absolutely everything. Its effectiveness is truly mind-blowing and, when you use it with an open heart and mind, it will create extraordinary change in your life and free you to be able to achieve things you never imagined possible.

One of my other favourite techniques is Sound Healing. As a Master Sound Healer, I have found sound to be one of the most powerful tools for changing consciousness and bringing people closer to their connection with their true selves.

This is why I've included a sound healing CD as a part of this book and I encourage you to spend time in meditation listening to it daily to help you reconnect with your true, limitless, magnificent self and discover the greatness that lies within you. The truth of who you are is so astonishing that it will take your breath away.

No matter what you have decided in the past, you can always make a new decision. So, will you decide to play it safe and live a life of mediocrity until you die feeling unfulfilled, regretful, disappointed and dissatisfied?

Or will you decide right now to create a vision worthy of your brilliance and give everything you have in its pursuit until you've achieved it?

It's your choice, all you have to do is decide!

7. What Have You Decided?

~ *Key Reflections* ~

1. Every result in life is preceded by a decision, either conscious or unconscious. Your decisions shape your destiny. Those who achieve great things decide they are going to go for their dreams and make them happen by taking deliberate, progressive steps toward their goal every day.

2. What stops us from reaching for the stars is our limiting beliefs, stories, paradigms and conditioning that tell us we're not good enough, it's not safe or we don't deserve to have what we want. The fast track to your success is to discover what these limiting stories are, and release them.

3. There are seven common blocks that stop most people from being all they can be. Once you know what they are you can use a variety of powerful mindset and transformation tools to set yourself free from being imprisoned by them any longer.

8. The Power Of Surrender

There is a powerful unseen force underpinning all of creation that, when we give it permission to work with us, for us and through us, helps us to transcend anything we have imagined we're capable of achieving.

When I speak of surrender, I'm not speaking of waving your little white flag, shouting "I give up" and walking away from your dreams. The only way to fail is to give up and not participate in life. That is the ultimate failure.

No. When I speak of surrender I'm referring to stopping the insane struggling and pushing against the Universal Intelligence that can see everything, knows exactly what we need, and provides it to us at exactly the right time and place. When we fight what is, we're exhausting our power in a futile attempt to force our will upon the Universe.

There is a saying, "What you resist, persists" which means, when you push against the circumstances you have in your life, you just give them more energy that continues the cycle. Judging 'what is' as wrong doesn't change anything. To the contrary, it creates an opposing force that lends energy to the situation, helping to perpetuate what you're resisting.

Mother Theresa famously said, "I will never attend an anti-war rally. When you have a peace rally, invite me."

We get what we focus on, so when we focus on what we don't want, we get more of what we don't want. When you make conditions, situations, circumstances and people in your life wrong, you are simply adding fuel to the fire of what you don't want.

Accept what is, whether you like it or not, and use all your energy to create what you do want from that place.

Esther Hicks and Abraham call it contrast, and from the contrast of our life we get to know what we don't want so we can create what we do want. Without contrast, we would never know what we actually want.

Here's an exercise that you can do quickly in a few seconds as you sit and read. Raise your hands to chest height and put them into the prayer position. Now push with both hands, exerting equal and opposite force. No matter how hard you push, your hands don't move. They can't because they're both met with equal resistance.

Now put your hands in the same position and push with just one hand. When that force is met with no resistance, the other hand simply pushes through and the force disappears altogether.

Use this analogy to think about the circumstances or people showing up in your life that you don't like. It's not that you let them railroad you and knock you over. Instead, you accept what is, and redirect your powerful focus and energy away

8. The Power Of Surrender

from what you don't want, and use the situation to fuel the creation of what you do want.

We have been conditioned that life is meant to be a struggle, and the only way to survive is to persistently and relentlessly endure the difficulties in our life and push against them.

Super achievers face challenges every single day and take massive action to solve them and bring their vision into existence. They have an innate ability to work with the forces that compel them to strive for more and more, not against them.

Whilst training as an opera singer, one day, I realised that it wasn't about 'producing' the voice and making it do what I wanted it to do, but setting up the instrument to 'allow' the voice to do what it knew how to do naturally. Strangely, after much of my years of training, I had to learn to undo a lot of what I had either learned to do or was just doing on autopilot out of habit.

As a singer, I can't see my instrument like other musicians. Just like you, I've learned from childhood to engage my vocal chords to produce particular sounds on autopilot. So to produce a particular note, I must trust my apparatus to know exactly what to do and I just focus on placing the particular note I need to sing to produce the purest sound I'm capable of with as little interference as possible.

It's surprisingly difficult to 'leave the voice alone' and allow it to do its best work, as it was divinely designed to do. At the same time, it's necessary to provide it with the best possible support by utilising the breathing muscles, facial muscles, resonating cavities and mouth, to facilitate the purest sound I possibly can. Doing this with one note is hard enough, then you have to do it with multiple notes in quick succession. It really is quite an art form.

This is the perfect analogy for the easiest and most effective way to live life and achieve more than you ever imagined possible.

Far from being a sign of weakness, surrender is something that takes courage, faith, and an understanding that transcends your current human conditioning. It is the process I am using to write this book, as I surrender to the higher power that has been calling me to pen this manuscript for many months. A calling I've been resisting and am finally ready to surrender to.

You are reading this because something within you called you to it. Surrender to the Universal Intelligence in you that called you to pick up this book. This is a time when you are greatly needed. Take whatever you need from its pages as I guide you through a journey to the deepest part of you. Then you will be able to access the truth and resources you require to be the best you can be, and unleash your greatness onto the planet.

When I refer to surrendering, I am alluding to the art of allowing that many great teachers have been preaching in various ways for many years.

From the time we are born, we're exposed to conflicting information about our existence. We're taught life is a fight and a struggle and that, in order to survive, we must wake up every day ready to go into battle. If we survive the day, we're doing a good job and we get to do it all again tomorrow.

8. The Power Of Surrender

Rarely are we taught to reach for joy in every moment, or see the perfection in our lives. Can you remember being trained how to love yourself and others unconditionally, be in flow, yield to life, and leverage the energy of the Universe to create your life effortlessly by design? I don't think so.

Some of the greatest teachers of our time, such as Eckhart Tolle, Wayne Dyer, Abraham Hicks, Deepak Chopra, Bob Proctor, Byron Katie and so many others have been teaching these principles for many years. Their teachings seem to be in stark contrast to everything we've been exposed to and worked with all our lives. Although our hearts and deeper knowing yearn to follow these teachings, we struggle to understand how it can be true when all the evidence we have suggests otherwise.

Having spent decades struggling through life, we're afraid to surrender and let go in case we get mowed down, trampled and beaten up by life because we've let our guard down. We're terrified to show our vulnerability because "It's a jungle out there" and "Life wasn't meant to be easy."

Like the dragon that protects its vulnerable soft spot from its adversaries, sharing our feelings and exposing our emotions to the world is perceived to be giving our enemies, who are apparently everywhere, ammunition to bring us to our knees and deal the fatal blow.

The process of surrendering to your higher self, to your calling, to the wisdom that resides within you, can be extremely confronting and challenging. On the flip side, its rewards are infinitely more satisfying than continuing to battle your way through life, gathering mere crumbs from the plate of abundance. Nothing can compare to what you're capable of achieving and receiving when working in harmony with Universal Intelligence and the power you have within.

Surrendering is an act of faith and true understanding of the nature of our existence. It's yielding to the highest power within us, around us, that works through us and gives us great power and strength. This act alone makes you far more powerful than any force that will come against you as you have greater clarity, access to your creativity, inspiration, and the ability to turn any situation to your favour.

A tree in a storm bends to the forces of the wind that blows against it, because if it attempts to stand rigid, the wind will surely break it in half.

Small seedlings find a way through cement just by surrendering to the power of Mother Nature's quest for life and growth. They don't use sheer force, but the power of intention to find a way, as their yearning for the light is greater than the rigid force of the cement that stands in their way.

As water flows downstream, it has an inbuilt intelligence that knows its destination and moves continuously toward it, all the while weaving around rocks and fallen logs and other obstacles in its way. It doesn't try to push back against those obstacles but works with the forces of nature to find the path available to it with the least amount of effort.

This is what surrendering is. Working with, and being guided by, the forces and intelligence of the Universe to achieve your vision with ease and grace. If you think this means you do nothing, or you won't have to face and overcome challenges, then you're mistaken. If you remain in a state of

8. The Power Of Surrender

inertia, forces will come to set you in motion because the Universe is in a continual state of growth and it stimulates growth and change in us.

Challenges are an inevitable part of our life on this planet as they are our invitation to grow and become more of who we truly are. If you are not growing, you are dying. If you are not evolving, you are dissolving. It's how you interpret and respond to the challenges you're faced with that determine the outcome you achieve.

High performing athletes driven to achieve the pinnacle of their sport will endure physical pain and torment throughout their career as they punish their bodies in the pursuit of achieving more and more. This is a result of our naturally competitive nature and spirit.

However, I don't believe this relentless quest, sometimes beyond our normal physical and mental endurance, is healthy, or necessary, to achieve greatness. When we drive ourselves beyond our breaking point, we are not working with, but against the forces of nature. But it is what our society demands and celebrates of those who want to achieve great things. The question is, how big a price is too big?

When sports became professional, and money, not personal achievement, became the prize, media became involved, and sports stars were pushed to achieving more and more. Some individuals and teams are even electing to resort to performance-enhancing drugs to achieve that elusive competitive edge.

Whilst obviously still fuelled by passion, and highly driven, amazingly gifted athletes are now part of a machine that is relentless in the almost impossible standards it is demanding of them.

Superstars like Lance Armstrong, Marion Jones, Ben Johnson and Maria Sharapova, revered champions in their respective sports, irreparably damaged their reputations and their careers, bringing shame upon themselves and their sports, when caught cheating by taking drugs.

One of our greatest Australian sporting teams, the Essendon Football Club of Australia Rules Football, has been embroiled in a doping scandal for the last couple of years that has not only rocked the club but the entire Australian Rules Football code. The players themselves were unwitting pawns in this obsessive quest for winning and they're the ones who have paid most dearly for the betrayal by the club they gave their careers to and trusted to do the right thing by them. Perhaps they should have asked more questions and be less trusting. Were they afraid if they asked too many questions, they would jeopardise the careers they had worked so hard for, particularly with so many other gifted sports people hungrily vying for their privileged position? If they'd asked questions, would they have been told the truth?

Did each of these athletes have a personal choice? Yes. Are they responsible for those choices? Of course. But there's something wrong with a system where elite athletes and sporting teams feel driven to take drugs to get that competitive edge. I believe it's another symptom of a world gone mad and out of control, constantly revering the competitive spirit and the obsession to win at all costs.

We loudly applaud those willing to risk everything and put their bodies and lives on the line, while 'losers' are quickly forgotten, if ever recognised at all. When even the highest achievers retire, are injured or just fall by the wayside, they too become absent memories of a bygone era. Once glorified, they become nobody. Often sports people who retire sink into a self-destructive cycle of depression and abuse because they're not prepared for a life beyond the competitive obsession of their sport. It has come to define them. Is this truly a system we can honestly say is for the good of humankind?

In the world of business, a vast number of people are over-stressed, anxious, exhausted, depressed, and suffering other mental illness, but it is still never enough. The rigours and demands of business and the corporate world, obsessed with gaining a competitive edge, have turned us into unwitting slaves; driving us into the ground in the quest for ever-increasing profits, without any care for our personal wellbeing. Only those at the very top are reaping the benefits for which we sacrifice our physical and mental health, our relationships, and our happiness. Is this a system you wish to continue to participate in and give your life for?

We've lost the art of balance and the ability to experience the satisfaction of just being in the moment and giving something our very best without the need to beat everyone else in the game.

Is it important to strive for excellence? Yes, but not at the expense of our long-term mental, physical and emotional health, or the expense of others. It should never be solely about competition with others but striving to be the best we can be in every moment and discovering the beauty and satisfaction of achieving our personal best every day.

The system is broken. It's time for a new system to emerge and it's up to us to pioneer that system and bring sanity back to an insane world. We each have greatness within us, and our true greatness cannot be realised under the extraordinary pressures we are placed under to constantly perform above and beyond our capacity.

Paradoxically, we are, in fact, capable of far more than we believe we are capable of achieving. Only by surrendering to the power within us will we ever realise our true magnificence and greatness. Living up to, or down to, the expectations of others won't cut it. It's when we set our own standards for the achievement of excellence that our true power and genius is revealed.

How do you do this? When everything you're exposed to and conditioned by is calling for your blood, sweat and tears just to climb the ladder of relentless achievement, how do you rebel against the tide of conformity? The answer is by yielding to the forces that lie within you waiting to be harnessed and released into the world, in a tornado of might you could not possibly unleash without collaborating with a connection to Source.

Don't get me wrong. Hard work, dedication, commitment, tenacity, persistence, resilience and going beyond our perceived limits are essential if you want to be the best you can be, and live a life that transcends your wildest dreams. The question is what are you working for? What vision are you dedicating your time and resources to? What cause are you committed to? Are your goals in alignment with your values and are they big enough to inspire you and yet still something you believe you can achieve given where you're right now?

8. The Power Of Surrender

In all honesty, I have spent most of my life in a relentless push to be better, do more and achieve more, according to impossible benchmarks and goals I would set for myself. I set goals according to what I believed to be acceptable, relying on society's high achievers to be my litmus test, and failing to acknowledge the achievements I had accomplished along the way because they didn't match up with my impossible standards.

Consequently, nothing I achieved was ever good enough. It would send me into a frustrating pattern of bursts of relentless hard work, dedication and striving, followed by periods of downtime, inertia and feelings of disappointment and hopelessness. It was tiring, frustrating, often unproductive and very disempowering. Talk about self-sabotage. It also meant that I remained stuck in a destructive pattern where I went nowhere fast. My external results were far less than I could have achieved had I started where I was and acknowledged my achievements along the way.

It's amazing how we fail to see our own patterns of self-sabotage until either someone else points them out, or we step back and surrender to the ever-present intelligence of the Universe that's always calling us forward into its grace. Interestingly, we never see them until we're ready to.

Grace is a powerful gift that can only be received when we're in a state of flow. This is when we ask for help and allow ourselves to be guided by Universal Intelligence in the direction we need to go. Grace enables the Universe to do eighty percent of the heavy lifting for us, but this help will not be provided until we ask for it, and allow ourselves to receive it.

I recently had a discussion with an extraordinary visionary who has created a large multi-million dollar business helping ordinary individuals and families to become wealthy through investment strategies. During this conversation, he surprised me by saying that people talk to him about flow, but he had never personally experienced flow and didn't believe in it.

This threw me initially and made me begin to question one of my fundamental beliefs. How could someone who had achieved so much and is such an incredible visionary, not experience, or believe in, the power of flow? Had I been wrong all this time?

Then, over the next several days, I observed his environment. It was chaotic and stressful and seemed to be at odds with itself every step of the way. Yet somehow, this incredible man, whom I greatly admire, was achieving things in spite of the fact that he wasn't in flow. Imagine what he could achieve if he was in flow and used the power of the Universe to support his vision? The stress would fall away and unseen forces would come to bear that, would pick up his vision and carry it onto as yet unimagined heights and possibilities beyond what even he had dared to dream.

When you're being true to yourself and surrendering to your highest power, work becomes play. You no longer count the hours spent on your work, but instead eagerly anticipate dedicating your time to sharing your gifts and talents in service of others. Your work becomes an

8. The Power Of Surrender

obsession, not because of the money you earn, or the awards you achieve, but because you're lost in the joyful pursuit of doing what you love the most: Utilising your innate abilities to transform the lives of others through satisfying a desire, or fulfilling a need, so they can enjoy life to the fullest.

Imagine a world where people were encouraged, supported and rewarded to serve others from a place of ease and joy, pursuing the endeavours they love the most and are gifted in. Is that a world you would love to live in? Is that a way you would like to live your life? If it is, then choose that for yourself, and encourage others to choose it also through your example. Decide right now to stop supporting and participating in a system that is on a path of the relentless pursuit of more and more, irrespective of the cost or personal and environmental destruction it causes.

It's time to surrender to the power within you and rise above the system that's been repressing you and keeping you from realising the incredible forces lying dormant inside of you. It is calling you to release the greatness within you and to show the rest of the world there is another way. A better way. A way that does not require painful sacrifice or hollow rewards. A way that means the liberation of all humankind, animals and Mother Nature to glorious heights of joy, love, peace and freedom.

Are you willing to dedicate your life to that pursuit? Is this a utopian ideal? Absolutely! I believe our life can be a utopian existence. Sadly we've unwittingly been conditioned to listen to authorities outside of ourselves, who don't necessarily have our best interests at heart, and seek to exploit us for their own gain. It's time to say enough! We're not playing by those rules anymore.

It's time for a revolution that requires you to surrender to your truth, your infinite power, and claim your divine right of freedom to live your life the way you choose, not by anybody else's ideals, rules, systems or principles. It's time for a revolution of your heart, mind and soul!

8. The Power Of Surrender

~ *Key Reflections* ~

1. There is a powerful unseen force underpinning all of creation that, when we give it permission to work with us, for us and through us, helps us to transcend anything we have imagined we're capable of achieving.

2. Surrendering is an act of faith and true understanding of the nature of our existence. It's yielding to the highest power within us, around us, that works through us and gives us great power and strength. It is working with, and taking inspired action on the guidance we receive from Universal Intelligence.

3. Trust and have faith that the Universe is conspiring in your favour, and surrender to it's infinite wisdom. Stay curious about what's showing up for you and how it is for your highest good and guiding you toward your purpose and achieving your vision. Take inspired action from the place of surrender and faith, and watch magic and miracles unfold.

9. What Is Seeking To Emerge?

This is a powerful question I recently experienced at a Think Tank in Brazil with 46 brilliant minds and social entrepreneurs called "The Unstoppables."

This question, along with others that I will share with you, will help you to uncover more of your brilliance. They will serve you for the rest of your life in navigating the great unknown realms of the subconscious mind, calling on it to bring the best possible outcomes for you.

The truth is, the future, your future, lies in you being able to tap into the unseen, unexplored magic that lies just beneath the surface of your conscious mind. You unlock your unconscious genius by asking the right questions because the quality of the questions you ask will determine the quality of your answers. It's simple. If you want better results, ask better questions.

The majority of people, either directly or indirectly, ask questions like:

Why am I always broke?

Why can't he / she behave the way I want them to?

What's wrong with me?

What's wrong with them?

Why doesn't anything ever work out for me?

What am I doing wrong?

Why are they so mean?

Why do I do such stupid things?

Why do they do such stupid things?

Why can't I get it right?

Why is life so hard?

Why me?

These type of questions will only serve to produce more of the results you're already getting, as the core of your focus is on the results you're already getting and how they're all wrong, instead of the results you desire.

Energy flows where attention goes. Earl Nightingale said, "You get what you think about most of the time." In other words, you get what you focus on. If you focus on what you don't want and everything that's going wrong, you'll create more of that. When you focus on what you do want, your world changes and you start to create and attract events and circumstances that get you closer to what you want.

The super successful and wealthy have used this principle, either consciously or unconsciously, for thousands of years. Now it's time for you to employ this powerful tenet yourself to create your life by design instead of by default.

9. What Is Seeking To Emerge?

Your subconscious mind has no judgement about your results. It only serves to produce what you focus on as its only job is to match where you place your attention, to your results. If you're focusing on something you don't want, it doesn't understand that and just produces more of what you don't want.

A list of empowering questions that will change your results are:

- Where's the perfection in this situation?
- What am I pretending not to know?
- What's right about this?
- What can I learn from this?
- How can I turn this situation into a blessing?
- What do I need to do to achieve better results?
- Who do I need to become to achieve my goals?
- How does it get any better than this?
- What else is possible?
- How much am I really capable of?
- What do I need to know to achieve my goals?
- What books do I need to read to change my internal and external game?
- Who do I need to meet to have a positive influence on my life and results?
- What's in it for them?
- What problem am I uniquely equipped to solve for others that will change their world?
- How can I serve?
- What is seeking to emerge?

Can you see how the nature of these questions shifts your focus and will help to change your results, and quickly?

Training the mind in this way requires you to be present and vigilant, particularly in the beginning. The mind is mostly on automatic. You think approximately 60,000 thoughts a day. For the average person, 65% to 75% of those thoughts are negative and 80% to 90% are the same thoughts you thought yesterday, and the day before that, and the day before that, and the day before that, etc.

When you consider our thoughts drive our behaviour and produce our results, it comes as no surprise why most of us aren't achieving what we really want. It feels like our lives are out of control, and no wonder when you realise where our minds are focused most of the time.

The truth is, our lives are always in our control and we are creating our lives every single moment of every single day. All it takes is a shift in perspective and focus to change everything in an instant.

Will everything we want turn up overnight? No. That's not the way our Universe works. But, when you change your thoughts and your focus, you will start to see slight shifts almost immediately. This will gain momentum and speed until you're seeing the things you want show up far more quickly than you anticipated, just from asking different questions and changing your focus from what you don't want to what you do want.

If you consider Unicorn companies like Uber, SpaceX, Pinterest, Snapchat and Airbnb, they launched into the global business space asking a powerful question similar to "What is seeking to emerge?"

9. What Is Seeking To Emerge?

Unicorns are private start-ups worth more than a billion dollars. They seek to solve a problem and disrupt an industry by creating a unique solution to that problem. Their founders are creative, bold, solution focused, innovative, disruptive and relentless in their pursuit of excellence.

The saying is, if you want to be a billionaire, solve a problem for a billion people. The way to create sustainable wealth is to solve a problem or fill a need. This is why disruptive companies are so profitable. They take an industry where they see limitations and potential for development and solve those limitations using creativity and ingenuity.

Highly successful entrepreneurs are lateral thinkers and don't allow the limitations of their perceived reality or popular culture to restrict their ability to come up with new ways to solve a problem.

Revolutionary companies like Uber and Airbnb don't need to build and maintain infrastructure, hire hundreds or even thousands of staff, apply for or issue licences, meet strict regulations and endure audits and inspections, implement complex systems and structures, etc. They took infrastructure that was already available and helped to make it available to the public. This simultaneously gave the wider population an opportunity to create another stream of income using the resources they already owned. Pure genius.

These companies bend the rules, and in some cases break them. Because Uber and Airbnb moved fast and grew virtually overnight, they caught the current monopolistic players in those industries napping. These industries had not changed significantly in decades and they were not asking, "What is seeking to emerge?" They thought they had it all sewn up. Uber and Airbnb would never have had a chance to emerge, and become so big so quickly if the current players had not become complacent about the service they were providing.

They grew so fast that, although they didn't comply with current laws and regulations, somehow they got away with it. Regulations have been changed and new laws introduced to accommodate them. Perhaps governments saw the benefits to the community and tourism and decided to let it slide. Or maybe, because they grew so fast, they knew the horse had already bolted and it was too hard to rein it back in. Either way, these companies managed to change the nature of entire industries.

What is seeking to emerge in your industry? What problems are you uniquely equipped to solve with your gifts and talents? What problems are crying out for you to step up? Start to get creative, think outside the square and come up with new solutions to an old problem and do something about it before someone else beats you to it.

There is another question I have found particularly powerful and I return to regularly and that is, "What am I pretending not to know?" We become so blinded by our paradigms and limiting beliefs that solutions to problems are often right in front of us, but we fail to see them because we aren't asking the right questions.

You can ask this question in relation to your health, your relationships, your career, your spirituality, in fact, with any situation or challenge that presents itself. It will help you to

9. What Is Seeking To Emerge?

discover the solution that's waiting to be discovered. It can also help you to head off problems before they occur.

When a problem occurs, there is nearly always a lead-up and warning signs before the problem actually becomes a problem. Imagine if you were to sit down each week and focus on an area of your life and ask the question, "What am I pretending not to know?" Most problems occur because we fail to see, or even ignore, the warning signs.

Take health for instance. If you're feeling tired, breathless, stressed or just generally not at the top of your game, don't dismiss these feelings as just 'getting older' or 'stress'. Instead, ask the question, "What am I pretending not to know?" Do you think you might be able to address any lifestyle choices you're making that could be damaging your health before it becomes a potentially serious issue in the future?

Remember, one out of every three people end up with either heart disease or cancer or both. These diseases are avoidable and if you're paying attention, you can prevent them from occurring if you change some choices that are potentially contributing to the condition before it arises.

One in two marriages end in divorce. Imagine if each person in the relationship were to take time out once a month to ask the question, "What am I pretending not to know?" in their relationship. Do you think you would have a better chance to prevent any disconnect, conflict, resentment and unhappiness, and rectify the problem before it ends in a bitter, messy, expensive divorce? Of course, you would.

On numerous occasions, I've heard people say they were getting on with their busy, stressful lives when suddenly, to their complete surprise, their partner said, "I'm not happy, I want out." Or a partner has an affair, which is a classic sign of discontent in the relationship. Rarely does this happen overnight and if you're paying attention, you'd be able to see this coming and potentially do something about it before it gets beyond the point of no return.

Back in the world of business, there are of course innovators such as Steve Jobs who solved a problem we didn't even realise we had. He was so creative he managed to provide a range of communication devices that, once we were presented with, we just had to have.

Smartphones revolutionised global communication and altered every industry and person's life significantly. We behave differently, work differently, play differently, relate differently and think differently all because of the smartphone. Entire industries were created because of smart devices, and we now have more access to information, technology and the world than ever before as a result.

It has, in turn, caused other problems like the fact that, whilst we may be now much more connected globally, we are further disconnected from each other locally. Not to mention the personal disconnect from who we truly are as we have the distraction of social media at our fingertips 24/7. They've also fuelled the growing problem of an inability to focus for any significant period of time. Either our devices distract us, or we're afraid we're missing out.

Seeing the world the way Steve Jobs saw it is an ability we all have, but very few will exercise. Visionaries like him are

9. What Is Seeking To Emerge?

few and far between. That doesn't mean you can't have a significant positive impact on the world. Utilising your knowledge, gifts, talents and unconscious competence you can have a significant impact on your industry, and provide solutions to problems in a way that haven't been provided before. Dare to be disruptive.

The trick is to keep asking questions like, "What is seeking to emerge?" and then keep an open mind and stay intensely curious. Decide not to be locked in by the paradigms that restrain the rest of the population and go beyond the limitations of what already exists. Do not dismiss any ideas or inspirations that come to you. What seems ridiculous may turn out to be a feasible idea when you begin to explore it.

I'm sure that when Steve Jobs pitched his ideas to his engineers, many of them thought he was crazy on more than one occasion. The same goes for Henry Ford, Thomas Edison, Guglielmo Marconi and Alexander Bell. In fact, Marconi's family tried to commit him to an asylum for thinking he could create a device to transmit and receive radio waves over great distances. Thankfully they didn't succeed.

Never underestimate your ability to be extraordinary. You were born extraordinary and the only thing preventing you from expressing that to the world are the limiting beliefs you've adopted. Replace them with the belief anything is possible and you're capable of achieving anything you put your mind to. You'll be amazed at what will unfold.

The idea and inspiration may not come to you for days, weeks, even months. What's important is you keep asking the question and staying open to all possibilities.

What you're destined to bring into existence is waiting for you to drop the illusion that you're not good enough, that something is missing and it has to be hard. What will make this journey infinitely easier is recognising your unconscious competence. This is your core genius, your gift to the world.

Discovering your unconscious competence is simple. Again, it's all about the quality and type of questions you ask. What do you play at that others have to work at? What do you do that people compliment you on but you've never considered anything special? What do you love to do so much that you frequently get lost in it and lose track of time? If there was one thing you could do for the rest of your life and never get tired of it, what would it be?

Write a list of the things you do well effortlessly, the things that come easily to you. Don't dismiss anything. You'll be surprised what you discover.

We all possess gifts and talents that were bestowed upon us when we arrived. These talents are a part of our divine mission, but because those things come so easily, we dismiss them as nothing special. We fail to see how unique and gifted we are in those areas because we assume everyone finds them easy, when in fact the opposite is the case.

This is why it's so important to work with your passion and your gifts and talents to create a life you love. What are you passionate about? What legacy do you want to leave? What difference do you want to make? What situation in the world breaks your heart that you would like to change?

The answers to these questions all point to your divine mission. As was the case with visionaries like Jobs, Bell, Marconi and Edison, who knows where your idea may

9. What Is Seeking To Emerge?

lead or how many lives it will change? We are living in extraordinary times where there are no limits or boundaries to what's possible. I'm continually amazed and in awe of the huge number of amazing innovations I see being brought into existence.

If you're struggling for inspiration, all you need to do is visit some of the crowdfunding platforms like www.indiegogo.com, www.kickstarter.com, www.gofundme.com, www.pozible.com, or www.rockethub.com. There you will find incredible innovations that will give you an idea of what's possible when you apply your creativity to a problem.

If you're not convinced you have the creative ability to do this, decide to put aside that limiting belief for a while and stay curious. Allow yourself to explore the possibilities. Pose the particular problem to your subconscious mind and allow that part of your mind to come up with a solution. Don't search for it. Wait for it to come. Release your impatience and trust the answer will appear when it's ready. Your job in all of this is to pay attention.

The answer will be presented to you, but possibly not in the way you expect. It could come from a book, a TV program, a workshop, a seemingly random conversation, in the shower, or on a walk. Steve Jobs is just one of the many entrepreneurs who was known to take long walks daily to focus, solve problems and receive inspiration.

Make a commitment to eliminate "I can't" from your vocabulary, and instead ask, "How can I?" Stay curious and open to the infinite possibilities of the Universe.

It doesn't matter if you're an entrepreneur, a visionary, or an employee, there is always a way you can rethink the way things are done in your field, and create solutions that will benefit others and a different future for yourself.

Never underestimate your greatness, your ability to make a significant difference. Just stay focused on service.

There is a story about a man who was walking along a beach. The beach was covered with thousands of starfish that had been washed up on the shore. As the man walked, he came across a boy who was diligently picking up one starfish at a time and throwing it back into the ocean.

The man was intrigued by the boy and stopped to ask him, "Little boy, why are you spending your time throwing these starfish back into the ocean? There are so many of them, you can't possibly make a difference throwing them back in."

The little boy didn't miss a beat as he picked up yet another starfish and threw it back into the water, looked up at the man and said, "It made a difference to that one."

You may not be able to solve the whole world's problems, but you can serve the person who presents to you at any given moment. It doesn't even have to be a revolutionary act. It may be as simple as a smile or a kind word. Yet, sadly, these simple acts are becoming increasingly rare in a world that seems to be becoming more and more insular and at odds with itself.

As you pay attention to the people around you, observe their needs, wants and desires. You'll learn how you can best serve, what is seeking to emerge, what you are pretending not to know, and what difference you can make that will not only change the lives of others but your life as well.

9. What Is Seeking To Emerge?

~ *Key Reflections* ~

1. The Universe is always providing answers to your questions. The quality of the questions you ask will determine the quality of the answers you receive. Most people ask poor quality questions and wonder why they get poor results. If you want to change your results, change the type of questions you ask.

2. The way to create sustainable wealth is to solve a problem or fill a need. If you want to be a billionaire, solve a problem for a billion people. Successful disruptive companies are profitable because they see an unfulfilled need and seek to fill that need using creativity and ingenuity.

    Highly successful entrepreneurs are lateral thinkers and don't allow the limitations of their perceived reality or popular culture to restrict their ability to come up with new ways to solve a problem.

3. You get what you focus on. If you're asking questions that focus on the problem, you'll get an answer that features the problem. When you ask questions that open space for a solution, and allow the Universe to guide you to the answer, solutions will appear seemingly from nowhere. This is how you engage infinite possibilities and leverage the power of your subconscious mind.

10. Ten Things I Learned From Millionaires In 10 Days

In February 2016 I was privileged to take a trip to Brazil with 46 extraordinary social entrepreneurs, philanthropists and business leaders who are dedicated not only to their own success but to making a difference in the world and solving some of the biggest problems we're facing.

Committing to this journey was a transformational decision for me, and the trip delivered on so many levels. Financially, it was the single biggest commitment I had ever made to my business and myself. This aspect on its own created a big mental shift for me.

Its effects continue to reverberate for me in so many areas of my business and my life. It's certainly been the catalyst for some daring leaps of faith to take my business far beyond where it has been in the past and into an exciting new future with new horizons.

The wonderful people I met, and now meet with on a regular basis, constantly inspire me, challenge me and help me to continue to up-level my mindset. There is always another level to move to and more to achieve and going on this trip really demonstrated to me that anything really is possible.

I learned so much being immersed in an environment of high wealth individuals referred to as "The Unstoppables". Following are ten of the things I learnt from these super high achievers, many of whom are multi-millionaires. I share them here so you can benefit from my experience, learn how these people think, and embrace possibility thinking so you can achieve anything you put your mind to and unleash your greatness.

1. Self Care Is Essential

In order to take care of others, you must take care of yourself first. I saw this first hand on my trip with these larger than life philanthropic entrepreneurs. Many of them have created multi-million dollar businesses, some of them several times over. Their attention is now focused on leaving a legacy through social enterprise and helping others in a variety of capacities, such as sanitation, education and sustainability projects in 3rd world countries; creating solutions to environmental crises; mentoring other business owners to get better results; and supporting a variety of organisations who provide help for others less fortunate than themselves.

Their philosophy is, if you want to give $1,000,000, make $2,000,000. We've all heard the safety brief on the airplane as it's taxiing down the runway. In case of an emergency, fit our own oxygen mask first before helping others, including children. Whilst for many of us it may be a natural selfless tendency to try and help others first and ourselves last, this approach would only render us useless, possibly dead, and completely unable to help anyone else. The advice to quickly fit your own mask first before turning your attention to others means, once your needs are met, you have the capacity to focus purely on others and help more people. Plus there's an added bonus- you get to live another day.

This advice is definitely true not only in an airplane emergency but in business and all areas of your life. This can be particularly challenging for women who play many roles such as mothers, wives, in the workforce, have their own business, volunteering for school duties, or other organisations, etc. They have a tendency to spread themselves very thin and try to look after everyone else before they look after themselves. This inclination can be very damaging and has the potential to bring them undone as it creates overwhelm, stress, and exhaustion. They feel progressively more depleted and have less and less to give.

When you attend to your own needs first and make sure your cup is overflowing, you have so much more to give, with peace of mind and joy in your heart.

In order to do this, you must be open to receive. This is a major block for so many people, particularly women and spiritual people. We're taught it's better to give than to receive. This is a very destructive belief as it causes a grave imbalance in the natural flow of the Universe. It doesn't serve the receiver either.

In order for you to give, someone has to receive. So, according to the essence of the original statement, the giver is the 'better' person. This potentially provides the giver with a feeling of superiority, the receiver one of inferiority, and blocks your ability to receive because you're convinced giving is better.

It's commonly acknowledged you'll be rewarded financially in alignment with the level of value you provide to others. This is absolutely true, but only when you're open to receiving.

Giving and receiving are both equally important as each other. In fact, it isn't possible for you to continue to give endlessly if you're not also receiving. When both are in balance, and your cup is overflowing, you can give and give and give from an endless pool of resources because you're in a flow of giving and receiving.

Returning to one of the essential principles of having a highly profitable and sustainable business, you must be providing a quality service to people that either solve a problem or fulfil a need. So it's important you offer a solution to a problem first in order to receive, but then you must be open to receive straight away. This is what opens the flow. In the case of delivering a product, to ensure a fair exchange is made, you may provide the promise of the product first, and receive payment in advance before giving the product.

For many service-based industries, the service is provided first before payment is received. If you are a service-based provider like a coach, health practitioner or therapist, I would suggest putting together a package for the client, such as paying for four sessions in advance and receiving the fifth one free. Now you're able to provide a long-term

10. Ten Things I Learned From Millionaires In 10 Days

plan to solve their problem and can ask them to pay for the package in advance, prior to providing your service. This will help you to maintain your cash flow and client retention, which is very important for any service-based business.

Not being open to receive is a problem I had for many years. I was always giving, but I wasn't open to receiving in abundance. My business was generating a sporadic trickle, not a constant, reliable flow of income. It all came back to my one-sided equation where I wasn't open to receive in return for the tremendous value I was providing. I coached many people for free and, whilst some of these coaching sessions were conducted in exchange for their services, which proved extremely valuable, many were just out of the goodness of my heart. Now, whilst this made me feel good, it didn't help me create a sustainable business or achieve my vision of having a much greater impact in the world.

Truly understanding the importance of both sides of the giving AND receiving equation was a catalyst to turn things around. I realised that if I wasn't receiving, I would never be able to have the global impact I intended. Suddenly it became a priority.

Another issue potentially impacting your ability to receive is your self-worth. How much you value yourself, your time, and what you have to offer will directly affect the receiving equation. Personal development work around this piece will significantly impact your earning capacity and ability to command what you're truly worth. The vast majority of people underestimate their worth and, as a result, never receive the financial reward they deserve. Don't let this be you.

This concept of giving and receiving being an exchange that needs to be in balance is a simple and logical principle. Remarkably, it's one many spiritual entrepreneurs fail to embrace fully and it often brings them and their businesses unstuck before they really get off the ground. Sadly, this means the positive impact they have the potential to make is never fully realised.

2. You Must Back Yourself

If you want to succeed, you must be willing to back yourself, take calculated risks and do whatever it takes. A half-hearted attitude of "I'll just give it a try and see what happens" will not produce results.

Yoda said, "There is no try, there is only do." If you decide you're going to 'do' then, like so many people who've been seduced by the idea of being an entrepreneur, you can flap around on your own for a while, maybe even a long while, and never get much closer to your vision. You'll become increasingly more frustrated with your lack of results, and maybe even give up and walk away from your vision altogether. Alternatively, you can dive right in and get the job done right at the outset.

How do I know this? Because I was one of those who flapped around for some time trying to do everything on my own, stuck in the excuse that I didn't have any money or resources to hire the professional help I desperately needed. I have a good mind, I'm good with technology and I'm perfectly capable of doing most things myself, so

10. Ten Things I Learned From Millionaires In 10 Days

I didn't give myself permission to get help. This held me back from realising my true potential for several years. I also missed out on hundreds of thousands of dollars, or more, in potential income.

Committing to this journey with "The Unstoppables" was a significant leap of faith for me as it was a significant financial investment. Add the fact that I'm really not much of a traveller, and the flights to and from Brazil were 30+ hours each way, it was a daunting prospect for me. I didn't actually know what to expect or what the return on investment would be. I just knew I had to be there. It was a risk I was willing to take because I had a gut instinct that the returns would far outweigh the level of commitment.

The impact this had on my mindset was enormous. Now I was playing at a level I hadn't played at before. This sent a powerful message to my subconscious that I was bigger, bolder and capable of achieving so much more than my conscious perception and belief systems had been allowing me to believe.

At first, I felt like a fish out of water. I questioned what I was actually doing there. But as I gained new friends and insights, observed how people at that level of business operated, and started having new expansive types of conversations, my belief in myself grew exponentially. I adopted a whole new identity that said I deserved to be there and I was one of 'them'.

The size of that shift in mindset and its impact cannot be overstated. I was in an environment with people playing a much bigger game, and the quality and type of decisions I started to make, the conversations I had, and the ideas that started to flow, shifted accordingly. When I returned, I was ready to play a much bigger game and the return on the initial investment will repay me many times over.

What are you willing to do? What are you prepared to sacrifice? To what lengths are you willing to go, to achieve your goals? Are you prepared to not just get out of your comfort zone, but smash your comfort zone? Where are you going to invest in yourself and your business? How are you going to stretch yourself, your thinking, your resources? Who do you need on your team to take care of the things that are not the best use of your time, whilst you concentrate on your core genius?

It's okay to bootstrap for a while in your business, at least in the beginning. But if you need to do marketing and it's not a part of your core genius, find someone who can at least guide you in that area. As soon as you're able, hand that responsibility over to someone who really knows what they're doing.

Other professionals who will be invaluable to you is a bookkeeper, branding specialist, social media strategist, graphic designer, admin assistant, photographer (for publicity shots), website designer, marketing consultant, mastermind group and networking groups. Many of these are only going to be relevant to you as your business grows. However, you can outsource some of these tasks for a fraction of the cost of hiring someone for your business, and the return on investment will be invaluable.

There are many online services such as Fiverr, Upwork, 99 Designs and 48 Hours Logo that can provide you with some services at a reasonable price. Just remember you get what

10. Ten Things I Learned From Millionaires In 10 Days

you pay for. I would not leave my branding or marketing strategy up to someone on Fiverr for instance.

One investment you must be prepared to make is in a coach or mentor. No matter where you're in your business, someone to help guide you, show you your blind spots (we all have them), keep you accountable, help clear your blocks to move forward, build your faith in you, pick you up when you're down and celebrate with you as you achieve your milestones is invaluable and essential if you're going to be successful and achieve your goals and dreams.

Having a dedicated coach providing one on one coaching can be a significant investment, and whilst you will gain the most value from this kind of coaching, this may not be an option for you right in the beginning depending on your resources. If not, join a good group-coaching program, or purchase a program that guides you through some of the essentials in mindset and business strategies.

Read books, listen to audio, go to seminars and attend workshops. Whatever stage you're, be prepared to stretch yourself and your resources to get the best help you can afford, and start where you're. Most important of all - implement, implement, implement! Where most people go wrong is they keep listening to copious amounts of information, going to seminars and workshops but fail to implement what they learn. Nothing will happen if you don't implement your learnings.

The bottom line is to stop saying, "I can't afford it" because the reality is, if you want to be successful, you truly can't afford not to.

3. Collaboration Is The Key To A Sustainable Future

Every multi-millionaire on "The Unstoppables" trip had partnered and/or collaborated with multiple people to get to where they are. They also built a team of people who support them in achieving their vision every step of the way. They're well aware of their strengths and weaknesses and appreciate they can't do it on their own.

The entire trip was a think tank expedition. Every day, there were collaborative and supportive discussions taking place. We were helping each other to find solutions to problems, providing investment in startups, partnering with each other to attain mutually beneficial outcomes for the parties involved. There was no sign of competition or chest beating on the trip, just people with open minds seeking to support each other and be supported in whatever way they needed in order to expand and achieve the outcomes they wanted.

Who's on your team? Who's supporting you? Who are you collaborating with to achieve your goals? As mentioned in step number 2, stop trying to do everything on your own. You'll end up burned out, broke and broken.

You might collaborate with your colleagues, friends, networking buddies. You could create a mastermind group to collaborate with. You may seek out an investment partner, or a joint venture partner to help you build your business to the next level.

You may even have a business partner whom you work with to build your business and your success. If you take this option, always work out the divorce strategy before you plan the marriage. The reason this is essential is because

10. Ten Things I Learned From Millionaires In 10 Days

people's circumstances and needs change. If you don't have a potential exit strategy for a partner things could end up getting very messy.

For any partnership, have all the roles clear cut and well defined and have a way to resolve potential disputes. This sounds like you're preparing for the worst and in a way you are. This planning is essential. I've heard of and experienced the result of partnerships going bad and the headaches and stress this causes, particularly on handshake deals.

We had this in one of our own businesses in the past where my husband helped to create a potentially very lucrative company but was hampered at every turn by one of the partners who was abusive and divisive. Eventually, after investing thousands of dollars and hours into the company, my husband decided to resign as director and walk away from the company altogether, cutting his losses. The partnership was extremely stressful, affecting both of us emotionally and mentally, and there was no sign of any resolution in sight. The alternative of hanging in there just wasn't worth it. It was a tough lesson and certainly not a mistake we'll make again.

Some business partnerships are a match made in heaven. Some of the people on the trip who had created billion dollar businesses said they couldn't have done it without their business partner. It's important you have all the necessary paperwork drawn up and signed before any money is invested or time and energy committed to the business. This could save you a lot of stress down the road.

You could also collaborate with other businesses who have the same customers as you but are providing a non-competitive product or service. These kinds of collaborations are called Joint Venture (JV) Partnerships and can be extremely lucrative and beneficial to both businesses.

The agreement must be a win-win for both parties, so if you're thinking of approaching local businesses in your area with this in mind, make sure you have an enticing proposal with an offer they can't refuse. In return for you obtaining access to their customers, what do they receive? It might be a percentage of the revenue generated, a free gift for their customers that promotes goodwill for their business, free access to your services or something else that would be of value to them.

You could form or join a Mastermind Group where other professionals and like-minded people come together to discuss solutions to problems, innovative ideas and products, marketing concepts and execution, highlight potential challenges, trade professional services and expertise, receive valuable support and encouragement, provide accountability, and more. The saying "Two minds are better than one" is absolutely true. When you have a panel of like-minded people who have a variety of skills, knowledge and expertise working on each other's businesses, the benefits are invaluable. It's important when joining or forming a mastermind group that the people involved are on the same page and open to respectful collaboration.

Ultimately, when you collaborate, you multiply your efforts many times over. Seek to collaborate with others in every aspect of your business and not only will you find the journey a lot more fun and enjoyable, you'll get to where you want to be a great deal faster.

4. Nice Guys Can Finish First

"The Unstoppables" were seriously nice dudes with big hearts wanting to make the world a better place. They care about others and have a vision of using their skills, talents and excess resources to make a difference to the environment and humanity in some capacity.

Their businesses are built on service and commitment to excellence. They value and look after their employees knowing they are their best asset.

So often, our environment programs us to believe rich people are greedy, selfish, criminal, rude, arrogant, narcissistic, ruthless, thoughtless, heartless, don't care about others and will do anything to make money regardless of the consequences. Does this sound familiar? Were you exposed to any examples of this during your childhood?

Even if your household didn't demonstrate this kind of thinking, there would have been pockets of your environment where you saw these kinds of thoughts about wealthy people. You only have to look to some of the television programs and movies to find old and new favourites like *Gilligan's Island, Days of Our Lives, Dallas, Revenge, 101 Dalmatians, The Godfather, The Corporation, Limitless, The Wolf Of Wall Street* and *Wall Street* in which wealthy characters range from thoughtless to downright evil. Characters we love to hate who will stop at nothing, including murder, to get what they want and protect their interests. Compared to the heroes of the plot who are ordinary characters with average existences, very relatable for most of us, and are typically portrayed as nice, considerate, caring and thoughtful.

Is it any wonder subconsciously we don't want to identify with the characters who have money? We love to hate and revile these characters and would gladly step on them if they fell down in the street. Why would we want to be like, or be identified as that kind of person?

Whilst there are some people who are really like this in the world, fortunately, they are not typical of the majority of people with above average wealth.

We are currently seeing the emergence of a string of documentaries such as *Inside Job, The Big Short, Vaxxed, The Truth About Cancer, Zeitgeist, Thrive* and other compelling and very thought-provoking movies and series that demonstrate the dark side of insanely wealthy mega-corporations and industries run by megalomaniacs.

It's important to be informed about this side of the equation in order to bring back balance and harmony. It's even more important to recognise that there are many more examples of heart-centred, wealthy people intent upon making a positive difference in the world. People who give generously to worthy causes and help those less fortunate by dedicating their time, money and resources to bring about positive change.

This is what I saw from all of the people on my trip to Brazil, no matter what stage of business they were at. They're compassionate, kind, caring people who just happen to make a lot of money, and I am proud and honoured to call them my friends and colleagues. What I find really encouraging is they are just the tip of the iceberg.

Whilst our money system is corrupt and must change, money itself is not evil and doesn't have a conscience. It only serves to bring out and amplify traits that already exist. A genuinely kind and generous person who is self-confident and knows their own worth, will not be corrupted and turn nasty because they become wealthy. In fact, they'll show even more kindness and compassion toward others and demonstrate it with their wealth.

The bottom line on this particular point is that nice guys can and do finish first!

5. Ask For What You Want

If you don't ask, you don't get. It really is that simple. If you dare to ask for what you want, you might just get it. If you don't ask, then there's little, if any chance you'll get what you want.

During our time in the Amazon, we were invited to pitch our innovations and ideas to potential investors in the room. We were given multiple opportunities to do this and receive constructive feedback, so we could hone and polish our pitches, and make mistakes in a safe, supportive environment.

We learned you must be well prepared with your 'pitch' to a potential investor, and be able to present your business models complete with succinct, definitive explanations of the project. This includes details like marketplace research and expectations, projected revenue, time frames, resources required, benefits for an investor, etc. You must also be very clear and precise about what you're asking for from the investor and how those resources would be invested. Confidence and an understanding of what it's going to take to complete your project were absolutely crucial to the outcome of whether you received investment or not.

This practice of asking for what you want doesn't just extend to potential investors in a boardroom situation. It applies to every relationship you have in every aspect of your life. If you're not clear in asking for what outcomes you want and sending that vision out to the Universe, it's unlikely you're going to get anything like what you want. I've mentioned it previously but I can't emphasise enough how important it is to be crystal clear about your vision for what you want for your future.

Your significant relationships are another prime example where this comes into play. If each person in the relationship isn't clear about what they want from the relationship, chances are one or even both people are going to end up dissatisfied and unhappy with the direction and benefits they're receiving. Sadly, this is all too common. The vast majority of people aren't taught to vocalise and communicate their expectations for the relationship. Some people may even perceive it to be crass or vulgar; as if you're treating the relationship like a business contract.

Here's the flip side. Everyone is different and you both intend to love each other and support each other, but how do you each know how the other person wants to be loved and supported if you don't ask? How can you possibly meet the needs of the other person if you don't know what they are?

It's not up to any individual to meet another's expectations or fulfil all their needs. However, in a relationship, there are naturally some expectations, and unless those are clearly communicated, unhappiness will be the end result. Don't you think open and honest communication, and a willingness for each party to understand the other person's point of view and agree to a compromise, is preferable to a messy, resentful, angry divorce? Sadly, many couples don't do this and grow apart with both parties blaming the other for the collapse of the relationship.

Let's move on to health. Let's say you engage a personal trainer to help you get fitter. Now, your desired outcome may be to lose 10kgs and slim down to fit back into your favourite jeans. The diet and exercise programme the trainer develops for you will be specific to that outcome. If, however, your desired outcome is to compete in a triathlon in four months' time, or to compete in the world body-building championships next year, can you imagine how different those diet and exercise schedules would look? They would each look vastly different and if you don't clearly communicate your desired outcome to your trainer, then the possibility of achieving the outcome you want is Buckley's and none!

Bottom line, know what you want, ask for it, and believe you can get it.

6. Your Environment Determines Your Level Of Success

In personal development circles, it's well recognised that your environment determines who you become and what you achieve. You are a product of your environment. From the day you're born, your environment determines how you think, how you act, what you eat, your opinions, your attitudes, how you relate to the world, your education, your relationships, your health, your financial status, your relationship with money, your goals and dreams, your values, your spirituality, your beliefs, your ideals and decisions. In fact, your environment shapes who you become and what you achieve in almost every aspect of your life. You literally are a product of your environment.

As has already been established, your subconscious mind, which is 92% to 96% responsible for your results, is mostly programmed between the years of zero to seven. This is when you have the least amount of control over what you are exposed to and how your brain is programmed. Your brain is like a sponge, particularly in the first two years of life, simply absorbing everything it's exposed to and filing it away. There's no critical reasoning or filter, just storing information and turning it into a library of tens of thousands of beliefs that will determine how you think, how you act and what results you achieve.

Our entire life is a product of this programming. Fortunately, with recent discoveries about brain neuroplasticity, we now know that by applying the right information, tools and strategies, we're able to alter our beliefs at any time in our life, and consequently change our thoughts, behaviour and ultimately our results. This is exciting news.

One of the most impactful ways to influence your programming is by analysing your current environment and changing what is not supporting your results. I experienced this first hand in the Amazon. I had never been in such an

10. Ten Things I Learned From Millionaires In 10 Days

intense environment crammed with so many high achievers in one place for an extended period of time. We were literally immersed in a high achievement environment, and it was almost impossible not to be influenced by the other "Unstoppables" in a positive way.

Following that experience, I have re-evaluated my direction and my goals and the way I am approaching my future. I'm now more determined, focused, and resolute than ever before about achieving my vision. My level of belief in myself and my ability to achieve my vision has also increased dramatically. Many of the people on that trip are now those I count as my friends and colleagues. People I can call on when I need help and vice versa. We socialise together and we're doing business together.

All this is a result of making an emphatic decision to change my environment and the circle of people I connect with. I still have the friends and contacts I've always had. This new circle of associates is a different breed of people I now identify with and I can recognise myself in them and them in me. It's a very humbling and liberating experience to be able to recognise the traits of someone you admire in yourself and how, by simply changing your behaviour, you have the same ability to achieve what they have, and even more.

There are many more aspects to your environment. Nine in fact, according to Success Coach, Jim Bunch and Mentor, Thomas Leonard. I'll dedicate an entire chapter to those environments later in the book as this is such a critical factor in determining your results.

For now, recognise all aspects of your environment are a powerful force in your life and start looking for ways you can change it so it is supportive, not destructive. Socialise with people who have already been where you want to go, and spend as much time in their presence as possible. Absorb their thought patterns and behaviours, choose the ones you see as beneficial and make them your own.

Your environment will make or break you, so it's time to pay attention to it.

7. Mindset Is Everything

Small minds produce small results, whilst expansive minds are capable of endless possibilities.

These hardworking, focused, super high achievers didn't get to where they are purely by accident or sheer hard work. They developed themselves over many years and conditioned their minds to be able to create the success they've achieved.

I've interviewed dozens of super successful high achievers, read many of their books and listened to hundreds of recordings. Everyone I've heard refers to mindset as being a critical factor that is the core difference between success and failure.

Of course, there are a lot of variables and actions you need to take to create the level of success you desire, but underpinning all of it is your mindset. Your mindset will dictate your behaviours such as whether you'll stay up to 2am or get up at 3am to finish a project or start a new one. It will determine whether, instead of watching the television, you will spend 2 or more hours researching, studying, marketing, creating, developing, learning,

10. Ten Things I Learned From Millionaires In 10 Days

mastering new skills and immersing yourself in information and developing new strategies to achieve your goals. Your mindset will dictate whether you have the discipline to declare an embargo on social media so you can stay focused and achieve your vision in the shortest possible time frame.

You must be willing to fail many times and have the fortitude and resilience to get up and do it all again, over and over, to succeed.

You must believe in yourself and your ability to achieve your vision, as well as believing in your vision.

Super successful people pursue spectacular goals and visions that seem almost impossible because they believe in themselves and they know that whatever they can conceive and believe, they can achieve. Super achievers make the impossible possible through the power of their mindset.

Millionaires' minds are wired for success. For these super achievers, it's a given that they can achieve whatever they put their minds to. They wouldn't entertain any other possibility.

Do they have doubts and fears? Of course they do! The difference is they don't give them oxygen. They only feed the thoughts and belief systems that support the achievement of their goals, and fulfilment of their potential.

You can turn your results around quickly, but you must be willing to do whatever it takes. Your mindset must be focused, determined, curious, constant, enduring, resilient, unshakable and uncompromising. Are you willing to be the person who will do whatever is necessary to achieve your vision?

Once you have a winning mindset, your success is inevitable.

8. It's Not About Your Resources, But Your Resourcefulness

OK. So, millionaires do have plenty of financial resources, but most of them didn't start out that way. Have you ever noticed that, no matter how much money you have, you can always think up an idea that requires more than what you have? This is our nature, to expand beyond our current level of achievement.

I observed this in so many ways during the trip with the "Unstoppables". It didn't matter what they had in the way of resources, their ideas and visions always extended beyond the resources they had. But they didn't sit there, arms folded, saying, "Well, that's that then. I don't have the money, skills or other resources I need, so I can't realise my vision." That was never even a consideration.

These people leverage the resources they have and their networks to find out whom they know who can help them, or connect them with someone who can, to bring their vision to life. There were people on this trip, like myself, who hadn't yet achieved the millionaire status, but there's nothing to stop anyone from dreaming big and finding the resources required to fuel their visions wherever, and however, they need to. Including you.

There was one story in particular I want to share with you that illustrates this perfectly.

One of the incredible women on the trip was the amazing Caroline Pemberton. Caroline was Miss Australia in 2007

10. Ten Things I Learned From Millionaires In 10 Days

and she has seen much of the world. Not only is she drop-dead gorgeous, she's intelligent, determined, funny, adventurous, entrepreneurial and incredibly resourceful.

Caroline loves adventure sports like skiing, white water rafting, mountain climbing and surfing. She's not the typical girly girl kind of model you would expect of a former Miss Australia. She loves to travel and during her time as Australia's Ambassador she experienced much of the world and saw many causes she would love to devote her time to. She's very philanthropic and devotes a lot of her time and energy to such causes.

Caroline has also had a lot of experience in front of the camera, even producing some shows and productions. This is her passion and she had a concept that she spent 5 years developing and filming around the world to take to the networks and pitch for a series. This took all of her resources to complete and none of the networks wanted it. She had missed the market with her idea.

But this didn't stop Caroline. Even more determined, she adjusted her idea and started again. This time though she'd exhausted all her resources. In true Unstoppable style, Caroline approached her contacts and leveraged her network to get the resources she needed to film and edit a 'Sizzler' to take back to the networks. It was filmed in the Himalayas and the corporations and connections she had nurtured and developed over the years provided everything she needed. She also completed the whole project in just a few short months. As I write this, Caroline is still in negotiations with networks to see if her idea will see the light of day. But one thing is for sure, even if it doesn't, Caroline will be back with a new project, concept or idea, because she is truly Unstoppable.

When you see this kind of attitude in action, it makes you start to think about how many times you've used excuses to stop youself from moving forward and you realise just how, by shifting your mindset and looking for solutions instead of allowing yourself to be stopped by your problem, you really can accomplish anything you put your mind to.

Whatever you want to achieve, stop thinking "I can't", and start asking, "How can I?" Who do you know that can help you to get to where you want to be? No great achievement is achieved alone and it's imperative you get very good at leveraging the resources and contacts you have to help you to achieve your goals and dreams.

9. Think Big! If You Can Dream It, You Can Do It!

"Whatever your mind can conceive and believe, it can achieve" – Napoleon Hill.

Unstoppable achievers don't dismiss wild, crazy ideas that are larger than life because they can't see how they're possible with their current resources or level of knowledge.

They entertain new possibilities, expand their level of thinking, embrace new concepts and are willing to transcend their current model of the world and pioneer new horizons.

Consider visionaries like Steve Jobs, visionary and creative genius who revolutionised our communication with the Smart Phone and other innovations; Guglielmo Marconi who invented the radio; Alexander Graham Bell created the telephone; and Thomas Edison the light bulb. These men

10. Ten Things I Learned From Millionaires In 10 Days

were considered by many to be foolish, peculiar, irrational, crazy and even insane. They had the capacity to envision something that had never been realised before and make the seemingly impossible, possible.

Elon Musk is a modern day visionary who is putting his brilliant mind to turn dreams into reality. The advantage he has is the visionaries who have gone before him and carved unconventional paths. Society is not quite so dismissive anymore of visionaries and their crazy ideas.

When most people have a big dream, they dumb it down because they don't believe it's possible or that they're capable of achieving it or it just seems too hard. When you create your vision, make it grand and outrageous. What do you really want? Don't worry that you don't know how. Your job is the 'what'. Leave the "how" up to the all-seeing Universe.

A big goal will inspire you and get your creative juices going. It will bring you alive. A goal that is ordinary, mundane or boringly doable, won't tend to excite or challenge you. When the right people surround you, they're also far more likely to be excited by a big vision than a small one.

When you focus on a big vision, you don't sweat the small stuff. Things that would normally bother you will suddenly seem insignificant because of the size of your vision.

It's important to understand that the bigger your goal, the smaller the steps you take toward it. This may sound contradictory, but this approach will keep you more focused and you'll gradually achieve your grand vision much more quickly if you break it down into smaller, bite-sized chunks you can gobble up, gain momentum and move toward the big picture. Remember, your greatest challenge is becoming the person you need to be to achieve any goal or vision you set for yourself. So your vision toward a big goal requires you to expand your thinking, and yourself, a lot more. If you try to do this too quickly, you'll sabotage yourself and your vision.

Thinking big with an attitude of "How is this possible?" is liberating and exciting. It's how our new world must evolve if we are to reinvent ourselves and transform our world into a better place where we solve the potentially catastrophic challenges we face and where all of humanity can thrive into the future.

10. Fundamentally, Millionaires Are The Same As Everyone Else

At the beginning and at the end of the day, each and every one of us is the same at the core.

We're conceived and born the same way. We all die. We all breathe, eat and sleep. We are all subject to getting sick. We all have the same basic physiology and mental capacity. The only difference between the average person on the street and a high net worth individual is their mindset and the way they view their world. Our environment shapes us mentally and emotionally, but with brain neuro-plasticity, we can change our present and our future anytime we choose by changing our mindset.

Wealthy people have fears, doubts and insecurities just like everyone else. They just don't allow them to rule their life and determine their results. They focus on their vision

10. Ten Things I Learned From Millionaires In 10 Days

and where they're going - not where they've been or all the reasons they could fail.

Begin to analyse those people whom you admire and aspire to be like. Who are your heroes and icons? The people who inspire you and make you feel proud to be a part of the same species? Map the similarities between yourself and these people. Look for ways in which you're like them and how those particular traits have contributed to their success. Now, look at the other desirable traits, characteristics and behaviours that have empowered them and been a part of the foundation that's helped them achieve their extraordinary results. How can you adopt some of those traits and characteristics to help you to achieve your goals and dreams too?

You have the capacity and ability to achieve just as much, if not more, than anyone you admire. When you start to see yourself in their likeness, rather than your differences, your entire world of possibility will expand and become so much more exciting than you've ever imagined.

You have everything you need to achieve what you want already inside of you. Recognise, appreciate, nurture and foster the greatness you have within you and you'll discover that all things are possible. It's just a case of changing your attitude and your mindset.

I learned so much that was invaluable from being willing to back myself, step up and put myself out of my comfort zone into an environment with super achievers and big possibility thinkers. The experience has changed the course of my life forever and will no doubt have far-reaching effects into my future. These are just 10 of the lessons I've recognised.

I know there are dozens more. I also learned so much about myself, and how small I've been playing. I came back a different person and I now know there is no limit to the positive impact I can have in the world. Life is an exciting opportunity of limitless possibility. My biggest challenge is which mountain to climb first!

10. Ten Things I Learned From Millionaires In 10 Days

~ Key Reflections ~

1. High achievers have a unique way of seeing the world. They live in the same world as us, but operate with a different blueprint, which is why they get different results. To get the same results, you need to adopt the same type of blueprint. Set yourself up for success by seeing the world through the eyes of a successful person, and you will act differently and get different results.

2. Think Big! If you can dream it, you can do it! Unstoppable achievers entertain new possibilities, expand their level of thinking, embrace new concepts and are willing to transcend their current model of the world and pioneer new horizons. They don't allow their resources, or the fact that something hasn't been done before to stand in the way of them achieving their visions.

3. High achievers are fundamentally just the same as you. Wealthy people have fears, doubts and insecurities just like everyone else. They just don't allow them to rule their life and determine their results. They focus on their vision and where they're going- not where they've been or all the reasons they could fail.

11. Eight Steps To Being Unstoppable

If you desire to live an extraordinary life, instead of the mundane existence most settle for, there are several things you must do to make that happen because, I can assure you, it's not going to fall in your lap.

Experiencing true abundance and success takes deliberate, specific action that puts you head and shoulders above the rest of the population.

Everyone is capable of achieving greatness. The only thing that separates those who do achieve spectacular results and those who live a life of desperate mediocrity is their mindset and the action they take.

Here are eight essential steps to set yourself up for success beyond your wildest dreams. The only thing between you and your goals is whether or not you take these action steps. All the information in the world won't guarantee your success. That part's up to you.

1. Decide

Nothing happens until you make a decision. Once you decide to achieve your dreams, no matter what, the rest is academic because then you will do whatever it takes. If you simply think, "I'll give it a go and see what happens", this will not be enough to carry you through the tough times.

Are you prepared to make the decision right now to achieve your dreams no matter what? When you do, you'll be amazed at what you're capable of and how the Universe turns up to support you once it knows you're serious!

2. What's Your Vision?

Clarity around what you want for yourself and the difference you want to make in the world is essential. Be specific when you dream about the future you want for yourself. It's very important to also make your vision bigger than you.

What does your perfect day look like? Who are you with? What are you doing? What does it feel like? What does your heart yearn for more than anything? What will make you truly happy? Adding emotion to the equation is an essential part of this equation as it multiplies the co-creative force many times over.

It's important to truly know yourself to realise what you truly want. I'm actually pleased I didn't manifest some of the things I thought I wanted because they would have been more of a burden than a pleasure. The better I came to know the truth of who I was, the more I realised some of my dreams were merely a replica of what society expects and how it measures success.

11. Eight Steps To Being Unstoppable

Big houses, fancy cars, expensive dinners, pricey jewellery and designer clothes are not things that make my heart sing. Had I realised that with the big house I used to dream of, the initial excitement of its acquisition would have quickly descended into the reality of cleaning, maintenance and the uselessness of having a tonne of space our small family doesn't need. It would have felt like an empty and hollow victory.

Understanding and appreciating yourself, and not feeling the pressure of society's expectations and benchmarks are important to achieving dreams that will satisfy you for many years to come.

When you know what you want to create for yourself, go further and think about what difference you want to make in the world. What legacy do you want to leave? What impact do you want to have? What difference do you want to make? What situation breaks your heart? If you could change one thing in the world, what would that be? This makes your vision bigger than you and will drive you forward beyond all the challenges you will inevitably face as you strive for your goals.

When you have a bigger purpose in mind, your creativity expands greatly, and you're better able to stay solution focused instead of getting stuck in your own problems.

3. Get Out Of Your Own Way

You have the ability to achieve so much more than you have even begun to imagine. The only thing stopping you from achieving greatness and realising your full power and potential are the belief systems (BS) that are running in your subconscious mind. Your belief systems stop you because the fear, self-doubt, self-worth and negative emotions crowd your mind and your energy system. These prevent you from tapping into your genius and accelerating your progress and your ability to be all you can be.

Any thought, feeling or belief system that stops you from experiencing joy, freedom, abundance, wealth, love, happiness, satisfaction, fulfilment, and all the riches life has to offer, is an outright lie. All your fears, doubts and uncomfortable emotions are based on lies.

You're so powerful, but the belief that you're insignificant, small or not good enough is stopping you from stepping into that power. There are so many tools and techniques available today to help release you from the grip of your BS. Once you've made the decision to go for your goals and not let them hold you back, you will do whatever it takes to clear them and get on with being truly great and powerful.

Fortunately, with all the progress in the personal development world, we now have tools, techniques and strategies that are exceptionally good at stripping away negative belief systems fast. The more you know what to target, and the more willing you are to dive deep into your subconscious, be vulnerable and decide to change, the better and faster your results will be.

I see a vast array of differences in results all the time. The major factor that determines the level of results is the person's willingness to change and do the work. Again, it comes back to whether you're willing to decide to stop making excuses and do whatever you have to in order to change your thoughts, belief systems and results.

If you're willing to play full out, you'll see results a lot faster than someone who isn't.

11. Eight Steps To Being Unstoppable

So, what are you willing to do? What risks are you willing to take to see results? How much work are you willing to do? How deep are you willing to dive? Are you prepared to back yourself? Are you willing to change everything about your life in order to achieve true abundance, fulfilment, freedom, abundance and joy?

I'm not saying you will have to change everything, but you must be willing to. Put everything on the table: your relationships, your lifestyle, your habits, your attachments, your behaviours, your belief systems, your identity, your opinions, your judgements and perceptions, your ideals and your values. Evaluate and question all aspects of your life and yourself. You must be willing to be uncompromising in your quest to uncover the belief systems that are holding you back and release them or 'change them'.

Your attachments to all these things are like anchors holding you in place. If you want your ship to sail, you must be willing to pull up the anchor, raise the sails and ride out the storms.

As mentioned previously, your environment is also an important part of this element. Surround yourself with the right people who will support you and be a part of your success dream team. Make sure your work environment is supportive of you doing your best work and you don't have any distractions. What are you reading? What are you watching? What are you listening to? Do you have the right tools to achieve your goals? Who are your mentors? Who are you hanging out with? Who's on your team? Do you have the right experts advising you and taking care of details you're not equipped or suited to?

You are a product of your environment so pay close attention to every detail associated with it and you'll find success a lot easier.

Attending daily to your mindset is essential to your success in any endeavour.

Your job is to seek out and release all the lies that are stopping you from experiencing the beautiful and effortless flow of life and unleash your power into the world.

How badly do you want change? Are you simply attached to the idea of change? Or are you committed to true and lasting change? The distinction between these two questions is the difference between achieving the pinnacle of success and living an exceptional life, and continuing to live in mediocrity and struggle.

In every moment you have the opportunity to choose something different and change your life. Are you going to decide in favour of yourself? I haven't said it will be easy, but I assure you, it will be worth it.

4. Values

Your core values will always be a driving force behind your actions and results. Do you know what your core values are? Are they in alignment with the goals and dreams you have for your life? Do your values conflict with your goals?

Doing an exercise to determine your core values will help you to determine if you need to adjust them to enable you to achieve what you want, or alter your goals to fit your values.

Here is a list of some common core values to give you an idea of what I'm talking about. Take the time to figure out your core values and align your goals accordingly, otherwise, you're just setting yourself up for continual disappointment.

- Freedom
- Security
- Love
- Connection
- Intimacy
- Safety
- Acceptance
- Achievement
- Wealth
- Recognition
- Making A Difference
- Support
- Fun
- Adventure
- Creativity
- Spirituality
- Peace
- Joy
- Health
- Success
- Money
- Community
- Impact

There are many different values, and everyone is different. Understanding your own values will help you immeasurably in your quest for success and living a rewarding and fulfilling life. Understanding others values will help you to have more intimate and fulfilling relationships.

5. Set Goals

Once you have a vision, it's important you set goals to keep you on track and heading in the direction of your vision on a daily basis.

People set goals differently. You may be a person who likes to set 20-year goals and then chunk your goals down from there. Or perhaps you prefer to set shorter term goals in alignment with your vision. These could be 12-month, 6-month, 3-month or even weekly goals. Whatever the term, just set some goals to help keep you moving forward. Regardless of your preference, always set daily goals in accordance with your vision. If you have big goals, but no immediate ones, you will flounder and struggle to get any closer to your vision.

Write your goals and your vision down. Studies have proven that those people who write down their goals are much more likely to achieve them. Review them daily to make sure you're on track and are reminding yourself of where you're headed, and why you're on this journey.

6. Commitment & Focus

There's a clear and critical distinction between being interested in achieving your goals and being committed.

11. Eight Steps To Being Unstoppable

If you're just interested, the latest television programme or Facebook post will be far more compelling than taking steps to achieving your vision. You will make all sorts of excuses and find all sorts of reasons not to take deliberate steps toward your goals. You won't make the sacrifices that are inevitably associated with success.

If you're committed, you will be willing to do whatever it takes and do what others aren't willing to do, so you can achieve and have what others will never have.

The ability to focus is an essential skill we are not inherently born with but must develop. Some people do find it easier than others, depending on their nature, but everyone must practice and be committed to developing laser-like focus if they want to succeed.

This takes discipline and commitment, without which, your grand vision will never be born, many people will not benefit from your expertise, wisdom and teaching, and you will never realise your dreams.

There's a lot at stake here, and we live in a society that is progressively turning us into people with ADD (Attention Deficit Disorder), unable to focus on one thing for too long.

Are you willing to make short-term sacrifices in order to achieve long term success? If not, this journey is not for you. It doesn't have to be hard, but it's not going to be handed to you on a platter either. You must be willing to take the hits that you will experience, and use them to fuel you to go further and farther than you've ever been before on a daily basis. The choice to be a high achiever is not for the fainthearted.

7. Planning & Preparation

If you fail to plan, you are planning to fail. Planning and preparation is the boring bit, but without it, you're doomed.

Put a plan in place, whether it be a detailed plan that reaches out to years in advance or one that just gets you through to the end of the week. Planning is an essential component to your success.

As for preparation, ask yourself what information you need to learn? What skills do you need? Is your environment supportive of your success? Who do you need to become to achieve your goals? How can you set yourself up for success and stack the odds in your favour?

You won't know every component of how to achieve your goals. If you did, you would have done it already. That's all a part of the journey and it will be different in every case for every goal. What's important is that you have some plan in place and you review it as you go, remaining flexible as you progress. You will come up against obstacles and challenges that cause you to adjust your plan, just never lose sight of your vision and remember the Universe is collaborating in your favour. Even when it looks and feels like you're up against it, know everything is perfect. This belief alone will help you greatly as you stumble your way forward toward success.

When everything looks like it's falling apart, breathe and consider that maybe it's falling together.

11. Eight Steps To Being Unstoppable

8. Go For It

Consistent daily action is the final critical component to achieving your goals. If you think about losing weight, preparing to run a marathon, the quest to win a gold medal or win the premiership, obtaining a promotion, building a business, wealth and success are no different. It is consistent, daily action steps toward your vision that creates massive success. There's no fairy dust, no magic pill, no secret sauce. If you want a different life, more than what you have right now, you've got to be prepared to take consistent daily action toward your goals and dreams. You have to chip away daily at your mindset, your vision, your dreams. Do you want it enough to do that? Are you committed enough to your vision for your future?

Take time now to write out five things you can do in the next 24 hours to get closer to your goals and dreams and then do them. Do that tomorrow, and the day after that and the day after that, etc., until you reach your goal.

It's not rocket science. The truth is so boringly simple and predictable, and yet that's why so many people don't do it. They don't want to take progressive, predictable, daily action, so they waste years looking for the elusive secret or quick fix, to discover there isn't one.

You now have a proven formula to achieve your goals and dreams, unleash your greatness and realise more than you ever imagined possible. Question is, will this be another piece of information you file away and don't take action on? Or are you going to do something about it?

The rest is up to you.

~ Key Reflections ~

1. The Universe loves structure. The reason most people never achieve their dreams or their potential is because they don't have a structured approach to their success. Experiencing true abundance and success takes deliberate, specific action that puts you head and shoulders above the rest of the population. The only thing that separates those who do achieve spectacular results and those who live a life of desperate mediocrity is their mindset and the type of action they take.

2. Having a clear vision is one of the first and most crucial parts to achieving a life that is fulfilling, satisfying and delivers the lifestyle you truly want. Clarity around what you want for yourself and the difference you want to make in the world is essential. Be specific when you dream about the future you want for yourself.

3. The final step in the eight steps to being Unstoppable is to Go For It! Consistent daily action is the final critical component to achieving your goals. We live in an energetic world, and in order to get a specific result, action is absolutely essential. The key is to take the right action. One of your priority actions should be to work through the eight steps in this chapter to set yourself up for success.

12. The 9 Environments of Success

According to Success Coach Jim Bunch and Thomas Leonard, there are nine environments that determine your health, wealth and happiness. They refer to these as "The nine environments of you". Understanding these environments has the potential to bring life-altering transformation to all areas of your life, so let's go through each one briefly so you can understand them and how they impact your results and your life.

1. Memetics

This environment is your belief systems, paradigms, conditioning and how you view the world. Your beliefs underpin every thought pattern and outcome you will ever experience in your life.

Your subconscious mind, which determines your results, makes decisions and drives your actions according to the belief systems installed, mostly when you were very young.

If you keep believing what you've always believed and doing what you've always done, you're going to keep getting the exact same results you've always gotten.

If you're lucky enough to have been exposed to and to have adopted predominantly positive beliefs about yourself and the world from a young age, you're going to achieve mostly positive results. The opposite is also true. Those raised in a mostly negative environment will achieve a lot of negative results in their life, until they change their memetics.

The good news is, when you change your belief systems, you immediately change your results. The really good news is we now have a wide variety of powerful transformation tools and techniques, like Emotional Freedom Technique, Peace Process, Instant Miracle Technique, Sound Healing and many more that can release negative belief systems and turn your results around very quickly.

The other environments and how you engineer them will also have a profound impact on your memetics, so let's have a look at those now.

2. Physical

Your physical environment is comprised of the tangible things you can see, smell, touch and taste. This includes your office, home, possessions, etc. This is one of the easiest environments for you to change.

For example, if you have a cluttered office, your mind will tend to be cluttered and your results unpredictable and haphazard. If your office is clean and tidy, you'll be able to think more clearly.

12. The 9 Environments of Success

I suggest surrounding yourself with things in your office that give you joy and make you feel at peace. I have plants and crystals in my office. My desk is relatively tidy with things neatly put away. I do tend to have a pile of things to attend to in my in-tray, but they're neatly arranged in the tray.

I have a vision board and positive affirmations, plus my word for the year on my wall as well as inspiring photos, and a photo of my husband in my office.

As I am fortunate enough to work from home, my dogs are always in the office with me. They are most dear to me, so it makes my environment perfect for me to feel comfortable, at peace and happy to be in it. From my computer, I see our backyard, which backs onto the environmental corridor at the back of our place and is rich with trees and wildlife. For me, it's pure paradise.

Does your office have any natural lighting, or is it purely lit by fluorescent lights? What kind of flooring does it have? Are there any distracting noises from nearby sources? Do computer screens and technology emitting EMF's surround you? All of these will have a direct impact on you physically, mentally and emotionally and it's important you make changes where you can to assist you to change your life to one you want. Declutter, update, chuck out old stuff you don't use, keep it simple, clean and inviting.

Your physical environments are a direct reflection of what's going on in your life, so pay close attention to them because they will impact your results dramatically.

Your bedroom is another room that's very important, as it should promote restful, revitalising sleep. If you have a television and other electronic devices in the room these are going to impact your ability to get all the quality sleep you need. Make sure your bedroom is free from all sorts of stimulation and helps you to relax and sleep peacefully.

Go into each environment in your home and ask if it inspires you. Do you want to be in that environment? Does it make you feel welcome, happy and comfortable? Or do you feel challenged and uncomfortable and would you prefer to be somewhere else? If the latter is the case, then you need to change it so it inspires and welcomes you instead.

Do you have toxic chemicals in your cupboards that are polluting your home and environment? Do you have over processed foods full of fats and sugars and empty of nutrition in your pantry? Do you have old clothes you know you'll never wear again in your closet? Are you hoarding old trinkets that don't add to your quality of life? If so, it's time to clean out and change your environments to be reflective of whom you want to be and the results you want to achieve.

You may want to re-evaluate where you live as well. Do you feel happy, content, fulfilled where you live? Or do you feel hemmed in, claustrophobic? Is there a lot of noise pollution or air pollution? Are there plenty of trees, water, or natural environment close by? If you're not feeling that where you live is reflective of where you would like to be living, maybe it's time for a move. Or, if that's not possible at this point, at least start dreaming about the ideal environment you want to be in and put it on your vision board so you can bring it to be.

There are many aspects of your environment to consider. Take stock of your physical environment and change what's not working for you. It has the potential to dramatically change your results.

3. Financial

Your financial environment includes the technology, systems and strategies you have in place to maximise your financial results. Do you have professional financial advisers helping you with investment strategies that get the best return on your income and set you up for the future? If you have a business, do you have a bookkeeper and accountant looking after your tax returns and advising you on how to increase your business turnover and reduce costs in your business? Do you have credit cards maxed out, or bad loans hanging over your head? If you do, do you have a plan in place to pay them out as quickly as possible? Do you have a plan to create a passive income in the years ahead so you can retire comfortably and still have a lifestyle and not have to rely on the government for support?

There's a lot to consider with your financial environment, and once you have the systems and plans in place, you feel more secure, stable and under control. You can relax and put your attention on how you can increase your income going forward and really boost your financial wealth in the years to come.

4. Network

There's a popular statement that your net worth is equal to your network. This simply means that the people you hang out with will directly impact how much income you earn and the financial results you achieve. The vast majority of people's income will be an average of all the people they socialise and hang out with.

If you're hanging out with nay Sayers and dream stealers, your chances of success are seriously limited. Being immersed in an environment with people who are possibility thinkers, know that every challenge has a solution, and who believe in you is very liberating and uplifting, and will greatly increase your chances of success.

Another observation is that money has species recognition. So, employees of a particular level will socialise with people at the same level. Millionaires hang out with millionaires, and billionaires will associate with billionaires. People with yachts will mix with other people with yachts. I think you get the idea.

Whilst I'm not suggesting you immediately go out and ditch all your mates, I am suggesting it would be worth your while cultivating a network which includes wealthy, successful people, and start spending a lot more time with them. Their way of thinking, behaving and the results they achieve will start to rub off on you. Your conversations will change and, amazingly, you'll find your results will change accordingly. It's like osmosis.

Make sure you surround yourself with people who are uplifting and will support your endeavours and fuel your ideas. People able to see and share your vision, and who will challenge you to overcome your perceived limitations. People who will lift you up when you're down, will call you on your BS, and celebrate your successes with you.

Seek these people out and spend as much time with them as you possibly can. They will help guide you to places and achievements you never imagined possible.

5. Relationships

This can be one of the most difficult environments to change because it is made up of your nearest and dearest. Are your relationships loving, supportive, intimate, safe and inspiring? Do they pull you up? Or are they pulling you down? Are they helping you to be the best you can be, and step into a bigger you?

If your relationships are detracting from your life, then it's time to take a serious look at them and take action to change them. Now, this doesn't mean you need to change the other person. Remember, as within, so without. You need to change yourself to change the quality of your relationships.

If your family is bringing you down, try spending less time in their presence and choose not to share your inner-most secrets, dreams and aspirations with them in case they say things to bring down your level of confidence.

If your significant other doesn't understand you and is not supportive of you, work quietly on your goals and dreams and be the quiet achiever.

By working on your self-esteem and self-confidence, self-love and your relationship with yourself, you'll find the nature of your other significant relationships will start to change. Never seek to change someone else, always seek to change yourself and see how your external relationship changes.

If you feel you need help with your significant relationships, perhaps getting a counsellor to help you navigate them would be a good idea.

Firstly, think about what is working in your relationships and express gratitude for that. Then think about what you would like to change with your relationships and start focusing on how it would look and feel to experience having them just the way you want them. What kind of conversations would you be having? How would you be interacting? Would you be laughing more? Would you be having more expansive and interesting conversations? Would you be more relaxed and open and connected? Would you be more intimate and loving? You can have whatever you want, but first, you need to know what you want so you can focus on that.

6. Body

This environment is largely self-explanatory, but I'm going to break it down in case there are parts of your body environment you're not paying enough attention to, and could do with improvement.

To analyse your body environment you need to look at several key factors such as:

- What foods are you putting into your body?
- What exercise are you doing each day?
- How much sugar are you eating?
- How many stimulants, such as caffeine, are you consuming?
- How much water do you drink?
- What kind of health practitioners are you seeing?
- How much sleep are you getting?
- How much stress are you under?

12. The 9 Environments of Success

- What kind of toxins and pollutants are you exposed to?
- How much alcohol are you consuming?
- Do you smoke cigarettes?
- What thoughts do you have about your body?
- Do you feel tired, stressed and overwhelmed much of the time?
- Do you treat pain by taking pain killers, or are you actively looking to find the cause of the pain and treating it?
- Do you use and abuse your body, or treat it with the love and respect it deserves?

The truth is, if you don't put time, effort and energy into being well now, you'd better make time for being sick in the future because it's inevitable. Our society is getting sicker and sicker and, while many will trot out the line that it's because we're living longer, this is only a small contributing factor to the global health crisis we're currently experiencing.

The overwhelming amount of toxic processed foods, hidden sugars, additives in our water, pollution in our air and water, chemicals in our personal care products, poisonous cleaning agents, pharmaceutical drugs, and yes, I'm going to say it, the bombardment of vaccines we're subjected to, are all contributing to making us sicker and sicker.

For the first time in history, children born today do not have the life expectancy of their parents. This is shocking and must be reversed for the sake of our children if we want them to live a long, quality life.

How you look after your body not only affects your physical health now and into the future, it affects your ability to focus and concentrate, your energy levels, your ability to solve problems, your clarity for making sound decisions.

It also directly impacts your self-image and self-worth. If you truly want to be successful, you must look after your body and make its health one of your top priorities.

This doesn't mean you need to have the figure of a catwalk model, the strength of Arnold Schwarzenegger or the fitness of a tri-athlete. In fact, many models are very unhealthy because they're not feeding their body properly. When was the last time you saw a strong, fit looking model? Whilst your weight is one indication of your health, it isn't the ultimate determining factor.

What's most important for you to focus on is:

- Eating a clean, balanced diet filled with whole foods rich in nutrition. Here's a hint: anything that comes out of a box or plastic is highly unlikely to meet this criterion
- Reduce your sugar and saturated fat intake. (The first step will help with this)
- Drink 1.5 to 2 litres of water a day
- Cut down on stimulants like caffeine
- Get regular, moderate exercise that increases overall strength, mobility and aerobic fitness to maintain healthy heart and lungs
- Reduce stress (Emotional Freedom Technique is great for this)

12. The 9 Environments of Success

- Get sufficient sleep regularly – whilst 8 hours is the guide, this doesn't work for everyone. Personally, I'm great on 6 hours sleep and I can't sleep more than that.
- Ask: "If I truly loved my body, what would I do differently?"
- Get out and connect with nature on a regular basis – daily if possible
- Gratitude and appreciation for life (essential for mental health)

Here's the ironic truth. If you bought a high-performance, prestige car, you'd make sure you put the best fuel into it, get it serviced on time, keep it clean and tidy, do everything to keep it functioning at optimum levels and generally treat it with respect, wouldn't you? Reality check: A car is something that can be replaced as there's millions and millions of metal boxes on wheels out there that all do the same thing – transporting people from one place to another. That's their job.

But you only have one body and you can't replace it! This is it. It's your vehicle to carry you through life and if you screw it up, you can't just order a new one. So if you're not treating your body with the utmost love and respect, WHAT THE BLOODY HELL DO YOU THINK YOU'RE DOING?

Seriously! The vast majority of people are insane the way they use and abuse their bodies and just expect them to keep functioning in spite of neglect and mistreatment. Look after your body, it's the only one you've got and if you don't you will eventually pay the price. Don't say you haven't been warned! Rant over.

7. Self

Your self-environment is not as tangible as the other environments. This is about your mission, purpose, talents and gifts. This environment, however, gives your life meaning and will be the single biggest contributing factor to the level of fulfilment and satisfaction you experience in this lifetime.

Those who know their purpose and mission in life tend to be happier, more focused, more resolute in the actions they take toward living out their visions and achieving their goals than those who don't.

Knowing what your gifts and talents are will help you to live out your mission, leave your legacy and live from a place of passion. This is the greatest possible gift for any human being to receive during their lifetime, and it's why you're here.

You aren't just some random being who accidentally happened to end up here on planet earth. You're a brilliant, amazing, talented, priceless human being who is part of the fabric of the grand plan. You have a destiny; it's up to you to own it, claim it and make it yours.

The ultimate goal is to identify your gifts and talents and how they contribute to your purpose and mission, and then design the rest of the environments around them.

How do you know when you're on purpose?

Do you feel like you're living from a place of inspiration and loving the work you do on a daily basis? Do you feel as if you're making a worthy contribution to society? Are your relationships supportive of what you're setting out to achieve? Do you notice the Universe conspiring to support you in your quest to achieve your vision? Do you feel a sense of flow and ease around what you're doing? Do you feel as if you're being the best you can be and doing what sets your heart on fire?

When you answer yes to all these questions, you will know you're living your life on purpose. If you're confused and don't know what that is, then set about studying yourself. Make YOU the subject of discovery until you've figured this piece out. Take the questions above and rephrase them by asking "How do I?" with each of them. Keep asking the questions, "What's my purpose? What am I here for?" and stay intensely curious.

Once you've nailed the self-environment, make sure you adjust the rest of the environments to be supportive of this one. Your life will be more magical, rewarding and fulfilling than you ever imagined possible!

8. Spiritual

With almost seven billion people on the planet, there are almost seven individual sets of spiritual belief systems. Even within organised religion, each and every person has their own interpretation of various aspects of the faith within those religions. Even if you're an atheist, and you believe in 'nothing', that is still a belief system.

Your spiritual beliefs must resonate with your soul and allow you to connect with your own internal compass as to what higher power you identify with.

I believe that we you and I are the ultimate Creator. We are an extension of Source Energy and we are Source

Energy. Although we may feel a sense of disconnection and separation in the human experience, that's just an illusion.

We are all connected, and we are all One. We are of the Universe and the Universe is of us. We are in a dance of co-creation with 'All That Is' moment-to-moment, day-to-day, week-to-week, month-to-month and year-to-year. If you want a different experience, you have the power to co-create a new experience. First, you must recognise, acknowledge and take responsibility for creating this experience you are currently living.

This belief system gives you the ultimate power over your life. To believe another entity outside of you has control over your present and your future experiences renders you powerless. It places you at the mercy of a force you have no influence over. That, to me, is a daunting prospect and not one I would like to entertain, particularly if that power is likely to punish me, or at the very least, abandon me if I choose to exercise my free will and do something that doesn't please the Almighty Deity.

If believing something outside of you has control over your destiny resonates with you and enables you to open your heart and soul to fully experience all the joy, freedom and happiness you have within you, then that's wonderful. I prefer to believe my destiny is a continual process of co-creation and I can decide at any moment, if I don't like what I've created, to begin again and create something new.

I am partnering with the Universe. I know as long as I'm clear and open to working with the Laws and Forces of the Universe, then what we create together will be magical. It's the best and most powerful relationship you will ever

12. The 9 Environments of Success

experience. Largely, this is because it's your relationship with yourself. Connect with your higher self and get to know who you truly are.

I believe the whole purpose of our existence on planet earth is connection. Connection with ourselves, with our soul, with others, with nature, with spirit, with every aspect of our environment. I believe we're not here to '*do*' anything, but to '*be*' all we can be in every moment and express our divinity to the world through our purpose and our mission.

If you drop the premise that you have to DO anything and focus on who you are BE-ing moment to moment, it takes a great deal of pressure off you as you no longer have to perform or prove yourself to anyone, including you.

Ask yourself; do your spiritual beliefs help you feel more connected, alive, empowered, like you matter, as if you're a significant part of the whole? Are there rituals or practices you perform or could perform that would deepen this spiritual connection? Are there books you can read that will help you to deepen your understanding of your faith and your place in the world in relation to that faith? Do your other environments have elements that reflect your spiritual beliefs? Are your spiritual beliefs giving you the return on investment you desire and deserve?

Exploring your spiritual beliefs, and adopting the ones which resonate with your soul, is a truly satisfying experience. It gives you a sense of connection we all crave in order to feel whole and complete. There is nothing missing within you, and whatever you believe will help you to experience that.

9. Nature

The nature environment is extremely important for the health of our mind, body and spirit. It has the capacity to nurture us, rejuvenate us, support us and sustain us. Living in a concrete jungle and failing to connect with nature can cause or add to feelings of discontent, unhappiness, emptiness and a sense that something's missing.

It's inconceivable to me how the vast majority of the human race treats our planet as if its resources are something we have the right to exploit, utilise and devour without any consideration for the impact on the source from which it came, or its other inhabitants. This attitude is fast destroying the very home that sustains us, gives us unparalleled beauty, and literally everything we need without asking for anything in return. The level of disrespect, disdain and disregard we have collectively shown this magical place we are lucky enough to call home, is unfathomable.

Mother Earth is a living, breathing being that, like much of the life she sustains and nurtures, we have treated with indifference and contempt. We continue to gobble up the environment at an alarming rate, poisoning it, reshaping it, destroying it and the life she sustains, with seemingly no acknowledgement of the delicate balance of the self-sustaining ecology that relies on all the components to function. Even whilst we're seeing her buckle under the pressure of our abuse, we're failing to take heed and correct the error of our ways. We're all waiting for someone else to provide solutions to the problem and regulate us into a sustainable way of life, expecting this will flick a switch, and nature will magically correct all of our sins of the past and recover from our abuse.

12. The 9 Environments of Success

News flash: It isn't that simple. Can Mother Earth recover? Yes. It will take her possibly thousands of years to undo what we have managed to do within the space of a couple of hundred years, but she can do it. Sadly, she will never be the same again. The species that have become extinct will never return. The Amazon forests that we have decimated will never regenerate as much of those landscapes have now turned to desert. The toxic waste we have dumped will take thousands and even millions of years to be turned back into a part of nature's garden.

What needs to happen is every single one of us must take responsibility for our consumption and the waste we generate. We need to reconnect with Mother Nature at a soul level and send her all the love and healing energy we can to assist her in her long recovery before it's too late. We must stop our greedy, selfish, unconscious consumption of all the stuff we continue to acquire that we don't need, and choose a more sustainable way of life that feeds Mother Nature and our soul.

The first step in this is to recognise your soul connection with nature. Make time daily to find a patch of grass and rub your bare feet in it. Go out into your backyard or a park close by and consciously connect with the energy of nature. Notice the stillness and effortlessness with which nature thrives when humans do not interfere with Her. Embrace nature and embody Her beautiful energy. Put some plants in your home and make a conscious energy exchange with them each day. Talk to them, sing to them and touch them.

Connecting to nature will help to reinvigorate and rejuvenate your mind, body and spirit. It will bring you back to you.

These are the nine environments you must attend to in order to stack the odds in your favour so you're able to be all you can be, and achieve all your goals and dreams. I encourage you to take the time to explore and understand each of these environments, how they relate to you, and then to go about optimising each of them and nurture and maintain them over time. Do not underestimate the importance of this exercise. You have been given everything you need to be the best you can be. It's up to you to make good use of those resources and set yourself up to express your greatness in the world.

12. The 9 Environments of Success

~ *Key Reflections* ~

1. Your environments have a measurable effect on how you think and behave, and on the results you achieve. Ensuring your environments are deliberately created to support your success could be the difference between achieving the success, wealth and freedom you desire, and continuing to struggle, experience failure and disappointment. There are nine environments you need to optimize for the best results.

2. One of these nine environments is your relationships. There's a popular statement that your net worth is equal to your network. The people you spend the most time with will directly impact how much income you earn and the financial results you achieve. The vast majority of people's income will be an average of the primary people they socialise and hang out with.

3. Another key environment is your self-environment. This is about your mission, purpose, talents and gifts and gives your life meaning. Getting this right will be the single biggest contributing factor to the level of fulfilment and satisfaction you experience in this lifetime. Knowing what your gifts and talents are will help you to live out your mission, leave your legacy and live from a place of passion.

13. Congruence

Your power and capacity for greatness are unlimited and the only thing standing between you and your vision is you. There are three fundamental differences between those who achieve things most of us would consider almost impossible:

1. Their mindset.

2. The actions they take.

3. Their congruence with their vision and goals.

Congruence is the mental, emotional and spiritual alignment of the individual with their goals. In order to achieve any big vision, you must conspire with the Universe because, as we've already established, to fight against it is counter-productive, exhausting and you end up being in a battle with the most powerful force that exists. Whilst you have unlimited power, putting yourself in a contest with another infinitely powerful source is going to hamper you greatly and you will experience constant setbacks and frustration on your journey. It's like a Goliath vs. Goliath contest, which is futile and no one wins, least of all you.

When you are congruent in all ways, Divine inspiration flows and your achievements become seemingly effortless in comparison. Universal forces become your virtual assistants and do 90% of the heavy lifting for you, while you take action on the inspiration you receive. Congruence is your magic carpet ride toward your goals.

Challenges will occur, as they are inevitable. You will even experience setbacks from time to time, but the ease with which you're able to navigate and resolve those challenges will astound you. People, information, situations and inspiration will show up over and over throughout your journey to carry you along your path to realising your vision. It's a truly rewarding and magical state to be in, and it's available to you right now.

So how do you create a state of congruence? There are several things you can do.

1. Be On Purpose

This doesn't have to be your grand life's purpose. If you know what that is, fantastic, definitely follow that. But for many people who haven't figured it out yet, the pressure of having to find their ultimate life's purpose can be paralysing. So, in the first instance, decide on a purpose that will give you a sense of meaning to your life and achievement as you journey toward its realisation.

In order to determine a purpose, think about a situation you would like to change in the world. This may be for one person, or for a group of people, or for other sentient beings,

13. Congruence

or for the planet. But the purpose must be grander than you and make a positive difference.

You're already living your purpose when you help the elderly lady with her shopping, comfort your friend in their hour of need, save that dog or cat from being euthanised, give someone a compliment or kind word. In other words, when you're being of service, you're on purpose.

I believe we all have a grand purpose and reason for being here. If you don't know what that is yet, ask the question, stay curious and just focus on being of service in everything you do for now. That is living your purpose.

2. Leverage Your Unconscious Competence

We're all born with specific gifts and talents unique to us and are a part of our reason for being on the planet. These gifts are our core genius and leveraging them is an essential part of this equation because it's what we're meant to be doing. Your unconscious competence refers to the things you're naturally good at and requires little effort for you to do well.

In order to be congruent, you must use the gifts you were born with and are destined to share with the world. It's all a part of the Divine plan. If you're not living in accordance with your Divine plan, you'll be out of alignment, and you won't achieve your full potential.

If you don't know what your unconscious competence is, think about the things you do effortlessly, without even trying.

- What do you do that people compliment you on?

- If there was something you could do all day, every day and never get tired of doing it, what would that be?
- What subjects do you love to read, learn and talk about?
- What fascinates you?
- What do you play at that other people have to work at?

Make a list of these things. One of your gifts may be as simple as putting others at ease, listening to others problems, recognising when someone needs support and encouragement. Are you able to take complex ideas and explain them in easy to understand terms for others? Do you have a natural ability for sales or marketing? Are you fascinated by different investment strategies? Are you good at telling stories or captivating an audience? Are you creative, or good at thinking outside the box?

We often dismiss our talents as nothing special because they come so easily to us and we naturally assume everyone finds them easy. This is definitely not the case. When you put pen to paper you'll discover that the things you naturally do well are things many people will have to work at, and they're in awe of how you do them so easily and effortlessly.

Sometimes they're blatantly obvious, like my singing voice and sound healing. But others, not so much. I used to have no idea why the people I meet, no matter where or when, openly share their troubles and reveal their life story to me. Now I know it's a gift of mine. It's the gift of trust. It doesn't matter if I've known them for five seconds or 20 years, people naturally trust me enough with their deepest secrets and problems. I would never have thought of it as a gift before I understood this principle of unconscious competence. It serves me very well in the work I do.

When you're leveraging your gifts and talents and you are on purpose, life takes on a new sense of meaning and problems no longer seem insurmountable.

3. Be Authentically You

From the day we're born we are learning to model our behaviour on our environment in order to survive. It's the way we're programmed and our existence has relied on this essential part of our learning and development for years. The modelled behaviour is not about being unique and different and expressing our true nature. It's about not upsetting the system, being a model citizen, playing by the rules and living up to everyone's expectations. We're taught to be the kind of person who is pleasing to others.

From the time in history where humanity evolved beyond simple community living for the good of all, to appoint leaders to determine what was good for us, we've been deferring our decisions about what's best for us to these appointed authorities, looking to them to tell us who we're meant to be and how we're meant to behave.

In theory, this model had the potential to work well, bringing cohesion and stability to our community. Sadly, the reality is, these leaders have governed us through fear and threat of retribution, punishing those who refused to play by the rules and who dared to be different and challenge the norm. Ultimately, this system results in people being pushed beyond reasonable limits to the edge of survival, which causes them to behave in ways that ultimately hurt others. We must break this cycle of destruction of the human spirit and psyche.

From being mercilessly imprisoned for daring to question authority, to being burned alive at the stake if accused of having magical powers, or being a 'witch', since early times of modern civilisation, we have been beaten into submission and forced to conform. Heaven help those who didn't because no one else will dare to come to your aid or defend you for fear of being implicated in your treasonous ways.

This may sound all a bit melodramatic, but when you think about it, this is exactly how our subconscious mind responds to things that are different. We're easily offended when people don't behave the way we want them to because it doesn't satisfy our own need for a life we can rely and depend on. We try to moderate our own and others behaviour so it doesn't upset the authorities or break the rules. We're afraid that if others rock the boat, we will be caught up in the fallout and the entire system will capsize.

Is it any wonder we're afraid to be our true selves and unleash our greatness and brilliance out into the world? We risk being condemned and crucified and being made an outcast. The very result we believe threatens our existence.

The question is, are you being true to yourself? Are you being fearlessly, authentically, uncompromisingly you? Or have you hidden your light away for fear of others reaction to it? Are you being who everyone else expects and needs you to be for them to feel comfortable?

13. Congruence

I invite you now to really sit with these questions. Are you afraid that, if you speak and demonstrate your truth, others would judge you, criticise you and maybe even reject you for making them uncomfortable and not following the rules society laid out for you? And what if they do?

What are the consequences of you continuing to be what everyone else expects you to be and not showing up as real and authentic in every area of your life?

As a society, we're very judgemental of others who aren't our version of 'acceptable'. We're quick to criticise. Think about it. I know I am at times, and I'm sure there are occasions where you have been too. We're all guilty of it because it's what we were taught we needed to do in order to survive. As we sit in judgement, we feel better about our mediocre lives and ourselves. If we force others to conform by judging them, the community continues to amble along, ensuring very few individuals ever achieve anything extraordinary, and everyone feels safe.

This programming and these paradigms are costing you your freedom. Until you're willing to shed all your fear, be authentically you, speak your truth, break the rules and question authority, you can never be in congruence with your Divine Destiny, and your results will never be anything but mediocre.

Imagine if we were to celebrate every person's differences and willingness to question the status quo and paradigms passed down from generation to generation. Entertain what would happen if we stopped being offended by others who are willing to challenge the system as it stands, and look deeply at what's not working.

I'm talking about a revolution of truth and human evolution of epic proportions. Are you willing to step up and lead the way?

The achievements of others you currently hold as extraordinary and quietly aspire to, whilst never believing you can actually achieve them, do not even scratch the surface of what you're capable of. If you truly knew what you were capable of, you would stand in awe of yourself, and the achievements of others would seem insignificant in comparison.

I recently had my own experience with the power of being authentic. I had been building an online business for several years and, after jumping around from one idea to the next finally birthed an online international summit called the Conscious Wealth Summit at the end of 2012. I was very excited about this and it consumed me for four months of my life. I had some fantastic speakers who were very generous with their time.

The Summit was not as much of a success as I would have liked. By the time I arrived on the Internet summit scene, the space was already quite crowded and I had no idea what I was doing. I made some fundamental errors that meant it never really took flight.

From the Summit, however, the Conscious Wealth Institute was born. With this new business, I created an international presence and built a tribe of loyal followers, some of whom became my clients. I focused on the CWI for three years and poured my heart and soul into it, sharing Emotional Freedom Technique, Sound Healing, Instant Miracle Technique and a variety of other transformation tools,

13. Congruence

techniques and information to really help people transform their lives.

This period of my life was incredibly rewarding and fulfilling, and I received many messages from people about how much my work had helped to bring big shifts in their lives. There's no feeling more satisfying than knowing you're making a real difference in the lives of others.

But after 2 ½ years, everything seemed to be stuck. I really wasn't moving forward at a rapid speed. In fact, no matter what I did everything seemed to be stagnating, including me. It was incredibly frustrating, and I felt lost and confused. It's interesting how that always seems to happen just prior to a breakthrough.

One day I was at a seminar and a friend introduced me to one of her friends. He was a highly successful businessman who'd started and run a thriving coaching school in Australia several years previously, before moving on to creating several multi-million dollar businesses. We had lunch together and were having a fabulous conversation.

Another woman sitting close by recognised us from the seminar and started talking to us about it. She wanted to invest in the program on offer but had reservations. Without even thinking about it, I went into coaching mode and guided her through her doubts and fears.

We finished lunch and began the walk back to the venue. My new friend said to me, "Holy crap! What do you call your business, Pitbull Coaching?!" Not knowing what he was referring to, I was a bit taken back and asked him why he would say that. He said I just slipped straight into coaching mode with that lady and didn't hold back. That I went straight for the jugular.

I was stunned by his comments and asked if I was I really that brutal? He reassured me by saying that no, he was actually quite impressed. Apparently, he hadn't often seen a woman use laser coaching as a technique.

Now, I didn't actually know what laser coaching was, as I've never heard of the technique, but it appears it's something I do naturally, and it's extremely effective.

This friend is Toney Fitzgerald and he's written several best-selling books on success including one called, *Don't Bitch. Get Rich*. It's a great book by the way and I highly recommend you read it. So, with that kind of book title, you can imagine this man likes to get the job done and doesn't want to mess around, so no wonder he likes a direct approach. For me, however, I was still quite confronted with the possibility that I had been so direct with this woman in public. I was actually a little disturbed that I had the propensity to do that to anyone.

Secretly though, there was a little part of me that loved the title *Pitbull Coaching*. As soon as we were seated at the venue, I got on to the Internet, checked if the URL was available, and registered the domain name.

It didn't take long to find out how naïve and delusional I had been for so many years. At first, I wasn't ready to own the name Pitbull Coaching as I felt it went against what I stood for and who I was 'supposed' to be.

However, I was curious. So, in the coming weeks, as I was talking to friends, I would jovially share the story of the

13. Congruence

encounter and throw the name out there. Much to my surprise and more than a little discomfort, my friends all said something like, "Oh my God! That is so you! You're always kicking my arse!"

After I got over my ego feeling bruised, I thought long and hard about who I was portraying to the world and whether I was being real. Truth is, I wasn't. I desperately want to make a difference in the world, and I thought, as a healer, I had to be all kind, mushy, soft and warm. In fact, this was how I identified myself. It was safe and comfortable and fitted the stereotype of who I thought I needed to be. I realise now just how laughable that was and how much of my true nature I was trying to hide.

I'm not an unkind person. At least, not most of the time and certainly not intentionally. But I don't let people languish in their stories. I have no patience for anyone who just wants to whinge and complain, and not actually do what's required and take direct action to achieve their goals and dreams. Whilst I was trying to hide away from this part of myself, my friends and family all saw me differently to the way I saw myself. I'm a kick arse coach, and when I work with people, I know I'm there to get the job done, not make friends.

So, I started to leave behind the Conscious Wealth Institute and built my new brand, PitBull. This was not an easy transition, and mentally and emotionally I really struggled with it. It seemed so incongruent with the sound healing 'angel' I had built myself up in my mind to be. Fortunately, I am blessed to have some incredibly talented professionals in my life and some friends who are just as real with me as I am with them.

One of my friends is a neuro-branding specialist, Lauren Clemett. It was through her personal and professional guidance and hand holding, as I worked through some serious mental health days, letting my old brand go and building the new one, that PitBull eventually came to be.

I had put so much work into my old brand, and was so attached to the Conscious Wealth Institute, that it was like letting go of an old friend. To embrace the new brand was very difficult in the beginning. Now I can honestly say it was one of the best things I have ever done from a business perspective.

Owning the PitBull brand has been incredibly liberating. Instead of having to hide some of my less endearing, but highly effective skills and traits, owning the new brand has enabled me to bring so much more of myself to the equation.

Contrary to some people's misconception, PitBull is not about tearing people apart or being aggressive and terrifying. It's about being uncompromising, relentless, committed, tenacious and doing whatever it takes to get results. The Pitbull is loyal, tenacious, determined, confident, calm and has courage in the face of adversity. It doesn't cower in the corner at the first sign of a problem, but will meet it head on and not back down.

I can now be all of me, not the shadow version of myself I was being. If people don't like it, I'm really ok with that. I'm obviously not their kind of coach.

I can be much more direct and cut through the stories and BS a lot faster. It's actually what my clients expect, and why they hire me. I'm able to hold the space for someone with

13. Congruence

empathy if and when they need it, but I'm not going to allow them to stay stuck in their story for long. I have a job to do, to help them move forward.

Now, attracting my ideal client is easy. I've never felt more excited about my future as I'm now boldly building a brand and a global presence that truly represents me, and what I stand for. I'm now standing tall, boldly and unapologetically sharing the message I want to get out into the world, to make the difference I was born to make.

The world needs more gifted healers, therapists, coaches and speakers who are bold, confident, boisterous, challenging, unapologetic, polarising, confronting and uncompromising when sharing their brilliance and helping individuals, and the world, to make a dramatic transition into consciousness. It's important to be kind and respectful, but this doesn't mean you have to be meek, docile or submissive.

Are you being a shadow of yourself and trying to please others and be who they want you to be? Or are you being truly, authentically and unapologetically all of who you truly are? This is not about being anything you're not, or adopting a persona that contradicts your true self. In fact, it's the opposite. It's about acknowledging and accepting who you truly are in all your brilliance, warts and all, and bringing that to bear in the world.

Decide now to be all of you, authentically, transparently, loudly, boldly, bravely and brilliantly! Even a quiet person will maintain a strong, commanding presence when they stand in their truth. Question everything you have been led to believe and dare to consider the possibility that it may be wrong.

This is a very confronting prospect because it means potentially giving up your identity and every belief you have been living by your entire life, since the day you were born.

The price of not doing this is high, for yourself and for humanity. We need people who are brave enough to explore the depths of their power and potential and be true to themselves in the face of resistance. Are you willing to pay the price of mediocrity and stay small in order to keep the peace? Are you prepared to continue to try to please everybody, be who they want you to be, and settle for never realising your true potential and your dreams?

Is this approach working for you? Is it working for humanity? The overwhelming evidence we have in front of us would suggest that it isn't!

4. Surrender To Your Greatness

Your brilliance, your genius, your greatness is already within you, waiting for you to be brave enough to share it with the world. You don't have to learn anything else, become somebody else, attain another qualification, gain someone's approval, or wait for someone else's permission to share it. These are just excuses you're hiding behind! I'm calling you out right now.

Surrendering to your greatness is the easiest thing you will ever do. It's being willing to admit you're a magnificent being of limitless power and potential, and taking action from that place of truth, knowing and strength.

13. Congruence

Your greatness is eager to launch itself on the world. Maybe you're scared to make others feel unworthy, less than, insignificant or, disempowered. You know others are already feeling the pain of powerlessness, and you have no desire to upset them and make it even more difficult to bear. So you continue to live the illusion that you're also powerless and unable to take control of your destiny or maybe even change the world.

Whatever the reason, and whether you're doing this consciously, or unconsciously, you're doing it! You're choosing to conform for the sake of your own comfort and ease and the comfort of others.

One of the greatest issues causing the many crises facing our planet and humanity is our willingness to conform and our unwillingness to challenge the status quo. Conformity is robbing us of our individual and collective future. We're all robots acting according to the way we've been conditioned and are expected to by society.

When you dare to let go of your inhibitions and reveal your greatness, you will challenge the current, long-standing paradigm and you will be in conflict with everything our society has been led to believe. For thousands of years, we've been taught to conform and fear the personal and collective consequences of disrupting the system.

If you have the nerve to unleash your greatness, you will stand out. All eyes will be on you. You'll be vulnerable to the judgement, criticism and hatred of others. Make no mistake, some of them will judge and criticise you and even hate you because it's easier to tear you down than it is for them to step up and unleash their brilliance. Because it's more comfortable to conform and not rock the boat than it is to risk the wrath of a society frightened to step out of line for fear of retribution.

We, as a community, are our own worst enemy. Instead of supporting and uplifting every individual to be more, do more, achieve more, we are prone to chip away at them and erode their greatness because of our own fear and our feelings of inadequacy and lack of self-worth. Any chink in the armour and we'll make sure we aim for the weak spot and tear them down.

The media will frantically scramble to whip up a feeding frenzy on some of our greatest and highest achievers if they dare to err, with little regard for the truth. They'll dish up whatever spin on a situation they know humans will eagerly gobble up because they want to feel better about themselves.

Whilst we admire the rare super achievers, we expect more and more of them, and if they fail to deliver and live up to those often impossible expectations, then they are diminished in our eyes and lose our admiration.

This is not meant to be a criticism of humanity. It is an observation of the conditioning that has taught us this is the way we must behave for the benefit of the community and ourselves. This is largely what has gotten us to this place where we're facing the catastrophic consequences of our actions, or inactions, in the modern era. The planet is in crisis. Humanity is in crisis. Unless we resolve to embrace radical change fast, it's unlikely we will make it as a species. The reality is that stark.

13. Congruence

In *A New Earth*, Eckhart Tolle stated that humanity must evolve, or we will die. His book was published in 2005 and yet, 11 years later, the train still appears to be going full steam ahead, and even gathering speed in the same direction it was going at the time with the same destination. What's the answer to this situation? How do we put the brakes on this speeding train before it plunges into the ravine?

The heart of this problem lies in the fact that we've been conditioned to conform. There are a select few who benefit from us being a compliant cog in their powerful machine. They lavish themselves from the profits of our labour and conspire to erode our will and keep us disempowered right under our noses. They tell us the things they're doing and imposing upon us are for the good of humanity, and we fail to question, even as the evidence mounts. They feed us the same old lines, while we blindly follow their directions and shut others down who dare to stand up and question by parroting their position.

We've been led to believe that not to conform is equivalent to mutiny and threatens our existence. That it's criminal and will tear at the fabric of society and bring the system, which apparently serves us so well, crashing down around our ears and everybody will lose. In this way, they enlist the majority who still believe what they want is for our own good to control the minority who dare to threaten the system.

I'm not writing this to make you feel hopeless and helpless, although it might feel that way. The system has already done that. The only reason this situation has been allowed to prosper is that we, humanity as a collective, bought into it and enabled it to happen. When you step into your power, your greatness, your truth, this system no longer has any hold over you, and you have the power to change it. It's imperative we rise up and stop conforming now. This book is your wake-up call.

Have you seen the movie *The Matrix*? This movie is a parody on our existence. The majority of the people plugged into a holographic representation of what they believe to be reality, whilst a few 'unplugged' / awakened individuals work in the background to disrupt and put an end to the programming and conditioning the establishment has so cleverly constructed, put in place and perpetuated to keep us under control.

The hero of the movie is named Neo. This name is cleverly chosen to represent the neocortex, which is the newest evolutionary part of the human brain. It serves as the centre of higher mental functions for humans and is responsible for sensory perception, complex language processing, and human cognition. It is what makes us human, and the dominant species on the planet. To step into our greatness, we must utilise more of our neocortex and frontal cortex the part that makes executive decisions, to determine our actions, and our future.

What if we were to look at unleashing our magnificence, our brilliance and our greatness in a different light? What if we dare to be bold enough to shed our fear and our willingness to conform, in order to show others just how brilliant and magnificent they truly are?

What if we each decide to lead the way out of conformity and be part of a revolution of empowered, conscious thought leaders to help trigger a mass awakening of our

13. Congruence

species and realise the power that lies within each and every one of us?

What do you think that would look like? Billions of people fully connected to the reality of who they truly are. There would be no more fear. No more need to control. No more slavery. No more oppression. No one left behind. Everyone equal. Everyone connected deeply with their truth and with each other. Everyone would have more than enough. Kindness, compassion, love, freedom, abundance, joy and wholeness would be where we lived from and would fill our everyday experience.

We'd all be aware of our own ability to heal others and ourselves. We'd return to the wisdom and healing powers of Mother Nature, and use our food as medicine, and let medicine be our food. We'd return to community, looking out for, and after, every member of the community. Honouring everyone as a valuable part of the whole. No one person would need to rule, as everyone would be recognised equally as part of the conscious collective. We would all work together for the highest good of the global and local community.

No one would want for anything or feel alone again.

Is this a utopian ideal? Absolutely! It's also one I believe is entirely possible. But only if we choose to step up, face our demons, unleash our greatness and stop waiting for someone else to give us permission or to lead the way. This activation of the collective consciousness has been happening and gathering speed over the last several decades. It may be happening fast enough to save us from ourselves, but it may not.

I'm calling for you to join the consciousness revolution and decide right now to unleash your greatness and be all you can be, so you can lead the way for others. Once you've decided, act on your inspiration as the Universe joins you in bringing transformation to your life and the lives of others.

Now you have the four things you need to do to be congruent with your vision and goals. When you are congruent, unseen forces will conspire to take your message and your brilliance to the world. Are you ready? Are you willing? Will you take action? The choice is yours. What do you really want?

13. Congruence

~ Key Reflections ~

1. Congruence is mental, emotional and spiritual alignment with your goals. When you're congruent in all ways, Divine inspiration flows and your achievements become seemingly effortless in comparison. Universal forces become your virtual assistants and do ninety percent of the heavy lifting for you, while you take action on the inspiration you receive. Congruence is your magic carpet ride toward your goals.

2. One of the most important steps to being congruent is to be authentically you. From the day we are born we're programmed to act in a way that conforms to what our families and society expects. Who we truly are is hidden away to make sure we fit in and are accepted. If you want to be truly successful, it's important you know yourself and are being true to you in all aspects.

3. Your brilliance, genius and greatness is already within you waiting for you to be brave enough to share it with the world. You don't have to learn anything else, become somebody else, attain another qualification, gain someone's approval and wait for someone else's permission to share it. Surrendering to your greatness is the easiest thing you will ever do. It's being willing to admit you're a magnificent being of limitless power and potential, and taking action from that place of truth, knowing and strength.

14. Emotional Freedom Technique

I've spoken of it many times, so I'd better tell you about one of my favourite as well as one of the most powerful transformation techniques on the planet.

Emotional Freedom Technique (EFT) is one of the most well-known forms of mindset transformation techniques in the new and exciting age of therapy today. It utilises our energy system, which is made up of a network of meridians, or channels, that move our life force through the body. These meridians were discovered thousands of years ago by the Chinese. A close cousin to acupuncture and associated with Applied Kinesiology, the energy psychology discovery statement declares: "The cause of all negative emotions is a disruption in the body's energy system."

Gary Craig, an American personal performance coach, pioneered EFT. It's been expanded on by many health practitioners, including some psychologists, to accelerate treatment of emotional trauma, relieve pain and release negative belief systems. EFT uses gentle tapping to stimulate the meridian points and clear the block in energy flow that is causing the continuation of the condition being treated.

By stimulating the meridian points while focusing on a problem, it is possible to completely eliminate blocks within minutes, even eradicating the problem permanently. This therapy is capable of creating transformation in a very short space of time, freeing the body's own powerful, natural healing systems to repair any disharmony that has resulted.

It has also been surprisingly effective at not only alleviating physical pain and illness but also, in some cases, actually helping to eliminate the physical manifestation altogether. This is probably not too hard to embrace for those who believe that physical illness is a reflection of some emotional distress. For those who find these claims hard to believe, I encourage you to try this technique, because you have nothing to lose and everything to gain. Once learned, the method is extremely easy to apply yourself and safe to use.

It's important to keep in mind that people who have severe psychological trauma or illness in relation to their issues should always be guided by a professional who is experienced with those disorders as release can be quite complex in such circumstances.

The important part of EFT is discovering what the core issue is that's underlying the physical or emotional condition. This may take some exploration, but once discovered and released, it will give you a freedom you never imagined possible.

On a following page is a diagram that outlines the main acupressure points utilised by the Emotional Freedom Technique. The 'Karate Chop Point' on the side of the hand,

14. Emotional Freedom Technique

is used for the 'setup phrase', which outlines the issue you want to address. The set-up phrase is repeated three times while gently tapping this point. There are some examples of set-up phrases on following pages to give you some clues about where to start.

Each of the acupressure points is then tapped on in succession using two fingers whilst repeating 'Reminder Phrases', which keep you focused on the issue at hand.

The trick to EFT is staying in the feeling of the issue you want to relieve. You don't have to be overwhelmed by it, in fact, that can be counterproductive. But the feeling needs to be activated within your energy body to have the best results from this technique.

Once you've determined the issue you want to work on, before you start the process, rate the intensity of the issue on a scale of 0 to 10, 10 being the most intense and 0 being non-existent. Then, once you've completed one round of EFT, rate the issue again to see if it has come down, and by how much. If the rating doesn't move after two rounds of tapping, there is either what is called a reversal, which needs to be de-activated, or there may be another cause such as dehydration, which can affect the effectiveness of this technique.

This process is organic, meaning it feeds itself. As you work with the process and explore different emotions and belief systems, you'll start to recognise other belief systems or emotions appearing that you would not have considered previously. Take note of these as they appear so you can keep breaking down the layers of belief systems and resistance and release them.

In The Presence of Greatness

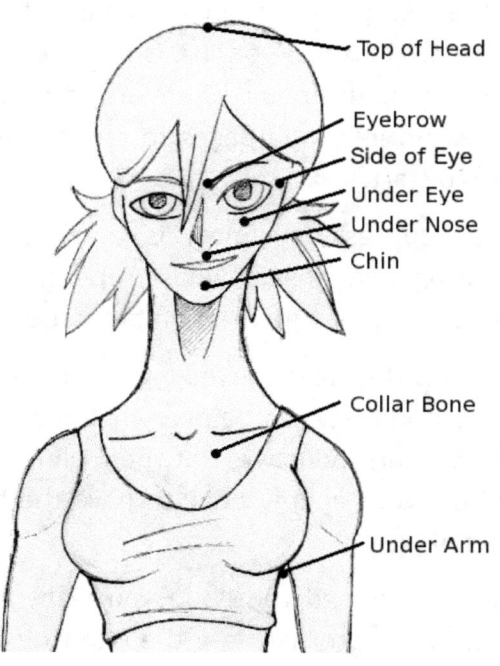

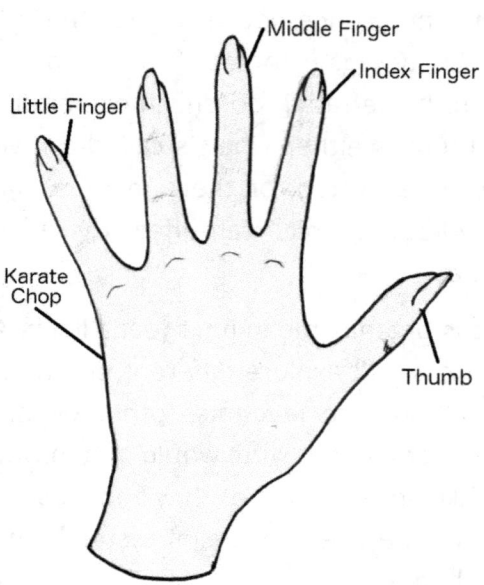

14. Emotional Freedom Technique

THE BASIC TECHNIQUE

1. The Set-Up

"Even though I have this/a.................. I deeply and completely accept myself"

Repeat the affirmation three times whilst tapping on the Karate Chop Point on the side of the hand.

2. The Sequence

Tap approximately seven times on each of the following energy points whilst repeating statements related to the issue and focusing on the problem you wish to address. (See diagram for tapping points.)

    EB, SE, UE, UN, Ch, CB, UA, TH, IF, MF, BF, KC

3. The Gamut Procedure

The Gamut Procedure is rarely used now as the simple EFT procedure is highly effective. However, it's good to know how it works for particularly stubborn issues.

Gamut Point – In between Ring and Baby Finger Knuckle (either hand)

Continuously tap on the Gamut Point while doing the following:

Eyes Closed; Eyes Open; Eyes Down Hard Right; Eyes Down Hard Left; Roll Eyes; Roll Eyes Opposite Direction; Hum a Happy Song- 3 Secs; Count To Five (5); Hum Happy Song

4. The sequence again

    EB, SE, UE, UN, Ch, CB, UA, TH, IF, MF, BF, KC

5. Then take three deep breaths

Here are some examples of set-up phrases that you can use:

Even though I................

    feel that I am not good enough

    feel angry at myself

    feel angry at

    feel guilty for

    feel abandoned and alone

    feel responsible for everything

    feel ashamed

    feel depressed

    am afraid of people judging me

    hate what he/she did to me

    feel powerless to change my results

    feel like the whole world is against me

    know nothing good ever happens to me

    feel like I am stupid

    feel that I will never amount to anything

    feel like a bad person

    feel like I don't deserve to succeed

    have a fear of success

    have a fear of failure

    have a fear of being alone

    have a fear of losing money

    have a fear of dying

    have a fear of heights

14. Emotional Freedom Technique

    have a fear of small spaces
    have a fear of spiders
    have a fear of public speaking
    have this pain in my
    am traumatised by this memory
    feel I can never forgive him / her for
    have this feeling
    feel despair and hopelessness
    my mum / dad told me I was no good
    have this craving for
    feel lonely
    have this deep sense of sadness

………………..I deeply and completely accept myself.

One of the best things about EFT is that once you've learnt the technique, you can use it anywhere, anytime on anything with great results. If you wish to improve those results, or you feel like you're stuck, then it is good to work with a practitioner as they will help you to uncover hidden belief systems and emotions that your subconscious is very clever at keeping from you.

From personal experience, I recommend working with a practitioner on a regular basis to ensure the best and quickest results. After all, you don't want to hang onto those destructive emotions and behavioural patterns for any longer than you have to.

Many people are apprehensive about using negative phrases as we have been encouraged for years to use positive affirmations and feel that by focusing on the negative, we're reinforcing it. This is where EFT flies in the face of convention. In order to target the issue in question, it must be triggered in the energy body, which is why it is focused on. The more you relate to the problem, without being overwhelmed by it, the better the results will be.

There are no words to express how grateful I am that I was introduced to this technique. Over the last few years, it has transformed my life on so many levels and has been one of the critical factors that helped me reach a deep level of confidence, mental fortitude and unstoppability. Not to mention a truly profound sense of inner peace and joy.

I urge you to learn this technique and use it regularly for the rest of your life. For the small amount of effort you need to invest, you will be as grateful as I am for the people who developed this extraordinary technique, and for having been introduced to its existence.

14. Emotional Freedom Technique

~ *Key Reflections* ~

1. Emotional Freedom Technique (EFT) is one of the most well-known forms of mindset transformation techniques in the new and exciting age of therapy today. It utilises our energy system, which is made up of a network of meridians, or channels, that move our life force through the body. These meridians were discovered thousands of years ago by the Chinese and have been used very effectively in the well-known therapy of acupuncture. Tapping on the major meridian points creates a profound effect in the mental, emotional and spiritual body.

2. The important part of EFT is discovering what the core issue that's underlying the physical or emotional condition is. This may take some exploration, but once discovered and released, it will give you a freedom you never imagined possible. It's simple but powerful process that you can use anywhere for anything.

3. To get the best results with EFT, work with an experienced practitioner who can help to uncover the major cause of your discomfort or distress, and help to bring relief quickly.

15. Build Your Wealth Muscle

One of the greatest, most common and most enduring challenges the majority of people struggle with throughout their lifetime is their relationship with money.

In today's society, it dictates so much, including our level of freedom. Money affects our significant relationships, our mental and physical health, our quality of life, and the lifestyle we choose, our emotional well-being, how we feel on a day to day basis, our spirituality, and the quality and nature of our experiences. Because our society has put so much significance on money, and how everything revolves around money, the vast majority of people in the world are suffering because they don't have a good relationship with it.

Regardless of what your judgements are about the monetary system as it stands, it is the system we have to work with right now. If you have a tendency to struggle financially, you can either change your relationship with money or continue to live in a state of lack and limitation because of it. Unfortunately, if you don't learn to master money, money will master you. And money can be a very cruel master.

Your situation around money is a direct reflection of your abundance mindset. If you feel any level of stress and anxiety around money, you will create and attract situations that cause you to have reason to be worried about money. Interestingly, it's not just your level of income that will determine your financial freedom, but also how you manage your money.

My husband's father was a labourer and a farmer on a meagre income. He had an incredible work ethic. He and Laurie's mum had four children and through hard work, he managed to pay off a working farm and provide for his family. He was incredibly frugal and even today, living on the pension, he manages to save about 50% of the benefit he receives, while still enjoying himself, whilst most pensioners are struggling to survive on the same amount of money.

He's never been short of a quid in spite of never earning a lot of money because he managed his money wisely. There are definitely easier ways to earn money and have plenty more of it. The point is you can actually live a good life with remarkably little, when you have the right attitude and mindset to money, and invest wisely to secure a wealthy future.

Studies show, no matter what someone's level of income is, when asked the question, "How much do you think you would need to be financially secure and have all your financial needs met?", the answer is typically double what they're currently earning.

For instance, if someone were currently earning $50,000, their answer would be they would need $100,000 to be

15. Build Your Wealth Muscle

financially secure and have all their financial needs met. If it is $100,000, the answer is $200,000. If the income is $500,000, the answer is one million and so on. Then, when the same person who was convinced $200,000 is all they would need reaches the $200,000 mark, guess what? Correct. Suddenly they now need $400,000 to be financially secure and have all their financial needs, wants and desires met.

It's not that there isn't enough money, it's that most of us always spend what we earn, and more, regardless of the level of income. When our money expands, so do our lifestyles to match, or exceed the income we now have.

There are plenty of instances of people on six and seven figure incomes who appear to have all their financial needs sorted and be living a fabulous lifestyle, when the reality is, their level of debt is so high, they're being crushed under a massive cloud of stress. They can't pay their mounting bills to sustain their lifestyle choices because they have no idea how to manage money.

Truly wealthy people do three things people who are struggling don't. Firstly, they have a positive and supportive consciousness or mindset about money and their relationship with it. Two, they don't emotionalise money but see it for what it is – a tool or resource that provides choices and leverage to do the things they want and live the lifestyle they want. Three, they understand the game of money and how to master it. There are three components to mastering the game of money they do very well: They know how to make money, keep money and grow money.

Let's look at the first part of this equation, the supportive consciousness or mindset about money. People who are truly wealthy have little to no stress about money because they believe it is plentiful and they deserve it.

Contrary to popular belief, money doesn't care if you're an angel of mercy or an axe murderer. Money doesn't have a conscience. We know this because there are very wealthy people out there who are doing incredible things with their money to help others and be of service, and others who are doing their best to screw up the world for all of us and don't seem to care who they hurt in the process.

What you will do with your wealth and success is of no consequence to money. It does, however, matter to you, and if you have a conscience, and don't do the right thing by yourself and others, you'll sabotage your success and wealth at some future point in time. I also believe the consequences of our actions are becoming more and more relevant as we move further into a new age of kindness, light, peace and community. If you're not being of service to others, the Laws of the Universe will eventually bring you undone one way or another.

If you're reading this book, you don't have to worry about that final piece because I know you want to make a difference in the world and you're on the earth at this time to make a positive impact that will resonate for decades and even centuries to come. It is your time.

So how do you change your consciousness around money? You decide to let go of your stress, anxiety and negative beliefs about money, and adopt positive, supportive feelings and beliefs instead. Spend time each day actively seeking out and releasing any negative beliefs you may have about money, yourself, and wealthy people.

15. Build Your Wealth Muscle

Your thoughts create your results, and positive thoughts around money and your relationship with it will produce positive results.

Your belief systems are what determine your thoughts, so the quickest way to change your thoughts is to change your belief systems.

You will have adopted the vast majority of your money and wealth belief systems from childhood, predominantly from the ages of 0 to 7. So analyse what thoughts and beliefs you were exposed to during these years in your home.

- Did your parents or primary caregivers exhibit a positive relationship with money or a negative one?
- What was said in the household about money?
- What was demonstrated about money?
- What was not spoken, but implied?
- What were the predominant emotions about money?
- What judgements and beliefs do you have about rich people? Did you grow up believing rich people are evil, greedy, selfish, mean, arrogant, rude, uncaring, difficult, criminals? As a society, we often downplay the good that wealthy people do, and focus on their negative traits and behaviours, which just reinforces our subconscious minds decision not to be wealthy because we don't want to be like 'those wealthy people.'

Next, you must address your worthiness about having the money you truly desire. Do you truly feel like you deserve it, or do you feel like you're not good enough? Let me remind you of something you knew when you were born and that you've just forgotten. You were born worthy and deserving of all the wealth, freedom and happiness in the world and everything your heart desires. What ensued after you were born was exposure to statements and experiences that caused you to forget this ultimate truth and start to believe the opposite, that you're 'unworthy'. This is a lie, and your soul knows it. Reconnect with your soul and embrace the truth: You're an infinitely powerful being with unlimited potential, and you're worthy of everything your heart desires.

The Universe loves you more than you can possibly imagine and wants ten times more for you than you want for yourself. Your job is to embrace your worthiness and change your belief systems, thoughts and emotions about wealth and success to positive ones that reinforce achieving your grandest vision for yourself and your life on planet earth as a human being.

I have prepared a mind map about money and a collection of positive and negative beliefs and forces which determine our relationship with money.

I wasn't able to include the map in the book because it would have been impossible to read. When you see this mind map, you'll get some sort of idea just how complex our relationship with money is. Use this map to give you some ideas as to the negative beliefs that could be holding you back and stopping you from creating the financial freedom you truly desire. No matter where you're financially, this resource will help you greatly in redefining your relationship with money and changing your results

15. Build Your Wealth Muscle

with it. Download the mind map here: www.PitBullMindset.com/money-mind-map.

The second part of the equation is to stop emotionalising money and see it for what it really is, that it is just a tool and resource to create the lifestyle of your choice and the positive difference in the world you desire to make. Releasing stress and anxiety around money is the first part of this equation. But there are myriad other feelings most people have about money that determine their results.

Most people believe money is scarce, elusive, difficult to earn and even harder to manage, and the cause of much of the problems they have in their life. There's a desperation that underlies and defines their relationship with money. For this large section of the population, it feels like they're frantically grabbing for money, but all they're getting a hold of is air. They're under a constant cloud of 'not enough'.

The vast majority of the population are in a state of lack or scarcity around money, causing a whole gambit of negative emotions. On the other hand, truly wealthy people have a predominantly neutral or positive emotional response to money and are free to enjoy the experiences and choices money gives them.

Money itself is not the cause of joy or frustration. When you take the negative emotion out of the money equation, suddenly your choices, your creativity, your ability to make good money decisions, your inspiration and the possibilities open up markedly.

Can you relate to feeling like there's never enough money? I know I certainly used to. I felt like, "What the hell? I'm doing good work, following my passion, helping others, making a difference, why can't I make good money? Why don't I ever have enough?" It wasn't until I understood how the way I viewed and related to money was a key factor influencing my results that I began to change my relationship with money.

The questions themselves were a clear and direct indication of my negative beliefs about money, and why I continued to perpetuate the same results. The quality of questions you ask will determine the quality of your answers and your results.

Truly wealthy people know, their results with how much money they earn, will be determined by the way they leverage their skills and talents to either solve a problem, or fulfil a need. The more people they do this for, the more money they make. They also know there's an infinite supply of money available for them to earn to fulfil all of their needs, wants and desires. They're proactive and put their minds to work figuring out how to funnel more of it their way.

Wealthy people experience money the way you experience air. Each time you take a breath, do you have any anxiety that there won't be enough air to fill your lungs? Of course you don't. You know there's plenty of air to sustain you and the other seven billion people on the planet and that it's all recycled and reused and it will never run out. This is the way the rich experience money.

Trillions of dollars change hands around the globe every single day. Money is not a static resource. It flows in and out, just like your breath. Being recycled, reused, reinvested day in and day out. By treating money like an abundant resource, there for those who want it and are willing to solve a problem

15. Build Your Wealth Muscle

or fulfil a need in order to have it, there will never be an end to its supply. For those who desperately keep chasing it, believing it's a source of torment and frustration that is in huge demand with limited supply, that's exactly the way they will experience it.

The third part of this equation is the three-step system wealthy people use to make money, keep money and grow money.

Let's look more closely at the first component, making money, which is commonly where most people's struggle begins. Making money is pretty easy really. Get a job and you can make money. You may not make as much as you would like, depending on your belief systems and conditioning, but you can make enough to get by if you manage your money properly. If you want to make more money, then you must increase your level of expertise and skill to get a higher paying job, or start your own leveraged business, if you haven't already. Having a business is the best way to increase your income capacity because then you are not limited to what someone is willing to pay you for your time.

If you're trading your time for dollars, this is the least effective way to earn money, as it relies on you constantly working in order to keep the money flowing in. In this model, you either have to get a better paying job, raise your hourly rate or work more hours to give yourself a pay rise. What happens if you get sick, or when you want to retire?

A more effective model is one where you can serve many people at the same time through creating a passive income stream. One way to do this is to set up a system to sell products and services automatically, without your direct involvement. Like an online sales funnel for an information product, which is one of the hottest ways to build a passive income stream right now.

If you're a coach or consultant, you can create a model where you sell programs that involve your time, but you're working with many people at once in a group situation. These group programs mean you still get to have the personal touch, but you're leveraging your time and earning capacity. Personally, I love running group programs because I still get to help people directly with their blocks and transform their lives, plus I get to experience impacting more people at one time. One-on-one mentoring has a greater impact on an individual, but group mentoring has a larger community impact. It's a very rewarding way to spend your time.

Another part of a leveraged business model is to sell DIY information and transformation products where people work through a pre-prepared program at their own pace. This provides an opportunity for a whole new tier of people who may not be able to afford to work with you in person, but can still take advantage of your skill and expertise at a lower price point.

It can be on sale 24/7, making you money while you sleep, year in, year out, once you set up the system to sell it. This will revolutionise your business and you can do this with multiple programs. It's a 'rinse and repeat' system with no limit to the revenue it can generate depending on how many people you can reach and how effective your sales process is.

15. Build Your Wealth Muscle

While these cookie cutter type programs cannot possibly provide the same level of quality service and results you can provide personally, it makes you available to hundreds and even thousands of people who might otherwise be denied the benefit of your brilliance and expertise. It's also a stepping-stone for those who eventually want to work with you personally. Like a 'try before you buy' system.

Having the group program and DIY programs in place gives you another advantage. Suddenly your personal time for one-on-one clients becomes a lot more valuable and you're able to charge a lot more for your time. People who want to work with you one on one will become premium clients. The irony is – the more people pay, the better the results they get.

This is a perverse but proven part of human nature. The more something costs, the more valuable they perceive it to be, and the more likely they are to take action and reap the rewards of the product or service they've purchased.

There was an experiment done with bottles of wine. Subjects were brought in and different glasses of wine at different price points were placed before them to taste. They were told how much each wine cost prior to tasting. They were not actually told the true cost of the wine, but falsified prices for the sake of the experiment.

The results showed, the greater the perceived cost of the wine, the better the wine tasted to the individual. Even if it was actually the cheapest wine, participants thought it tasted the best when they were told it was the most expensive.

So your brain will alter your experience according to the price of a product as you have a tendency to assume it's better quality when it costs more.

It's an intriguing fact that the more you pay for a program or service, the more likely you are to take advantage of it and utilise it. A colleague of mine called it 'hurt money'. When you pay a significant amount for something you want to get the most out of it, whereas if it's an amount you can afford to let go, you're not as likely to put the effort in and see it through to the end and get as much as you can from it.

A perfect example of this is the amount of free downloads and information available on the Internet. If you're like the vast majority of the internet savvy population in search of solutions, you will have signed up to download a gazillion different free reports, e-books, audio programs, and video series. How many of those downloads do you have on your computer that you've never even opened? You probably have more than enough information in your computer library to help you create a multi-million dollar business, but because it's free, you will have taken advantage of very little of it because you haven't paid for it.

In contrast, if you had paid something for it, you will have been more likely to utilise it and get the best results from it.

This, of course, is not always the case. We've all experienced times where we've paid good money for a product or service and it hasn't lived up to its sales promise or just hasn't created the results we wanted. This sets up something called 'unwarranted buyers resistance', where we lose faith and are afraid to take advantage of genuine opportunities in

15. Build Your Wealth Muscle

case we get 'ripped off'. We become reluctant to purchase because we've been disappointed and felt betrayed from one or multiple 'bad' experiences.

One of two things has happened; either the sales process has over promised and under delivered, or, you haven't leveraged and utilised the product or service to its greatest level of effectiveness. If you've experienced lacklustre results from several programs, the reality is, the common denominator is you. I suggest revisiting some of those programs and bringing a different, more open and pro-active attitude to the equation. Be willing to go deeper than before, get out of your comfort zone and take positive action on what you learn and the information contained in the program.

Many people seem to think that once they buy a product or service, they've done their bit and the rest will just happen for them. The purchase is just the beginning of the process. You've demonstrated your willingness to invest financially in your future, which is very important. Now, you have to be willing to also invest significant time and energy to capitalise on whatever it is you just purchased.

It took me a long time to realise that it doesn't matter how good my mentoring skills are. If the person I'm working with isn't willing to take responsibility for their results and put in the work, there's little I can do to help them. I take great pride in the quality of service I provide and know this is one of the determining factors of the results my clients get. Ultimately, however, the responsibility lies with the client and their willingness to participate in their own success. I can't *do* the transformation or physical work for them. I can only do my best to guide them, influence them, help them release their blocks and up-level their mindset, whilst they're working with me. What they do with that is ultimately their responsibility.

To create a successful business that serves a lot of customers and makes a lot of money, it must either solve a problem or fulfil a need. I recommend you focus on building a business you love. For most people, 95% of their lives are spent doing the stuff they 'have' to do so they can look forward to enjoying the other 5%. Wouldn't it be great if you could create a life where you could enjoy the other 95% as well? That's what successful entrepreneurs do.

Business is not an easy road. If you're not doing something that makes your heart sing and you have a passion for, following through and doing what it takes to be truly successful is going to be extremely difficult. It's unlikely your vision for your future will ever see the light of day.

More than anything, your heart and soul yearns to make a difference and help others. If your mind is busy trying to solve your own day to day problems, even feeling stretched beyond your own reasonable limits, you probably won't feel like you have anything left to give. However, the essence of who you are is crying out to help others in some way.

Making a contribution is food for the soul. Making money is the leverage you require to make a significant impact to more people around the world. When you combine the two, cosmic forces come together and a new and powerful force enters the equation.

15. Build Your Wealth Muscle

Far from being mutually exclusive, doing good things in the world and making lots of money make perfect business partners. There's no doubt we're facing a truckload of problems in the world that need solutions. Unfortunately, the vast majority of people are too busy struggling with their own personal demons to think about them. What if you could be one of those people who are a catalyst for positive change, helping to ease the suffering and end the erosion of peoples' liberties? What if you could release your own demons, achieve the dreams and lifestyle you want for yourself, whilst making a positive difference?

What would you do if you knew you had all the necessary resources and could not fail? Before moving on to the next part of the money equation, think about this for just a minute. Write down an expanded vision for yourself in answer to this question. Dare to dream big and don't settle for what your conscious mind thinks is possible.

Done that? Great. The next component in the money equation, which most people don't understand and are not programmed to do, is to keep or save money. The vast majority of the population have been conditioned to be good little spenders. As they spend money on stuff they don't need, the wealthy get wealthier. Meanwhile, they remain disempowered and stuck in jobs they don't like, doing the bidding of their employers, to earn more spending money. The unnecessary spending cycle that enslaves people serves the system but doesn't serve the individual.

This conditioning means, as soon as we have more than enough to meet our needs, the rest gets spent on superfluous 'stuff'. Trinkets we hope will make us feel better and satisfy the hollow empty feeling we have inside, only to be sadly disappointed, again. This recurrent cycle of retail therapy is like an addiction that only produces a short-term hit and requires feeding all the time. In spite of its lack of effectiveness, we never seem to realise the error of our ways. We continue to repeat the same cycle, hoping in vain that the next hit will bring lasting satisfaction.

What if you were to analyse your spending to see where you're being extravagant, or where you could cut back on things you don't need, and keep a certain percentage of your pay cheque or income every week? This habit of putting a certain percentage aside in a savings account every week is a very effective way to take control of your money instead of your money controlling you. If you're up for it, start tracking where your money is going. Don't ignore any of your expenditure. If you buy a cup of coffee, record it. If you're buying a cup of coffee each day at $4.95 a cup, it doesn't seem like a lot each time, but that adds up to $24.75 by the end of a five day work week. And that's just one item.

In order to take control of your money, you must know where you're spending it. This doesn't mean you have to keep a budget. Some people are very good at this whilst others find it to be torture. Personally, I'm in the latter category. However, I pay close attention to my expenditure and where my money is going.

When you spend the time documenting your expenses, you will be amazed, and possibly shocked, at where you're 'leaking' money. A little bit here, and a little bit there quickly adds to a payment on an investment property or other

15. Build Your Wealth Muscle

investment strategies that could reap you hundreds of thousands if not millions of dollars in the long term.

The way you spend your money is an indication of what you value. If you value yourself and your vision, you'll spend money on things that will help to secure your future and long-term wealth. It fascinates me when I speak to potential clients who 'can't afford' to invest in themselves to work with me personally, or participate in one of my programs, but will spend the same amount or more on buying a brand new car or going on an extravagant holiday the next week. One investment will appreciate in value many times over, whilst the other depreciates quickly over a few short years. Which investment makes sense to you?

How savvy investors like Warren Buffett think about expenditure is in the amount of lost income they would have made with the money spent. In spite of being a multi-billionaire and one of the richest men in the world, Warren Buffett leads a relatively simple existence. He doesn't live in a big mansion or drive fancy cars. Buffett's last car was a Cadillac, which was 9 years old when he auctioned it off for charity. His next car was... guess what? Another Cadillac! Now, while a Cadillac is obviously a nice car, it's not one of the much more expensive makes like a Porsche, Ferrari, Bentley or Mercedes Benz, which he could easily afford.

Why does Warren Buffett choose to be thrifty with his personal expenses? Because he understands the true value of money. For every dollar he spends, he knows that's a dollar he could have invested, and with his success in investing, that dollar could have become $5 or even $10 within a few years. So, instead of seeing the direct cost of the purchase,

Warren Buffett sees the real cost of a purchase is what he would have made if he'd invested the same amount. $100 spent is actually viewed at potentially $1,000 in lost investment revenue. $1,000 becomes $10,000 and $10,000 becomes $100,000.

This is a smart way to view your expenditure as it will encourage you to stop spending indiscriminately, save those hard earned dollars, and do something wise with them to make them work for you. This will enable you to eventually have a passive income covering all your expenditure, giving you far more choice about how you spend your time. Anything above your regular expenses can be spent or invested, how you choose.

Now we come to the third component of this equation, knowing how to grow money; where to invest it and when for the best possible returns, so your money works for you instead of you working for the money. If you haven't learnt how to keep money, you'll have no idea how to invest it for the best possible returns.

Getting a professional to advise you in such matters is important, but be careful whom you decide to work with in this field. Financial advisers and investment brokers for this kind of advice are provided with financial incentives from investment companies to sell their particular product.

So, unless your adviser is independent of this system and not receiving commissions, the salesperson isn't impartial and doesn't necessarily have your best interests as their highest priority. They will want to sell you the type of product that makes them the highest commission, regardless of whether that particular product is what's best for you.

15. Build Your Wealth Muscle

They also have a range of fees for their service that add up really quickly when you analyse the bill. This costs you, the investor, a monumental amount of money by the end of the cycle, particularly when you consider the lost potential returns on the money in question.

Educate yourself about the investment landscape and find an expert, preferably via a referral, who gets above average results for their clients. The industry average for investment returns is very poor when compared with what's possible. So it's essential you find a reputable company or advisor with a proven track record that gets significantly better results than the average investment system.

There are plenty of great books out there to help you understand the various investment strategies, their yields and how to protect yourself from someone stealing your returns. One such book is *Money: How To Master The Game* by Anthony Robbins. It's quite a comprehensive look at money in a variety of aspects and includes a detailed investigation of investment options and their returns. It also provides you with access to investment strategies that, until now, have only been available to the elite and super wealthy. If you want different results, you're going to have to take different action and arm yourself with knowledge that empowers you to change your results for your sake, and the sake of future generations.

Another part of this equation is the fact that our money system is rigged. It's deliberately structured in a way to make the rich richer, and keep the poor and middle class forever hungry. We hear this all the time and we complain about it, but the truth is we're our own worst enemies. We keep playing the game according to the rules and roles we've been assigned within it.

If you want different results you're going to have to start playing the way the wealthy play. They're playing in the same game, but with an entirely different set of beliefs, skills, strategies and tactics. Some of them don't want you to know about this because you can then turn the tables on their game, start playing by their rules, and stop lining their pockets.

Money isn't corrupt or evil, but the money system most definitely is. It's deliberately constructed for you to lose. The question is, are you going to keep playing on the losing side, or are you going to choose to play on the winning team?

Money doesn't have a personality, characteristics or a conscience, but most people give it all of those things. Money doesn't care if you have it or not. It doesn't care if you're a good person or a bad person. It doesn't care if you work hard or don't. It doesn't care if you're generous or stingy. It doesn't care if you're fat or skinny, educated or uneducated, smart or dumb, short or tall, nice or nasty, etc., etc., etc. Money doesn't care about anything at all.

In your life, what money will do is accentuate who you truly are. So, if you're a generous person, you will be more generous. If you're selfish, you'll be more selfish. If you're compassionate, you'll be even more so. Conversely, if you're mean, nasty and a bully, more of those qualities will shine through. Money does nothing but show to the world more clearly who we truly are in all our splendour (or otherwise)!

15. Build Your Wealth Muscle

All money is, is an energy exchange between two or more people for something of perceived value to the purchaser. That's it. So drop the whole story around money and it being something it's not because it's just a load of BS (belief systems).

The only thing determining whether you have money or not is your money story, and you can change it anytime you like, starting right now. Again, the biggest part of the equation is for you to make the decision to change your results and do something different to what you've been doing before.

If you want the money system to change, there's only one way that's going to happen. It's up to people with a conscience, like you, to make a collective effort and get their act together, make a tonne of money, then, when you and a bunch of others have enough leverage, you can change the rules of the game. Currently, the machine has become a massive monster and you cannot fight against it on your own. Better to use the system against itself so it eventually implodes.

How would that look? I have absolutely no idea, but there are plenty of underground organisations working on creating a tipping point where the current financial system will cease to exist and a new system will emerge that's fair, balanced and not driven by greed, war and narcissistic psychopaths. (If you want a really raw look into what I'm talking about, read *Revolution* by Russell Brand.)

It's extremely important you pay attention to your money. Most people are not in a great financial position, so they tend to ignore their numbers at their peril. They're not keeping track of their expenditure so don't know how much is coming in compared to what's going out. Whether they realise it or not, they don't want to know, because often they're spending more than they're earning on things that won't provide a financial return. This is why so many people end up in all sorts of trouble financially.

No matter how uncomfortable this exercise may be for you, get all your statements and bills, and information on any loans you have, and get real about your money position. Go through your bank statements in detail and see where the money is going. Analyse where your spending habits are hurting you and devise a plan to cut spending in those areas.

While you're analysing your financial position, do the work to release your emotional attachments to it. As you're looking at your numbers, what emotions come up for you? Are you disappointed, sad, angry, ashamed, frustrated, anxious, stressed, afraid, confused, resentful or guilty? Using tools to release your emotional attachment, such as EFT tapping, will give you access to more creativity and inspiration to empower you to change your situation. When you're steeped in negative emotion, you lose much of your ability to think clearly and positively to come up with solutions to change anything.

Holding on to negative emotion also keeps you stuck in the same old pattern or cycle that created it in the first place. Stay present and focused. Let go of your judgements and emotions around your position, and you will see how you can create a whole new reality.

Now you have a clear picture of your money position and where you could alter your spending habits to have more

15. Build Your Wealth Muscle

money to save and invest. The next step is to educate yourself about money and how the wealthy see money, make money, spend and invest money.

What is a wealthy person's relationship with money really like? Wealthy people are always seeking out new opportunities to make more money, keep more money and grow more money. That's the way they're wired. It's neither bad nor good, it just is. To fight against it is to go back to fighting on the losing team.

What investment strategies are the wealthy using, and how can you take advantage of these systems yourself? How can you get the best return on your investment and make money work for you? Is there a way to get a substantial return without a huge amount of risk? What do you need to learn to make better investment decisions? Who do you need to speak with to understand the money system and how to win the game of money? What books can you read to educate yourself about money?

These are all examples of better quality questions to help you achieve much better results than you're getting right now and alter the game for you forever.

Almost everyone I speak to wants to have more money. Who doesn't? But most don't read any books or information about money. If you're truly intent on having more money in your life, you must become interested in learning about it. Read books and articles about it. Go to seminars about it. Listen to interviews of wealthy people about it. Register for online summits about it. Remember, "energy flows where attention goes."

Surround yourself with positive money role models, inspiration and information. The more you focus on money in a positive light as well as adopting positive beliefs and emotions about money, the more you will change your results.

We're conditioned to believe we're bad people if we focus too much on money. Let's get one thing straight. If you're focusing on money purely for your own gain and pleasure to the detriment of others, this is not a healthy relationship with the world. But what if focusing on money and improving your relationship with it helped the planet and its inhabitants in some way? Wouldn't that be a good outcome for everyone? How could it possibly be bad to focus on money to improve your outcomes with it in these circumstances?

Here are some simple direct actions you can take straight away to start changing your relationship with money and consequently your results:

- Write out positive affirmations about money and your relationship with it and place them around your house so you see them everywhere you go.
- Put up pictures of happy people and role models with money. A vision board with representations of what you will do with the money is very powerful for changing subconscious beliefs.
- Script out what your life looks and feels like in detail when you have the money you want in your life, and read it daily.
- Change your money habits like respecting what ends up in your wallet and ensure it always has some money

15. Build Your Wealth Muscle

in it so whenever you open your purse or wallet you see there is money in there. This sends a powerful message to your subconscious that you always have enough money.

- Say the mantra "Thank God I'm rich" in a variety of circumstances. For instance, when you have a bill come in, instead of allowing yourself to experience that familiar sinking feeling, or your heart racing unchecked, smile to yourself and say, "Thank God I'm rich." Then write the due date in your diary and go about creating a strategy to pay it by the due date, or make arrangements to pay it off with the company. You can also use this phrase as a positive affirmation that you state to yourself all the time. Bring as much emotion into the equation as you can each time you say it. Using it in conjunction with Emotional Freedom Technique is also powerful. This exercise is easy to do and produces amazing results.

- Immerse yourself in information about wealthy people, money and the money mindset. Read books and publications that teach you what you need to know and get your brain thinking differently about money.

- Pay attention to your conversations and your thoughts around money and make a conscious effort to change them.

Now that you're changing your mindset around money, you need to make a plan to create the financial freedom you really want. Here are some steps to assist you in doing that.

- Write down ideas on how you could make money from doing what you love and take action on those ideas.

- Analyse your spending patterns and see where you're leaking money.
- Create a savings plan to keep the money you have coming in and to pay down your debts.
- Educate yourself about investments and return rates and devise an investment plan that will bring about the kind of returns you want.

If you want to change your habits and your results, you must make a conscious effort to do everything you can to stack the odds in your favour and change your psychology around money. In a relatively short space of time, these little habits will transform your results. What you're willing to do to create change all depends on how badly you want it. Expecting it to arrive in your lap instantly by taking one or two positive actions for a few days is living in a fantasy. Wealthy people become wealthy, and remain wealthy, because of a strong and positive money mindset combined with deliberate, consistent strategies and tactics they employ over time. Their behaviour is driven by their thought patterns and belief systems.

You can alter the game in your favour forever if you're prepared to do what it takes to do so. If you keep thinking the same thoughts and doing the same things you have been, then you'll keep getting the same results.

Many people don't take positive action, like the steps I've outlined above, because it all seems too hard. Let me ask you which is harder. Employing some discipline, mental energy and plain old hard work now? Or being old, broke and filled with regret, with a reduced ability to change your situation in the years to come. What if your situation is the same in five

15. Build Your Wealth Muscle

years' time? Ten years' time? Forty years' time? How hard and painful would that be?

Exactly. I knew you'd come to see it my way. So you've got the information to start getting different results, what are you going to do with it? Unless you do something within the next 24 hours, the likelihood is that you won't do anything at all. Start right now. Just take ten minutes to think about what action steps you can take immediately and write them down and put them at the top of your 'to achieve' list. Make them an absolute priority. I'm not kidding. If you don't do this, I can just about guarantee you'll never do it and your results will not change.

It's time to get serious about money. Over to you, Maestro.

In The Presence of Greatness

~ *Key Reflections* ~

1. Your situation around money is a direct reflection of your abundance mindset. If you feel any level of stress and anxiety around money, you will create and attract situations that cause you to have reason to be worried about money.

2. Truly wealthy people do three things people who are struggling don't. Firstly, they have a positive and supportive consciousness or mindset about money and their relationship with it. Two, they don't emotionalise money but see it for what it is – a tool or resource that provides choices and leverage to do the things they want and live the lifestyle they want. Three, they understand the game of money and how to master it. There are three components to mastering the game of money they do very well: They know how to make money, keep money and grow money.

3. Let go of your stress, anxiety and negative beliefs about money, and adopt positive, supportive feelings and beliefs instead. Spend time each day actively seeking out and releasing any negative beliefs you may have about money, yourself, and wealthy people. Your thoughts create your results, and positive thoughts around money and your relationship with it will produce positive results. Your belief systems are what determine your thoughts, so the quickest way to change your thoughts is to change your belief systems.

4. If you really want to have more money in your life, you need to educate yourself about money. The reason wealthy people have managed to create wealth is because they understand how the game of money works, and play it very well.

16. What Is Abundance?

Abundance is a word that's been thrown around indiscriminately in recent years almost to the point where its true meaning has been forgotten.

The truth is, abundance is about so much more than just money and seems even more elusive. Certainly, in a society that revolves around money as the primary source of exchange, it's an important component of living a life of abundance. Without money, society as we know it would cease to exist.

But money does not provide you with freedom. Just ask the large numbers of financially rich people on the planet who still feel trapped by their own minds and life situations. Money provides you with a freedom to make choices you would not otherwise have. It gives you access to better health care, richer experiences, bigger houses and toys, more stuff, greater opportunities, spiritual enrichment, better technology, world travel, etc. Money can make life a lot more fun when you have it than when you don't, not to mention relieving the stress you may feel from not having it.

True freedom, however, comes from within and doesn't rely on any external condition whatsoever. It is a condition of the mind, body and spirit, and comes from letting go of your attachment to conditions and circumstances in life, and accepting what is. Resisting 'what is' is a futile exercise because you're in disagreement with something that has no quarrel with you, and just 'is what it is'. This resistance robs you of your energy, creativity, inspiration and your happiness. When you accept what is and stop offering resistance to it, you give life the space it needs to grow, expand and collude in your favour to bring you what your heart desires.

Accept what is, then take responsibility for every situation and condition in your life. Come back to the present moment and, instead of reacting to life, choose to respond to life from a place of presence and acceptance. Suddenly you have access to resources you never knew you had before.

When you stop judging the conditions and situations in your life as wrong and choose to see the perfection in everything, you see life for what it truly is. Every situation is simply an opportunity to expand and to demonstrate your greatness and brilliance through each event that presents itself. The greater the challenge, the greater the opportunity to expand and step into your greatness.

True abundance is a frequency which, when you align your own frequency with it, will empower you to experience an incredible flow of love, freedom, wealth, fulfilment, contentment, health, peace of mind, security, happiness, and a host of other desirable emotions. Abundance is all these things. To achieve all this, you must have an abundant mindset.

16. What Is Abundance?

Abundance is an attitude, a feeling, a knowing. Abundance is not something you have to create or an external condition. It's a powerful force of the Universe that flows through everything, including you. Abundance is the essence of who you truly are.

Once we acknowledge completely that abundance is of us, for us, by us, and flowing through us, our entire experience of life changes in an instant. No, it doesn't require our external circumstances to change for this to happen. Our experience of life changes first, then the external circumstances we have in life change to match and reflect our internal condition. As within, so without.

Tuning into the frequency of abundance is like tuning in a radio to a particular frequency on the receiver. The frequency is constantly transmitting a signal, and in order to receive that signal clearly and without interference, you need to adjust your own frequency. You will know when you're tuned into the right frequency by how you feel. It's like being in love. You may remember thinking as a teenager or even later, "How will I know when I'm in love?" and the truth is, if you have to ask, you've never experienced love. When you're in love, you know you're in love.

Just as you could never adequately describe the taste of honey or chocolate to someone who hasn't tasted it before so they could understand the experience of it, or biting into a sweet, juicy mango for the first time, or the feeling of your heart opening when you're in love, feeling truly abundant is indescribable and cannot be truly understood until you experience it.

Fortunately, the frequency of consciousness is all-encompassing. So when you increase your level of consciousness, your frequency naturally raises. Once you reach a particular frequency, all the highest vibrations such as love, joy, freedom, abundance, fulfilment, contentment, peace, bliss, gratitude and acceptance, are embodied at that level of consciousness.

The real skill is to then work at maintaining that frequency more and more often as initially, your experience of it may only be fleeting. This is because we're experiencing life through our external senses. We've been taught to allow the feedback we're receiving from our environment to dictate our frequency and our emotions. When you master your emotional response to your environment, you have the ability to maintain your high vibration through conscious choice, rather than it being determined by external stimuli. This is the point where you become a master of your own destiny and you have ultimate control over the results in your life.

The first part of this adjustment to your frequency is letting go of the illusion that you aren't already abundant. Look at the environment you live in. Even in a desert, you're surrounded by an abundance of sand. In our everyday life there is:

- An abundance of infrastructure
- An abundance of nature
- An abundance of people
- An abundance of health
- An abundance of experiences

16. What Is Abundance?

- An abundance of life
- An abundance of ideas
- An abundance of innovation
- An abundance of construction
- An abundance of entertainment
- An abundance of information
- An abundance of education
- An abundance of food
- An abundance of water
- An abundance of energy
- An abundance of love
- An abundance of opportunity
- An abundance of time
- An abundance of resources
- An abundance of technology
- An abundance of 'stuff'
- An abundance of money

Everywhere we look, there is abundance there for us to experience in so many forms. We are literally surrounded by, and immersed in, abundance. So how come we aren't seeing it? How come we feel stuck in lack and can't seem to get past what we don't have?

It's because our brains have been wired and conditioned to focus on and respond to what's wrong instead of what's right. This is why you're experiencing lack, and why you will continue to produce exactly the same results until you change your thoughts, feelings and conditioning.

You get what you focus on, and the vast majority of the population are immersed in the thoughts of what they don't have and how it's causing them pain, suffering and discontent.

When you decide to drop the illusion that you have lack in your life, and choose to immerse your mind, body and spirit in truly experiencing the abundance which surrounds you, you'll experience abundance in every area of your life.

What do you think will change when you acknowledge, accept, embrace and choose to embody the abundance that surrounds you? Outwardly, very little will change at first, but as you hold that frequency consistently everything will change. Inwardly you'll start to feel abundant and vibrate at the frequency of abundance. When you emit the frequency of abundance, the Universe responds by giving you more abundance. This is the Law of Attraction, one of the most powerful laws of the Universe and it never fails.

The reason you may not have experienced this yet is that you've been working predominantly with your conscious mind, which only has the ability to influence between four and eight percent of your results. When you start to engage the subconscious mind and truly feel abundant with every fibre and cell of your being, your results will transform and the lack you once thought you had will be a distant concept and a condition of the past.

This is when your external results will start to change and as you actively adopt habits that deepen and expand the feeling of abundance, the momentum will grow. It will grow to the point where you will hardly believe you ever even considered a concept of lack could exist in your life at all.

16. What Is Abundance?

When you reach the tipping point, it all feels like a snowball picking up speed and gathering momentum all on its own.

You're still taking consistent, deliberate action toward your goals and actively being involved in getting the results you want. It's as if a different force enters the equation and starts to carry you along. The forces that used to feel like they were holding you back and stopping you before, seem to have now changed sides and are fuelling your success, not hindering it.

This is when the much spoken about phenomenon that is rarely experienced called 'flow' occurs. Miracles will start to occur and seemingly random events that you cannot explain will happen to help you on your mission. You'll be in the right place at the right time, meet the right people, opportunities will present themselves and you will naturally make better decisions that produce the results you want.

Many refer to this as luck. I don't believe in luck. I say it's a combination of right mindset, right focus, right frequency and right action. This is the gift of being on mission, on purpose, in flow and having the right subconscious blueprint for success. It isn't a struggle or difficult.

Sometimes these miracles come as challenges and you're not able to see the true gift in them at the time. But if you're willing to open your mind to the possibility that everything is a gift and an opportunity to get you closer to your dreams and your destiny, you'll experience your journey in a whole new way. You start to see that life is not happening to you, but for you.

Suddenly you'll stop being afraid, angry and frustrated, and you'll use the energy you used to waste on negative emotions of resistance to help you create new solutions. You'll utilise your infinite power and leverage your inspiration to carry you through and beyond any challenge you'll ever face.

The biggest challenge you face is that you were conditioned to believe life's a struggle, a battle, and you must fight to win. Because of this, you've been setting up this battleground your whole life when all you needed to do was pay attention to what Universal Intelligence was showing you and allow it to work through you and with you. Where you used to feel like all of life was resisting your efforts to achieve what you wanted, in fact, you were resisting life.

Don't get me wrong. When you stop meeting life's events with resistance everything will become a lot easier, including achieving your goals. But don't think for a moment you won't experience any challenges or difficulties. These are all a part of life's rich tapestry, and its invitation to you to be more of who you truly are and step further into your greatness so you can realise your true magnificent power. It's working with these challenges, not against them, that flips the equation on its head.

Any resistance you feel is always your resistance. The forces of the Universe are always conspiring in your favour and working to bring about your success. The negative feelings of struggle, adversity, brokenness, separateness, aloneness, frustration, disappointment, etc are all coming from within you, not any external source.

This is why surrendering is such a powerful strategy to employ in order to fuel your success. But we're conditioned to believe that surrendering is weak and it means admitting

16. What Is Abundance?

defeat. When you surrender in the field of battle, you are conceding defeat to the enemy. This is far from the truth in the case of your success.

To surrender to the forces of the Universe is to simply give up the battle you set up, and have been perpetuating for yourself. It's yielding to the infinite intelligence of the Universe and deciding to join forces with it, rather than fight against it. To surrender is to lean into life, not push against it.

You've been fighting against the most powerful force in the Universe. Is it any wonder you feel tired, confused, powerless and frustrated? You're fighting a battle you can't win. As it's been working to conspire in your favour, you've been resisting it at every turn.

You may be feeling defiant and wanting to reject this concept right now, which is normal and natural. You've invested a lot of time and energy in this struggle, and it's almost depressing to think that all this time you've been in a "push me, pull you" struggle against yourself, and the very forces that actually want you to succeed more than anything else.

This all sounds so easy in theory. Unfortunately the movie *The Secret* fuelled this idealistic notion that all you have to do is focus on abundance and you will have abundance.

That is one essential part of the equation and something you must, must, must do to have abundance. As is releasing the belief systems, lies and conditioning that are causing you to see and experience lack. Again, I come back to my favourite transformation technique of all, Emotional Freedom Technique, which has the unique ability to quickly release negative beliefs and install new, positive beliefs.

The easy part is the actual release of the emotions and beliefs. The difficult part is finding the specific beliefs which are locking your current results in place and setting up the eternal struggle you're experiencing. I highly recommend working with a coach or mentor who is skilled at uncovering the hidden unconscious beliefs causing you to sabotage your results and stopping you from realising your goals and dreams.

The next part of the equation is to take specific, deliberate action toward drawing more abundance into your life so it fills you up, and flows over to the point where you cannot believe you ever had lack in your life. When you're tuned into the abundance frequency, thoughts, ideas and inspiration about what action you need to take to attract more abundance will flow effortlessly and, you guessed it, abundantly. You will see solutions and be inspired to take particular action to open up the floodgates to abundance.

When you're in a lack mentality, you're transmitting and receiving the message of "lack" out to the Universe constantly. You won't be open to receive the inspiration or see opportunities that exist at the frequency of abundance. You can't receive inspiration to create abundance if you're not tuned into the frequency transmitting those messages. Consequently, nothing you do will produce abundance. The opposite is also true. A truly abundant mind that is transmitting the frequency of abundance cannot help but receive abundance.

16. What Is Abundance?

I've set out some action steps below to guide you to create the abundance you want. You must take action on these steps whilst simultaneously working to release the stories and conditioning that have been keeping you stuck in lack and limitation all your life.

It's impossible to describe what living a truly abundant life is like. So few people get to experience it. Even many multi-millionaires never get to experience true abundance. Whilst their financial needs, wants and desires may be met, many are still left with a deep hollowness and emptiness that causes so much confusion. They thought money, success or fame was the answer to all their problems. Sadly, they achieve some or all of these to find out they're not.

To achieve financial success, you must learn about money, how it works and how you can master the game of money. If you want to win the game of life, you need to go deep within your heart and take a soul journey of abundance and love.

I invite you to not stop at following through on working toward financial freedom but apply the steps and principles discussed here to your health, your relationships, your career, and any other area of your life you feel could do with improvement. By adapting them ever so slightly, you can live a truly abundant life that fills your heart and soul to the point of overflowing.

This is the pinnacle of living an abundant life. There's nothing that can substitute for it. It's rare and it's the most precious thing in the world. The great news is it's accessible for everyone, and is waiting for you if you want it and are willing to do the work to realise it.

Below are some phrases you can use as positive affirmations to open yourself up to abundance. Adopt them as a mantra and really feel them emotionally and integrate them into the depths of your being. Imagine the statements as a part of who you are as you say them. I say these as I'm walking around Tamborine Mountain each morning walking my dogs and noticing the incredible abundance in my environment.

I recommend you get out into nature, even if it's just your back yard or a local park, to feel the truth of these statements in the depths of your spirit. They'll be even more effective if you use them with Emotional Freedom Technique. As you focus on them for five to ten minutes every day, even longer and more often if you can, you will notice a significant shift in your life around abundance.

> I see abundance everywhere
> I embrace abundance
> I embody abundance
> I am attracting more and more abundance into my life.
> I am swimming in an ocean of abundance
> I am immersed in abundance
> Abundance is the essence of who I am.
> I am the essence of abundance
> I feel abundance within me
> I feel abundance flowing through me
> I absorb the abundance that surrounds me.
> I notice abundance everywhere I go
> Abundance is evident in every part of my life.
> Abundance is who I am

16. What Is Abundance?

Abundance is the essence of my life.

Abundance is flowing through me.

Abundance is washing over me

I am nestled in the womb of abundance.

I live and breathe abundance

I allow abundance to flow through me

I allow myself to flow in effortless alignment with abundance

I naturally make decisions that help me experience more abundance

I was born abundant.

I deserve abundance.

I am of abundance

I am for abundance.

I am by abundance.

I am abundance

You can increase the power of this exercise by adding the phrase "I am so happy and grateful that" before all of those phrases. Gratitude is a powerful practice that will magnify your results even further.

Another practice is to create a vision board or mind movie that helps you to get into the feeling of abundance. Focus on it for several minutes a day to help tune into the feeling and frequency of achieving your goals and dreams. As your frequency shifts, your goals and dreams will start to materialise.

I did a fun exercise recently that I also found very effective. I was sitting as a pillion on my husband's motorcycle on a Sunday afternoon ride and I went right back to when I was a child playing the game 'I spy'. I adjusted the game slightly and started with the phrase, "I spy with my little eye an abundance of" and finished the sentence with anything I could see three or more of. Riding around the beautiful Gold Coast Hinterland, I was able to continue this exercise for 30 minutes easily without running out of things I could see in abundance. I rarely repeated anything.

You can be as general, or as specific as you wish, noticing an abundance of bushland, or of a particular kind of tree or flower. The exercise became so addictive, after about 30 minutes it became annoying because I couldn't shut it off! It was a lot of fun however, and it had the added benefit of bringing me fully into the present moment and feeling gratitude for my beautiful environment as we travelled along the hinterland roads. My abundance frequency was through the roof.

See the abundance you're literally immersed in every day and know you're the essence of abundance. You were born abundant and you are the embodiment of abundance. Embrace abundance and connect with it fully knowing it is for you, with you, of you and by you, allowing it to flow through you without any interference, and enjoy the coming tsunami of abundance in your life!

To receive free access to my 21 Days of Tapping Into Abundance Masterclass, visit: www.PitBullMindset.com/Abundance-Tapping/.

16. What Is Abundance?

~ *Key Reflections* ~

1. Abundance is an attitude, a feeling, a knowing. Abundance is not something you have to create or an external condition. It's a powerful force of the Universe that flows through everything, including you. Abundance is the essence of who you truly are.

2. You get what you focus on. We are immersed in abundance and live in an abundant Universe. Source does not know lack, this is a human condition created by the human mind.

3. The key to living a truly abundant life is to focus on abundance and take specific, deliberate action toward drawing more abundance to you. When you're tuned into the abundance frequency, thoughts, ideas and inspiration about what action you need to take to attract more abundance will flow effortlessly and abundantly.

4. Drop the illusion that you have lack in your life, and choose to immerse your mind, body and spirit in truly experiencing the abundance which surrounds you, you'll experience abundance in every area of your life.

17. The Seven States of Wealth

The model of wealth we've been reaching for has been misguided, misrepresented and is, in fact, keeping the human race very poor. It is one-dimensional, incomplete and very unsatisfying.

True wealth is multi-dimensional. It is about wholeness, fulfilment, freedom and liberation of the mind, body and spirit.

True wealth is the ultimate state of wealth as it includes everything and leaves out nothing. It is about having it all.

Now I am going to share with you what I call the seven states of wealth. None of these states of wealth are any more important than any other. Each is part of the whole and is required to be in harmony with the others in order to experience a truly rich, satisfying life filled with experiences beyond your wildest dreams.

The First State of Wealth - HEALTH

There is a general view that if you don't have your health, you don't have anything. Those who have chronic health conditions would probably agree emphatically with this statement.

After all, a terminal illness is a terminal illness. You can have billions of dollars in the bank, but apart from affording you the best medical care, if you're going to die it's not going to be of much help to you. You only have to think of Steve Jobs, Patrick Swayze, Kerry Packer, Rock Hudson, Walt Disney or dozens of other wealthy people who've died well before their old age due to terminal illness.

Unfortunately, the world is currently in the midst of a deepening health crisis. As medical science continues to make advances to increase our longevity, so our interest in taking an active approach in maintaining our health seems to dwindle. More and more of our population are taking an "I break it and they'll fix it" approach to their health, sadly to their ultimate detriment and demise.

As incredible as modern science is and as resilient as our bodies are, continual abuse and lack of care over a period of years cause untold damage to our body cells, tissues and vital organs. Beyond a certain point, this damage is impossible to repair, and all that's left are desperate attempts to prolong life and reduce pain. What a way to go.

Of course, death comes to us all. At least, death from this form of life. It's inevitable, as we were never designed to exist in the human body for eternity. It is but a fleeting and rich experience in our infinite existence. But why wouldn't you

17. The Seven States of Wealth

want to make the most of this experience and give yourself the best chance at living a rich, fulfilling, long and pain-free human life?

Personally, I want to be running, jumping and skipping till the day I die if I can, and I am doing everything I can to achieve just that. I can think of nothing worse than living out my final days, weeks, months, or God forbid years, in a hospital bed, or palliative care, in pain and anguish, barely existing!

When you are physically and mentally healthy, you are able to take an active approach to creating the life you truly want. You can dive out of bed ready to take advantage of all the opportunities and rich experiences that come your way each and every day.

Being healthy means being able to really live and enjoy your relationships to the fullest. It also means you can use your financial wealth to do whatever you want, when you want, how you want, without any considerations about physical limitations.

When you are physically well, pain does not dominate your thoughts and you're free to be creative, innovative and proactive in creating the life you truly desire.

So why wouldn't you want to have the best possible health you can? Fortunately, there are so many options available to us now for physical healing that go beyond anything we could have imagined 50, 20 or even 5 years ago.

Energetic and holistic healing is rapidly growing. There seems to be nothing that cannot be achieved or healed with the right intention and attention in the realms of this new wave of the healing evolution.

If you're not on top of the world physically, and conventional medicine is not offering you a complete solution to your problem, leave no stone unturned. There are thousands of powerful healers and healing modalities out there very capable of helping you to regain your health, vitality and physical freedom.

Physical wellness is a wealth state that cannot be ignored, underestimated or overemphasised. Your body is your vessel for this lifetime. Ignore it at your peril and look after it wisely, because if you don't make an effort to be healthy now, you better be prepared to experience dis-ease and some level of discomfort in the future.

The Second State of Wealth - EMOTIONAL

Emotional wealth itself is complex and has multiple elements to it.

Firstly, it is my firm belief that we came here to experience the wide variety of emotions on our human spectrum. Without emotion, our human experience on this planet would be pretty pointless as we'd be like robots. Every emotion exists within us, rather than the external conditions imposed upon us.

Emotions are a series of chemical reactions that happen within our body and are induced one of two ways, either as the product of our reaction to a particular circumstance, situation, event or person, or as the result of a conscious decision and deliberately induced state. This event we call 'life' is a rich experience largely because of our emotions.

17. The Seven States of Wealth

The sad truth is, for most of us, our emotions are in control of us rather than us being in control of our emotions. When our emotions are in control, they determine the way we experience life. When they're in control, we go through life in a reactive state, rather than a responsive state.

The fact is no event is determined by the nature of the event, but by our perception of what that event means to us and then by our reaction to it. It's our judgement of a particular situation that causes us to experience whether or not it is 'good' or 'bad'. This judgement comes from our past conditioning. When something happens, we take the limited information available to us in that moment, and we quickly formulate our opinion about what it means for us based on our past history and our limiting beliefs. This then determines whether we feel 'good' or 'bad' feelings, and we react accordingly.

What if we were to take every situation and consider that maybe we don't have all the available information? Perhaps there are things we don't know which could mean this event is actually not a bad thing, or a good thing, it just is. Every situation has a blessing in it for us, even when we can't see it immediately. Each event that happens in our lives also holds tremendous opportunity for us to grow, discover, explore, experience, transform.

By staying present in the moment, we're less likely to judge according to past experiences. We're not overcome by emotion or spontaneous, irrational behaviour that will not necessarily help our cause.

Next time an event happens, big or small, stop and breathe. Instead of operating on autopilot, and allowing your conditioning and the limited information you have to decide what it means, take the time to carefully consider how it might be a blessing instead of a curse. Then respond from that place.

What if, instead of immediately reacting emotionally, you pause and look for the hundreds of possibilities and opportunities that could be presented because of the situation or event? What if you were able to take any event or situation and define what it means to you through your carefully considered response to it, rather than your automatic reaction?

When you're in this state of presence and awareness in life, you're emotionally conscious, which means you're more capable of responding to life rather than reacting to it automatically. It means when something happens, even if it looks bad at the time due to our limited perspective, we are able to stop, take a breath, consider many options, possibilities and potential outcomes. We can then decide consciously how we will respond, rather than getting drawn unconsciously into a reactive state.

Being present means you have ultimate control over the final outcome of the event or situation. You're able to take something that may seem catastrophic, see the blessing in it and turn it into something meaningful. You have the upper hand.

Obviously, if the event involves loss of a loved one or an accident of some sort that changes our lives beyond recognition, we will undoubtedly experience grief, sadness and emotional discomfort. This is an inevitable part of our rich human experience. It can also be quite wonderful when

17. The Seven States of Wealth

we embrace the full range of emotions available to us and don't make any emotion 'bad'. It's how we process our emotions and interpret the event that determines how we feel about it, and how it affects our lives in the long term.

Most gun deaths in the US happen in the heat of the moment during some form of domestic violence incident or confrontation. Do you think the person who pulls the trigger and kills or seriously wounds their partner or their kids is in control of their emotions at the time? Do you think they might regret their actions later and wish they could have done something differently? That's an extreme example of what happens when people react to life from an emotional state.

We're not emotionally conscious because we haven't been taught to deal with what we've been taught are our 'negative' emotions. Generation after generation has perpetuated this travesty because no one feels comfortable with the 'negative' emotions. The reason those emotions don't feel good is that they're the ones that are lower on the vibrational scale (see page 276).

We're taught to repress our emotions rather than find a healthy way to process and express them. Any emotion not fully experienced and expressed is going to cause emotional, mental and even physical distress at some point because it doesn't go anywhere. It gets trapped in the emotional and physical body. If this happens over and over, we get to the point where we're all full up and we can't push any more down. Eventually it all has to come out and will then be expressed as rage, depression, despair, or other extreme emotion. If it still isn't processed, eventually it will manifest as some form of disease within the mind and/or body.

The beautiful thing is that when you get comfortable being uncomfortable, and when you're not afraid to feel your emotions fully, they actually dissolve quite quickly. They have to because there is nothing to hold them in place. Feeling emotions never killed anyone. Not feeling emotions can be deadly. They build to the point of complete overwhelm, and we become reactive or develop a physical condition.

When you understand your emotions and use them as they were intended, they become your guidance system that lets you know when you're in vibrational harmony with your purpose, your spirit and what you want in your life.

If you're familiar with Abraham and Esther Hicks you will have heard this plenty of times. Your emotions are what let you know when you're on track. If you're feeling content, satisfied, happy, fulfilled, joyful, at peace, free, relaxed, you're in a high vibrational state and your frequency is in alignment with what you want. In this state, you're offering no resistance to receiving everything you truly want and desire and it is able to manifest in your life.

Now here's the part where most people come unstuck. You can't wait till you get what you desire in order to feel that way. That's all backward. If you want to achieve your goals and dreams and manifest great things in your life, you have to be feeling that way to get it.

Most people wander around feeling upset, angry, frustrated, disappointed, guilty, ashamed, depressed, anxious or

17. The Seven States of Wealth

stressed and wonder why their life isn't turning out the way they want and they're not getting what they think they're focusing on. They're missing the most important piece of the puzzle – their vibration is all wrong! And actually, when we're feeling those emotions, we're not focusing on what we want, but what we don't want. Our guidance system is always right.

If you're feeling stressed, anxious, afraid, sad, angry, guilty, doubt, ashamed or any other negative emotion about a particular situation, it's unlikely you'll be able to turn it around whilst you're in that state. In fact, in that vibrational state, you're actually repelling what you want.

This is why I work with people using powerful transformation tools like EFT, Sound Healing and other modalities that take the charge out of the emotion around a particular condition in their lives. Once the emotional charge has been released, and you're feeling at peace with what is, you're in a higher vibration and a more resourceful state to be able to change a situation and create a desirable outcome from it.

Have you ever felt a sense of absolute certainty about something in your life that was so strong that nothing and nobody could convince you to change your mind or your course of action? We've all felt that at different times right? How often, when things didn't turn out the way you expected the first, second and third time, have you started to doubt?

How often have you kept trying for what seemed like a pretty long time, when in reality it was only a few weeks, or maybe even a few months, only to give up thinking it's not meant to be, or it's never going to work? Of course, all of us have!

It's imperative you believe in yourself and have absolute faith. You have the power to create anything you truly want and desire in your life. As long as you have clarity and faith as you take action, whatever you focus on will eventually manifest in your reality.

Faith and trust are essential if you are to achieve great things in your life. Think about having complete faith and trust that you can achieve anything you set your mind to. Will you falter? Will you ever give up? No. If you have complete faith, you will keep going no matter how long it takes, how many times you fail or how many challenges you face. This is what separates the winners from the wannabes.

There is one final thought I want to leave you with about emotional wealth.

One of the things becoming a Deeksha (Oneness) Blessing Giver taught me is there are bliss and joy in every emotion. It is our resistance to what we judge about our negative emotions which creates the suffering, not the emotion itself. When we're fully present, loving and accepting toward our negative emotions, they cannot continue to exist. They just dissolve under the intense focus of love, appreciation and understanding. All you're left with is pure joy. So your way to joy and bliss is by being fully present and accepting all your emotions.

The reason so many law of attraction experts, teachers and coaches like myself encourage the use of tools like

17. The Seven States of Wealth

visualisation, vision boards, mind movies and meditation is because these are powerful tools designed to get you into the feeling state of having what you want. Using other transformation tools like EFT and Sound Healing, in conjunction with those, are an incredibly powerful way to transform your life. You're working on multiple levels to alter your vibration, your consciousness and your emotional state.

Unfortunately, most people miss that part. They look at their vision board or they visualise and all they feel is frustrated, sad and angry because they don't have it yet. Then they get even more frustrated, sad and angry because it never turns up, and instead, their life gives them more stuff to be frustrated and angry about.

I understand just how hard it can be to get into a peaceful, joyful state of gratitude when the bills are piled sky high, or your relationship is toxic, or you're feeling lonely, or you've got some disease in your body. We haven't been taught how to feel the bliss when life isn't perfect. It's a skill that has to be developed, practiced and mastered. Fortunately, we now have a wide selection of tools and techniques available to us to help us become a master of our emotions. These enable us to release the charge and resistance from our negative emotions, move our way up the emotional scale and get into alignment vibrationally with what we want regardless of what's going on outside of us.

Use these tools every single day to gradually and continually move closer and closer to what you truly want and desire in your life. As you do this, baby steps will turn into giant leaps and, in a relatively short period of time, your life will look completely different and magic will become a constant companion.

Below is the emotional guidance scale from Esther Hicks and Abraham. Find a way to gradually move your way up the scale so you can become a master of your emotions and create your ideal life by design.

**Emotional Guidance Scale

1. Joy/Appreciation/Empowered/Freedom/Love
2. Passion
3. Enthusiasm/Eagerness/Happiness
4. Positive Expectation/Belief
5. Optimism
6. Hopefulness
7. Contentment
8. Boredom
9. Pessimism
10. Frustration/Irritation/Impatience
11. Overwhelm
12. Disappointment
13. Doubt
14. Worry
15. Blame
16. Discouragement
17. Anger
18. Revenge

19. Hatred/Rage

20. Jealousy

21. Insecurity/Guilt/Unworthiness

22. Fear/Grief/Depression/Despair/Powerlessness

** Esther & Jerry Hicks – "Act As If"

The Third State of Wealth - RELATIONSHIP

I believe the other reason we choose to have a human experience is to be in relationship.

Just like if you take emotion out of the equation of our experience, if you take away our relationships, our lives are empty and meaningless.

Relationships are another aspect of life that adds immeasurable richness to our experience here on Earth. There is our relationship with others, with our environment, and most importantly, with ourselves. Ironically, the better our relationship is with ourselves, the better our external relationships will be.

So, if we want to improve our external relationships, we must change our internal relationship first.

Sadly, we're programmed to put the blame outside of ourselves when our relationships aren't as fulfilling and satisfying as we would like. We habitually point the finger and say it's somebody else's fault that we feel a particular way and if they hadn't done what they did, or had treated us differently, then our relationship would be better.

This is giving all your power away to an entity outside of you, and when you do this, you're completely powerless to change the nature of the relationship. By paying attention, going inside and seeing how your external relationships are merely a reflection of your internal relationship with yourself, you have the power to have a significant impact on those external relationships by transforming the internal one.

You will undoubtedly have heard that when we love ourselves deeply, we will attract loving relationships with others. When we are highly judgemental and critical of ourselves, we will attract people who are judgemental and critical of us and we will be critical and judgemental of them as well. When we are angry with ourselves, we will attract angry relationships.

Of course, we can't control other people. But when we improve our internal relationship, many people will naturally and automatically respond to and treat us differently. It appears quite miraculous. People who aren't capable of meeting us in that higher vibrational place will no longer be in our presence to provide the source of challenge for us. Either they'll choose not to be a part of our lives, or we'll choose not to be a part of theirs. This transition will often unfold naturally.

Having wealthy, healthy relationships means the ability to engage with our fellow humans, animals and our environment in a way which is understanding, forgiving, considerate, compassionate, loving, caring, fulfilling and satisfying. It's not possible to give that to others if you're not able, or willing, to give it to yourself first.

Relationships are an essential part of your complete wealth equation. Pay attention to them, nurture them and, most of all, nurture your relationship with yourself. You're the only one who is guaranteed to be present in your life 24/7 for your entire life. You might as well learn to love and appreciate yourself!

The Fourth State of Wealth - FINANCIAL

Of course, this is the state of wealth most people identify with when we mention wealth, prosperity and abundance. Unfortunately, it's the one that appears to cause the most suffering as we live in a society where money is essential to our survival on this planet and we all have to be in a relationship with it all the time.

It's also one of the most consistently frustrating and elusive parts of our existence, as the majority of us are conditioned with a consciousness of lack, scarcity and unworthiness around money.

If we're in a toxic relationship, we have the choice to end it. Of course, until we deal with our relationship with ourselves, it's likely we'll just attract a similar toxic relationship. However, at least we can have temporary relief from the angst and frustration of a personal relationship.

Our relationship with money, however, if it's not a good relationship, never seems to give us any respite. For the majority of people on the planet, there never seems to be enough to go around and the mere thought of the subject creates a tightening in the stomach, jaw, chest, shoulders or some other part of the body.

Money is often deemed to be the cause of a large percentage of relationship break-ups as well. It's a subject that evokes so much tension, anxiety, fear and overwhelm, that it's not surprising it tends to bring out the worst in us.

Most people will dismiss money as unimportant – "Money won't make you happy." Well, they're right, in part. Happiness is not reliant on anything except your decision to be happy. But having lots of money sure can make this human experience a lot less stressful and a lot more fun.

There are an infinite number of wonderful experiences and resources we have available to us on this planet. Most of them require money to enjoy them. Why do we dismiss the importance of money when it has the potential to save many people from suffering and death? Money builds hospitals and schools; churches and Universities; entertainment centres and theme parks; roads, bridges and parks. It buys clothing, food, shelter and other essentials.

When we have money, we can expand our spiritual experience by going to spiritual workshops, retreats and locations. Money helps us to travel the world and expand our understanding of the human race and condition. We need money to create solutions to the current environmental and health crises we've caused. Why do we continue to dismiss the importance of money in our own lives when it is a critical element in the lives of pretty much everyone on the planet? It just doesn't make sense!

We have given money a lot of power in our society. It enables us to experience more joy, fun and freedom. It's a powerful tool for leverage to help you to reach more people with your

17. The Seven States of Wealth

gift and your message. It's the must-have tool philanthropic wealthy people use to find and provide solutions to suffering and pain the world over. It can also be the cause of great suffering when people have an experience of not enough money.

Never, ever dismiss how important money is. It is no more important than any of the other states of wealth, but it's no less important either. It's a powerful tool to accomplish many good things in the world, and it can be extremely liberating and freeing in our own personal lives.

We tend to give money power by giving it characteristics that mean it gets to determine how much of it we have in our lives. Just like everything else in the Universe, money is just energy. It doesn't have a personality or a conscience. It doesn't decide who deserves to have more of it than anyone else. It's you who's deciding how much you have and how much you have to struggle. Only you can decide, and take action to change it.

The Universe does not decide who gets more air than others. Air is available to all of us in infinite amounts. It's the same with money. There is an infinite source of money available to you; it's up to you to let more of it into your life.

The good news is, like all the other states of wealth, our relationship with money, which is determined by our belief systems, paradigms, subconscious programming and self-worth, can be changed when we alter our consciousness around it and our relationship with it. This is an incredibly liberating realisation because now the power is back in your hands.

But until you change your consciousness around money, your situation will never change, or if it does, it will only be temporary.

You see, you have a financial set point, and regardless of any fluctuation, big or small, you will always come back to that set point. This is why eighty percent of people, or more, end up right back where they started, or even worse off within the space of two to five years after they win the lottery. Your subconscious is programmed for a certain amount of money and it will always conspire to bring you back to that until you change it.

This is where transformation tools and techniques have the ability to shift your consciousness, negative belief systems, paradigms and your vibration around money so you can enjoy attracting and maintaining a money flow greater than you have ever dreamed possible.

Many heart centred entrepreneurs, spiritual leaders and healers have a conflict between spirituality and money. While this is just one of the possible blocks for people, it's a very powerful one that prevents many from ever living a financially comfortable existence doing the work they love and have come here to do.

There are also hundreds of other reasons people block money such as:

1. Criticism and judgement about rich people (greedy, selfish, rude, etc)
2. Belief that there is never enough money
3. You have to work hard for money
4. Money is a struggle

17. The Seven States of Wealth

5. Money is the root of all evil
6. Money doesn't grow on trees (i.e. isn't abundant)
7. Money causes arguments (did your parents argue about money?)
8. It's greedy / selfish to want more money
9. You should be happy with what you've got
10. If I have more, others will have less
11. If I'm rich, other people won't like me / will reject me
12. If I'm rich other people will be jealous of me
13. I'll be lonely if I'm rich
14. I won't know who I am if I'm rich
15. I'm not good enough
16. I don't deserve to be rich

These are just a few of the hundreds of negative belief systems I've encountered working with people on their money blocks that stop people from allowing money to flow in their lives. It's a complex combination of multiple negative beliefs and conditioning that keeps them in a constant relationship of struggle around money.

These negative beliefs and paradigms aren't exactly shouting from the rooftops that they're there. They're hidden in the depths of your subconscious mind, lurking deep under the surface, cleverly avoiding detection.

Your belief systems are designed to protect you, or keep you safe. Consequently, they aren't advertising their presence when you're attempting to eliminate their presence from your subconscious. This is why it's so important for you to find a coach, healer or mentor you can work with to uncover the belief systems that are holding you back and keeping you stuck.

When you work with someone who can help you to uncover whatever blocks and belief systems are keeping you stuck, you will take quantum leaps in your progress.

Coaching is the most powerful force for change on earth. I strongly encourage you to find a coach you resonate with, who uses powerful transformation tools and techniques, and work with them. It will be by far one of the most transformational, powerful, rewarding and life-changing investments you will ever make.

The Fifth State of Wealth - INTELLECTUAL

Intellectual wealth doesn't refer to your level of intelligence or education. This state can also be referred to as wisdom. You could be the most intelligent and educated person on the planet, but that doesn't make you wise.

There is an age old saying that states knowledge is power. I disagree. Knowledge only has power when you do something with it.

Even if you're the most knowledgeable person on the planet, until you do something with that knowledge, it's virtually worthless.

Believe it or not, you have a unique body of knowledge which, when combined with your unique understanding and view of the world, is priceless. It's this unique combination that will provide great value to others, and it's what you

17. The Seven States of Wealth

need to use to create the financial freedom and lifestyle you truly desire.

Wisdom is something that comes when someone is able to carefully consider all the information they have available to them, without judgement, and come to the best possible conclusion about a situation. It's the ability to be completely present and make the best possible decision about a particular set of circumstances with the knowledge you have.

Wisdom is the ability to apply compassion, consideration and understanding with all people and situations.

Intellectual wealth also refers to the ability to tap into the biggest bank of knowledge that exists – Universal Intelligence.

Every piece of information that ever has, or ever will exist, resides in the realm of Universal Intelligence to which we all have access.

In our physical human experience, we access new knowledge and information through books, audio programs, video, direct human communication and various other physical forms. The reality is, all of that information originates within Universal Intelligence, and all we're doing by accessing it in physical form is remembering what we already know. So there's nothing we don't know, we've just forgotten, and we need to remind ourselves. It's pretty clever really when you think about it.

Have you ever been asked a question and you've known the answer without knowing you knew it? And you're surprised by the answer that comes out of your mouth before you've even thought about it? One explanation is you learnt it some time ago and have just forgotten about it until that moment. Another is that you accessed it directly from Universal Intelligence. I'll leave it up to you to decide.

In the way our society is structured, the more expertise you have in any particular field, theoretically the more money you can command. So it pays to become highly knowledgeable in a particular field if you want to make more money.

It's wise to choose something that really excites you. Something you're passionate about. This will mean your study and delivery of whatever it is you're becoming an expert in will bring you such joy that mastery of it will come easily to you.

But here is where many people become stuck. You don't have to know more than you know right now to be of service to others and create a highly profitable business you love.

In fact, as I said earlier, you already have a unique body of knowledge, divine gifts and an unconscious competence that you can implement right now to be of service to others and create the life of your dreams. It's up to you to unlock whatever is inside of you and share that brilliance with the world. You'll find the world is a magical place with more abundance and joy than you ever imagined possible.

You have a purpose. Do whatever you can to discover your mission and live it! You deserve it, and so does the rest of the world!

The Sixth State of Wealth - SPIRITUAL

Being spiritually wealthy is not confined to the 'gurus' among us.

Spirituality means different things to every single person. With almost seven billion people on the planet, there are almost seven billion versions of spirituality. There are as many different interpretations and forms of spirituality as there are people.

Your spirituality is your relationship with whatever higher power you believe in. It's a connection no one else, except you, has the power to define, determine and deepen. Religious doctrine and philosophies can provide you with guidelines and education, but your relationship with your Creator is yours alone to decide.

Organised religion certainly brought in a 'standard' that is adhered to by sometimes millions of people having similar beliefs. But it's impossible to confine the human spirit to have exactly the same spiritual beliefs as we all interpret information through our own filters, judgements and perceptions.

If we all learned to respect each other's spiritual beliefs, and not seek to impose our beliefs on others, there would be a lot less conflict and suffering in the world.

For me, spirituality is a meeting of the heart, mind and soul and a connection with my higher self, or higher consciousness. It is a connection with my spirit, my infinite being. This feeling of connection brings me incredible joy and the more I nurture this connection, the easier it is to access.

I believe we're all one being, existing in an illusion of separation so we can remember who we truly are – one with All That Is.

Unfortunately, some organised religions have actively sought to disconnect people with their higher selves in an attempt to control and manipulate them in a misguided quest for power. Fortunately, many people are now waking up and breaking free from this mass indoctrination and rediscovering their own infinite power and potential.

Helping others to rediscover and connect with their infinite power is something I'm extremely passionate about, and I've realised is part of my mission.

Take the time to explore any spiritual teachings you're drawn to. Decide for yourself what resonates with you and what doesn't, and embrace spiritual principals, beliefs, practices and community that brings you freedom, joy, liberation and personal power.

Nothing and nobody should ever seek to diminish you, control you, tell you what to believe or how you should relate with or worship your deity. Spiritual fulfilment is a highly sought after prize, and many have believed that a life of austerity, self-denial, laborious practices and suffering are the only way to true spiritual connection and liberation.

Emotional detachment from personal possessions, conditions and circumstances is the way to unconditional happiness, but that doesn't mean you have to deny yourself any and all pleasures life has to offer.

This state of detachment merely refers to an elevated state of consciousness where you're not reliant on anything in your life to make you happy. You can be happy regardless of what is going on in your life.

This is an incredibly powerful state to attain. It's absolutely achievable once you let go of your reliance on your life having to be a certain way for you to be happy. It comes back to your perception and judgement of everything in your life and whether it's good or bad.

Let go of your attachment to earthly things. You came here with nothing, and you will leave with nothing. Everything in between is simply an opportunity to experience what is provided for you in this rich playground.

Enjoy what comes your way, know that you are an infinite being with infinite power and potential and be happy with what is!

The Seventh State of Wealth - CONSCIOUS

Up until now, each state of wealth I have mentioned is just as important as any other.

The seventh state of wealth, however, is the ultimate, all-encompassing state.

You can focus on each of the other six states of wealth individually and work feverishly to keep them all in balance. Or you can focus on being in a state of conscious wealth and all of the other states will naturally fall into place for you.

Conscious wealth is a state of being, not a state of having. This is the ultimate state of wealth that will bring freedom, harmony, joy and balance to all areas of your life. Conscious wealth is coming from the inside out. It is your level of consciousness.

It is the embodiment of all the other states of wealth and coming to a place of deep understanding that you are 'All That Is' and there is nothing you are not. You ARE joy, peace, abundance, health, wealth, freedom, happiness, fulfilment, compassion, understanding and forgiveness. You are the Creator and the Destroyer.

When you're in a state of conscious wealth, external circumstances have little to no importance or influence on your state of being. This is when you can command life and its outcomes.

You're an extension of Source Energy and connected to everything that exists. You are One with the Universe.

When you realise you are 'All That Is' and everything you want is a part of you, there is nothing you can't be, do or have. It's impossible to be denied something that's already a part of you. When you embrace this belief, you will no longer be in a state of wanting because you'll recognise that wanting is based on the lie of separation.

By holding the belief and vibration of inclusion, you allow what you desire into your experience. Because of the nature of our existence, it may take a small amount of time: hours, days or even months depending on what it is you wish to include in your experience. By releasing the wanting and the illusion of separation, you drop into a state of allowing instead of resisting. In that state, inspiration will flow for you to take the action you need to take to cause circumstances and events to align and bring it into your existence.

17. The Seven States of Wealth

Conscious Wealth is a state where miracles are commonplace, joy is effortless and freedom is a permanent state of existence. Achieving this state could take you years, months, or merely seconds. There are no hard and fast rules about how to expand your consciousness to this elevated state. There are no specific practices you must do, or courses you must take.

For most of us, achieving this state, even for a moment, does take a certain amount of practice, being a part of a movement that promotes and assists the attainment of higher states of conscious awareness, and a dedication to achieving higher conscious states.

Almost everyone has experienced higher states of conscious awareness at some time. It is maintaining them on a consistent basis that is the elusive part.

I suggest you seek anything that brings you joy, peace and fulfilment, and be fully present to it. Investigate deeply your subconscious conditioning, negative beliefs and paradigms that could be preventing you from realising you're an infinite being with infinite power and potential. Know that you have the ability to achieve anything you put your mind to. Then do whatever you can on a daily basis to release those blocks from your physical, mental and spiritual body. This is what will bring you more and more into this most important state of wealth where you will be able to manifest the life of your dreams and more than you ever imagined possible.

~ *Key Reflections* ~

1. True wealth is not just about money. It's about wholeness, fulfilment, freedom and liberation of the mind, body and spirit. True wealth is the ultimate state of wealth as it includes everything and leaves out nothing. It is about having it all.

2. There are six primary states of wealth, and each is equally important to create a holistically fulfilling and rewarding life. They are health, emotional, relationship, financial, intellectual and spiritual. When all of these are in balance, you are truly wealthy.

3. The seventh and ultimate state of wealth is conscious wealth. The state of conscious wealth is when all six of the primary states of wealth being balanced and in harmony. Conscious wealth is a state of being, not a state of having. This is the ultimate state of consciousness that will bring freedom, harmony, joy and balance to all areas of your life. Conscious wealth is coming from the inside out. It is your level of consciousness.

18. Stack The Odds In Your Favour

There's an enormous amount of information out there offering recipes for success. Every version is a little bit different and every one is valid, depending on what has worked for the person it originates from.

You can do this the easy way or the hard way; it's your choice. Personally, my preference is to do the things I know will stack the odds in my favour and help me to achieve my goals with as much ease as possible. I've created a list of things you can do to give yourself the best chance of being all you can be and living a life beyond your wildest dreams.

I started with the intention of compiling a small list of things to help you, and it just kept growing and growing. There are so many actions you can take that will make a positive difference, and even these are just a small sample of what you can do.

Some of these have been mentioned previously, but are worth summarising here as an action list you can refer to whenever you need to.

You don't have to do all of them, at least not all at once. Run through the list. Think about what's relevant for you and where you're at right now. Then take action on the ones you feel will have the greatest impact on your results, implementing them one at a time. They're all appropriate and relevant.

If you want to change your current circumstances, the time to start taking action is now.

1. Define What Success Means For You

Success is often elusive, intangible and different for everyone. So the first thing to do in order to set yourself up for success is to define what success means for you.

Respected American radio personality, author and speaker from the mid-20th Century, Earl Nightingale, was referred to as the 'Dean of Personal Development'. Nightingale states that success is: "The progressive realisation of a worthy ideal. If a man is working toward a predetermined goal and knows where he is going, then he is a success." I think this is a pretty comprehensive and appropriate definition.

Success isn't just about the final achievement of a vision, but taking the steps necessary toward it. This immediately removes the stigma and judgement we put on ourselves when we look at our results and see ourselves as 'failures' because we haven't achieved our goals yet. This definition means as long as we're taking consistent action, we're successful. Doesn't that take the pressure off?

The main requirement for this definition is to know where you're going and to have clarity around your vision. So the

18. Stack The Odds In Your Favour

first step to setting yourself up for success is to have absolute clarity around your vision and what you want to achieve. This theme has been a constant throughout this book. I won't make any apology for it because it's important enough to warrant reiterating it time and again. It's also one of the primary reasons people fail. If you haven't got this piece in place, you have virtually no chance of success. How can you when you don't know what success looks like for you?

Sadly, our society has a general preconceived idea, that those who are super wealthy, or famous, or both, have the ultimate version of success. We cling desperately to this whimsical idea in spite of us also witnessing time and again via the media, the emotional and mental destruction of many of those we would hold as the most successful according to this definition. These people seem to 'have it all' when their achievements have left them hollow and empty, confused and lonely, sad and desperate. They've chased the long upheld ideal of success and wonder why they're not fulfilled. Some of them tragically take their own lives either deliberately, or accidentally in a drug and alcohol dazed stupor.

You've seen the headlines. You've mourned their passing. Are you sure you want to hold on to that idea of success? The likes of Michael Jackson, Amy Winehouse, Robin Williams, Whitney Houston, Kurt Cobain, Michael Hutchence, Philip Hoffman and Prince, all considered exceptionally talented geniuses in their professions and all still with bright careers in front of them. They seemed to have it all, so what on earth went wrong?

There are all sorts of conspiracy theories about their deaths, and there may be some truth to them. I really don't know.

But certainly, in some cases at least, in spite of all their success and fame and fortune, there was a hollowness and emptiness that consumed these people and ate away at their souls. Nothing could satisfy that sense of barrenness they experienced and, either on purpose or accidentally, they took their own lives. And it's not confined to the famous.

I've heard this likened to racing greyhounds chasing a mechanical lure on a racetrack. These dogs are trained to chase a representation of what they are convinced is a live animal to get them to run faster. If the mechanical lure breaks down and they catch up with the lure, they are quickly disappointed when they discover it's just a piece of fluff, or stuffed toy, anything but the live animal they thought they were chasing.

This false premise is what happens more commonly than you realise to so many high flyers and super achievers who think the answer to their ultimate happiness and fulfilment is contained in the success and money. I'm sure they experience a great deal of satisfaction when they achieve their goals and have lots of money, but it's not the whole story, and the satisfaction is fleeting. There is a vital part of this picture that's missing, which is the way they've treated their humanness like it's one-dimensional. As if being successful in one area of their life will fulfil them in all areas of their life, and this is definitely not the case. But it's the dream that society sells us: a dream that destroys many lives.

So what's the answer? You must know what true success means for you. Not just the money and the glory and the acknowledgement. Not the representation society would have you believe is the ultimate success. What will give you true meaning and help you to create an exceptional life that you're not only proud of, but fills up your cup to overflowing? What makes up that picture? What makes your heart sing? Include your relationship with others and with yourself. Your health. The difference you make. Create a complete picture of the kind of life that will give you inner peace, contentment, satisfaction and leave you knowing you truly lived and the your being here mattered.

Having clarity around your compelling vision is essential to first achieve true success by knowing what it is, but by also having something you can refer to so you can enlist the help of the Universe in your quest for success. Regardless of what success looks like to you, you must have clarity around your vision and refer to it often to remind yourself and the Universe of where you're headed.

Are you prepared to determine your own version of success and take responsibility for creating a truly fulfilling, satisfying and joyful life in every aspect? I believe the 7 States of Wealth are the essential pillars for achieving this. When you have all these 7 states in balance, you've mastered life. Ultimate success is achieved through continual growth in all of these areas simultaneously.

2. Connect Deeply With Your Vision

In order to realise your vision, you must be intimately familiar with and connected to it. You must embody it and constantly remind your subconscious where you're headed so it has a clear idea of what your new reality looks like so it can assist you to create it. Remember your subconscious is your most powerful ally and co-creator, so it's smart to engage it in the creative process to avoid years of frustration, disappointment and struggle.

There are a variety of ways to connect with your vision. I strongly recommend you have a vision board with a visual representation of what your goals look like. Choose pictures that evoke an emotion in you and get you into the feeling zone of realising your vision. Your feelings and emotions directly affect your vibration and ability to align your frequency with the frequency of your new future. Once they're a match, your actions will naturally lead you in the direction of where you want to go.

You can also create a moving representation like a video that brings up the pictures for you with appropriate music in the background. This will help stimulate the good feelings connected with the achievement of your vision and assist you with the visualisation. This is quite a fun, creative process and your feelings of having achieved the goals you want will be amplified many times over with the use of music.

There are several programs, such as Animoto, that make this very easy. This service is very affordable and will ramp up your efforts to achieve the goals and dreams that have eluded you so far.

3. Don't Let The 'How' Get In The Way

Let go of your need to know how it's all going to happen. Many people don't take action because they don't know how to achieve their goals. This is a common block for people and one that is completely irrelevant. If you did know how you would have already done it. Not knowing how is part of the delicious mystery of this process and it's not your job to know how. Leave the how up to the forces collaborating to help you realise your vision because they already know everything that needs to happen and will orchestrate it for you, if you allow them to.

Your job is to focus on the 'what'. Be very clear and specific about your vision and what it is you want to achieve. What will your life look like when your vision is birthed into the world? What will the end result look like? Who will you be with? Where will you be? What will you be doing? How will you feel? Be very specific and don't hold back. Let your imagination run wild with ideas and dreams. If you can dream it, you can realise it. Write down what this is like in specific detail and review it daily. Allow your vision to be front and centre of your mind morning, noon and night. Use it as your driving force to inspire, empower and enable your consistent action toward it.

Take action from the inspiration that comes to you. Often, this inspiration will not seem logical. Follow it anyway. The process of realising your vision will be far from logical. You cannot orchestrate its realization purely from the perspective of logic and reason. That would discount the existence of magic and miracles that make life wondrous, mysterious and exciting. It would be a pretty boring existence if everything was based on logic and reason.

4. Show Up

Another critical factor is to show up. Sometimes your progress will seem light, easy and fast. Other times it may seem slow and arduous, like trudging through quicksand. You may feel like the Universe has abandoned you and like everything is falling apart. Again, trust and know that when everything appears to be falling apart, it is actually falling together.

At times when things seem difficult is when it's most important for you to show up, and take whatever action you feel inspired to take. Or if inspiration isn't coming to you, do whatever you can to take just one step closer to your goal in faith.

Sometimes it doesn't matter what you do, just show up and do something constructive and positive, because when you show up, so do the forces of the Universe. At times it will feel like nothing is happening. As long as you show up consistently and resolutely, underneath the surface of your conscious perception, there are people, situations, events and miracles being orchestrated that you're unaware of. Chains of events are happening somewhere else in the world that will ultimately culminate in entering your experience, and being a part of your vision. Trust in that, focus on your vision, and always show up for yourself, for your vision, for your future. That's your primary job.

5. Set Goals (The right way)

There are many different formulas out there for setting goals and none of them is a 'one size fits all'. When I get my clients to set goals, I give them simple guidelines such as: make sure your goals frighten you a little, stretch you and get you out of your comfort zone. If your goals are too mundane, they won't inspire you. Also, if they're too

18. Stack The Odds In Your Favour

grandiose for where you're at right now, then you'll find it difficult to get started on them. So make sure you feel connected with your goal and, even though it stretches you, it's important you feel on some level that it's doable.

If you have a very big vision, make sure you chunk it down so you don't feel overwhelmed and become paralysed. I encourage you to think big and don't hold back. Big goals are achieved by consistently taking small steps in the direction of their fulfilment.

Set goals which inspire you and make sure you ask for what you really want. Heaven forbid you might just get it! What so many people do is they think about their ultimate dream and what they really want, then, because their belief systems and fears and doubts are telling them it's not possible for them, they dumb their goals down and settle for something they think is possible for them.

I'll say it again – ANYTHING IS POSSIBLE! Think about what you really want and ignore all your doubts and those nasty little voices in your head. This is your life. Make it count, and don't settle for anything less than what you really want.

Be very specific with your goals. When you're vague the Universe can't help you achieve what you want. It needs clarity.

Have a clear date you want to achieve your goals by and again be realistic and stretch yourself at the same time. Set a date that gives you something to work toward, excites you, and is something you can connect with and believe in. It's imperative you are able to connect with your goal on some level.

Write your goals down and use positive language. There is a great formula I like for writing goals and it goes like this:

Write them in the present tense to tell your subconscious mind that you know with absolute certainty this is going to come to pass:

"It is now *(the date you achieve your goal)* and I am so happy and grateful that *(what it looks like now that you've achieved your goal – what are you doing, how are you feeling, etc)*."

When you frame your goals in this way you're sending strong, positive messages to your subconscious and it will go to work on helping to make it happen.

6. Make A Plan

A plan is non-negotiable if you want to achieve your greatest vision for yourself. I know this may seem like a boring part of the process, but it is an essential part of the process none the less. 'If you fail to plan, you are planning to fail'.

While some people like to make detailed plans so they feel secure knowing they've got their bases covered, others like to make a plan that just includes the next few steps they need to take.

Either way of planning is perfectly valid, one is not necessarily any better than the other, it's just whatever works best for you. For the person who likes to have a detailed plan with everything mapped out, you must realise you're going to need to be flexible. Remember, you can't possibly know exactly how this is going to work out, and as events unfold you will need to review and adjust your plan according to how things progress.

18. Stack The Odds In Your Favour

For the person who prefers to have a few steps mapped out at a time, you must keep adding to the plan along the way, possibly daily, so you always have at least two or three steps mapped out for your progress. Just scribble a plan down on a napkin if that's the way you like to plan, just don't lose the napkin!

With either method, daily, weekly and monthly goals are advisable to keep you focused and moving forward. If you don't have at least daily and weekly targets, your efforts are going to be a lot less efficient and your progress a lot slower. Efficiency and effectiveness are key to you producing the best results in the shortest period of time. Get into the habit of setting weekly targets, perhaps on a Sunday before the typical start to the work week on Monday, and each morning, or even the night before, set daily action steps and goals for the day and stick to them. Keep them close to you and refer to them several times a day to make sure you're on track.

Failure to do this will see you wasting a lot of time procrastinating and doing things that are irrelevant and you'll be more easily distracted. Your goals will keep stretching further and further out into the future, which can be very demoralising and potentially bring you undone.

7. Who's On Your Team

Ensure you have a team working with you to help you to bring your vision to the light of day. I'm not necessarily referring to an army of employees. If you're a seasoned veteran in business and your vision requires employees in your team straight away to carry you forward, then employ a team. But don't try to run before you can walk.

In The Presence of Greatness

We've been conditioned into thinking that doing it on our own is the way to glory. Ever heard the saying "if you want a job done well, you have to do it yourself"? But no great achiever has ever achieved anything by themselves entirely. Lone crusaders simply don't exist. Behind every great achievement is a team of people supporting, guiding and collaborating every step of the way. From the time the idea is born to its realisation it requires a team to bring it to life.

When you're starting out, your team will be made up of friends, family members, mentors, colleagues, outsourced personnel and other people you enlist in your vision. You must surround yourself with positive people who will encourage you, champion you, believe in you and support you every step of the way. Make sure you spend as little time as possible, if any, with people who will try to steal your dreams or bring you down. We all have those people in our lives, but you must either refrain from sharing your dreams and what you're working on with them, particularly if they're likely to discourage you, or just not spend time with them. At least until you've accomplished what you set out to achieve.

Your team will be people who believe in you and your vision. This is essential because, until you build an unshakable belief in yourself, sometimes you're going to need to borrow that belief from elsewhere, and this is where the people you socialise and mastermind with will be some of your greatest allies.

Typically, your income will be the average of the people and friends you have around you. No, you don't need to

18. Stack The Odds In Your Favour

immediately ditch all your friends who aren't doing so great financially. What it means is, you need to include in that mix successful people who are doing well financially and know how to play the game and achieve great things. When you associate regularly with people who've been where you want to go, their habits and thoughts rub off on you. It's like osmosis. You automatically start to model their behaviours and thought patterns, and you start to get different results.

Some of the most successful people I know and now call my friends were smart enough to understand this principle early in their careers. They took deliberate steps in the very beginning to put themselves in environments with highly successful people. Some of them worked for and did internships with Personal Development icons like Anthony Robbins, Chris Howard and Brian Tracy.

If an internship isn't on the list of options for you, buy recordings and motivational programs and listen to them over and over. Make sure the voices in your head are those of successful people who will uplift you, and inspire you to do anything and everything you need to, in order to achieve your goals and dreams. Jim Rohn, Zig Ziglar and Jack Canfield are other very popular success gurus and there's plenty more where they came from. Choose someone you can easily relate to, and immerse yourself in their material. It will shift the way you think, behave and the results you get, which is the ultimate goal.

I'm all for blessing people and letting them go from my life if I don't find their contribution positive and supportive. I have big things to achieve and my own mindset to master, the last thing I need is people who are going to contribute to those sometimes very loud negative voices in my head and make it even harder for me to succeed.

Always be kind, but decide in favour of you and in favour of your dreams. You deserve it!

8. Immerse Yourself

Immersion is a very powerful way to change your results quickly. Many personal development workshops and spiritual retreats are immersive experiences. You spend 2 or more days with like-minded people discussing and exploring concepts and strategies to improve your results in a variety of ways. You're immersed in an environment that's safe and conducive to you exploring yourself in relation to the experiences you're having, and the information you're receiving. Then you're able to integrate them, make them a part of your being, and ultimately implement them in your life. This is an experience of deep transformation.

The realisations and awakenings that happen during this kind of immersion are much more likely to stick than when you read a book, watch a webinar, or listen to an audio program. This is because the subconscious has a direct experience of them and they become a part of who you are.

It means you'll be better equipped to adopt the new information, habits and awakenings, and take the 'New You' back into your regular environment and everyday life, than if you read a book or watch a webinar.

You can create an immersive experience in your everyday life as well by changing different aspects of your

18. Stack The Odds In Your Favour

environment as we have discussed previously. One of the most impactful environments is the people you have in your circle of influence. By surrounding yourself with successful, expansive, creative, solution-focused, like-minded individuals, you're more likely to adopt similar traits, thought patterns and behaviours of those people that are conducive to your success.

Consciously immerse yourself in an environment that helps you to feel abundance. Nature is one of the best settings to connect with this. You could be at the beach or in the bush, at a park or even in your own backyard. Either way, you can very easily connect with the experience of abundance when immersed in nature.

Explore the other eight environments as outlined in Chapter 12 as well, and make sure they are supporting your success, not sabotaging it. Just this step alone will make a dramatic difference to your results.

9. Be Of Service

As Wayne Dyer said to me all those weeks ago when I asked him for guidance, "Drop your agenda to save the world and just choose to be of service every moment of every day."

Surprisingly, the more you focus on how you can be of service in the world and take your attention away from just making money, the more success you will have.

It's important to have an intention and goal to bring in the amount of money you want to support the lifestyle you desire and your vision, but don't let it be your main focus. Money isn't a great motivator for the vast majority of people. If you're reading this book, I would hazard a guess you're more motivated by the level of contribution you're making than you are by how much money is rolling in.

Turn your focus to making a contribution and make sure you have a system in place to monetise your gifts and talents so you can create a profitable business doing what you love. Your gifts and talents are highly valuable and should be treated as such by you and others. Give of them generously everywhere you go and allow people to have a direct encounter with your core genius. Then, for people who want a more intense experience of your gifts, you direct them toward your business.

The more you give, the more you will receive. Giving and receiving are co-dependent on each other. It is a loop that feeds itself and as you give, so you must be open to receive. Where many people go wrong is they wait until they receive before giving. Giving comes first, so give generously of your time and your talents and be open to receive and you will be opening up the magical flow of reciprocity.

10. Appoint The Universe As Your Co-Creator

Neale Donald Walsch puts this so beautifully when he says, "You are never alone." You are in a constant state of co-creating with the Universe. When you consciously focus on having this powerful force as your co-creator you will feel so much more empowered, and your faith will grow exponentially. When you think that it's all on you and you have to do it all, it can be overwhelming and even crushing, depending on the challenges you are facing.

18. Stack The Odds In Your Favour

By appointing the Universe as your co-creator and acknowledging you have a partner in your dreams every step of the way you will feel much more inspired, powerful and able to achieve anything, even in the face of adversity.

You have powerful forces at your disposal every single moment of your existence. When you consciously connect to those forces and engage them in your dreams, you'll suddenly become an unstoppable force of unimaginable power. This is the place you want to create from. Create your dreams, vision and goals on a day-to-day basis because from this place, you become creation itself. You become who you truly are!

11. Mind Your Language

Your internal and external language is an extremely important part of your success equation. There's a saying "Your thoughts become things" and this is so true. You get whatever you think about and focus on, so you must pay attention to the mental chatter in your brain and the words you say, and change them if you want to create a new reality.

Is your mind running a negative commentary on your life and your situation? Is it critical of yourself and others? Is it telling you that what you want isn't possible? Is there a stream of complaints coming from your mind about other people, the government, yourself, your situation?

For the average person, the thoughts and constant mental chatter is 65% to 75% negative. And 80% to 90% of it is repetitive. The same thoughts, or same type of thoughts you had the day before and the day before that and the day before that.

If you get what you focus on, and what you focus on is largely negative, it stands to reason you're going to get negative results.

You can start turning this around at this very moment by paying attention and becoming aware of the mental chatter and conversations you're having. When you're conversing with others, do you complain about the state of the economy, how bad things are, problems in your life, how hopeless everything is, how broke you are, about someone in your life and how you don't approve of their actions, or maybe how they're causing you distress?

For example, some people say they're always broke and they've never got any money. They'll blame external circumstances for this and not take responsibility for where they are right now. If they simply changed their language and said "I'm temporarily financially challenged and I'm working on a solution" then they would start to take their power back. By changing the language, or reframing, they send a message to the brain that they currently have a problem and they're figuring out how to overcome it. It's no longer a permanent condition they have to endure forever.

If you're prone to speaking about how difficult your relationships are or your partner is, start focusing on the person's good qualities and talking about those. If you really can't find any good qualities then maybe it's time to rethink your relationship and whether it's serving you.

If you often complain about your health or your pain, change your language and talk about how good you're feeling, even when you're not. Focus on the parts of your body that are pain-free and functioning well and offer gratitude for that.

18. Stack The Odds In Your Favour

The mind is incredibly powerful. Thoughts and words are strong vibrational frequencies that are creative forces. Be mindful of what you're thinking and saying and change your negative thoughts and language to positive ones.

Positive thinking alone will not change your entire life overnight, but it is a significant part of transforming your experience because your subconscious mind has no judgement about what you think. It just works tirelessly in the background to match your external world with your internal world.

To add power to your positive thinking, create vision boards, stop watching the mainstream news with all its negativity and biased reporting, script your vision for your future and read it daily. Use transformation techniques such as Emotional Freedom Technique to release the negative thoughts and beliefs.

Stop focusing on your problems and pay attention to your dreams and the Universe will conspire to help you create a life you love to live.

12. Stay Focused and Disciplined

We live in an ADD (Attention Deficit Disorder) world. Attention spans are getting shorter and shorter with all the technological and environmental distractions we are bombarded with daily. It's getting increasingly more difficult to focus on one task for any length of time. If you can imagine what it would have been like even 100 years ago where technology was limited and there were few distractions, there would have been little trouble focusing on a task at hand.

Today, we constantly have phones ringing, social media addictions calling for our attention, sound pollution disrupting our focus, multiple demands on our time and attention. The skill of focus is becoming something we must both work to develop, and constantly strive to maintain, so we don't allow ourselves to be diverted from our task or vision on a daily, and even moment-to-moment basis.

Even writing this book I have struggled to maintain a focus for any considerable period of time as my mind is darting off in multiple directions thinking about what else I need to be doing, people I need to call and new ideas I want to implement. I've been horrified to discover just how addicted I've become to social media.

Something I have a huge objection to is our obsession with social media and I am now acutely aware of my slide down that slippery slope. It's very disturbing, particularly for our younger generation who have less capacity for moderation and awareness about how destructive this obsession can be, and how social media is potentially stealing their dreams.

'Shiny Objectitis' is a tongue in cheek reference to a well-recognised propensity for people, particularly creative entrepreneurs, to jump on the next craze or the next best thing. Allowing those ideas and trends to distract us from our real purpose and passion spells death for many visions.

Opportunities are like buses. If you miss one there's always another one coming. FOMO, or the Fear Of Missing Out, is part of the cause of 'Shiny Objectitis'. Desperation, boredom, and lack of faith and trust are others.

18. Stack The Odds In Your Favour

If you want success in your life, you must be ready to grab opportunities when they come your way, but not indiscriminately, without analysing if they're in alignment with your vision and where you're headed. Beware the mind that gets bored easily with the task at hand and wants to jump to the next best thing with big promises.

This is something that plagued me for many years. When a project didn't appear to be working, or not as quickly as I wanted, because I'm impatient, I would drop that project and move onto something else. When this is a consistent pattern, you will never realise your goals. You must, must, must follow through on your vision and your projects.

Single-minded focus is essential, and whilst a fear of failure is easily recognised in people who don't get started on their big ideas, a clear indicator of a fear of success is the inability to follow through on something.

To achieve your goals, you must practice focus, and exercise discipline to get stuff done and follow through to the realisation of your vision. I don't suggest you dismiss opportunities outright, but before you jump, ensure they're in alignment with where you're headed and will help you to realise your vision. Are they another piece that will contribute to completing your puzzle, or are they a whole new puzzle?

If you don't develop the skills of focus and discipline, you could potentially waste precious days, weeks, months, years or even decades on activities and opportunities that are negatively impacting your future and robbing you of achieving the lifestyle and vision you desire.

13. Know Yourself

If you truly want to be successful, you must know yourself intimately. What do you REALLY want? So many people think they want all the trappings society tells them defines success. Is the big home, fancy car, expensive bling, designer clothes, trips to the spa, and all the stuff money can buy really going to make you happy? OK, the trips to the spa are certainly a nice trapping, but as I've grown older, and hopefully a little wiser, I've come to understand there's no 'thing' I can own that will make me happy.

I know what makes me the happiest is spending quality time with my husband, fur family (pets) and friends, and making a contribution. Speaking and singing from the stage for me is when I feel the most alive. All the money and stuff in the world could never make up for the feeling I have when I'm connecting with an audience and contributing something unique and special to their lives.

It's also important to know your strengths and weakness. When you know this, you can leverage your strengths and outsource your weaknesses.

What is your core genius? Your unconscious competence? Your gifts and talents? Your mission? Your purpose? What makes your heart sing? What contribution do you wish to make to the world? What skills have you mastered and which do you need to improve? What are you pretending not to know?

When you get to know yourself intimately you can create a life beyond compare capitalising on your core genius and constructing dreams that will make you truly happy and fulfilled. Many people spend years working hard climbing the ladder of success, only to find it's leaning against the wrong wall! This is a mistake that will ultimately leave you hollow and empty inside and wondering what it was all for. You do not want to make this mistake.

So, who are you? What do you want? What are you here to accomplish? Drop all the filters you see yourself through and the masks you wear in order to portray yourself in a certain way. Be authentic, real, unapologetically you. Dance to the beat of your own drum and sing your song, not someone else's. There is no one else like you in the whole wide world. In the Universe in fact. Be all of you, all the time and have a blast. You only get one shot at this life. You may as well be who you were born to be while you're here!

14. Don't Sweat The Small Stuff

So often we get caught up in our first world problems and waste precious time and energy on things that, at the end of the day, don't contribute significantly to our lives long term. When something happens and you feel like losing your nut, think about whether it's really going to matter in five or ten years, or even in five minutes. Let go of the things that really don't matter and focus on the big picture. You'll find most of the things you're worrying about aren't worth your time and energy.

15. Choose Your Battles

I'm passionate about a lot of causes, but getting caught up personally in those causes doesn't help me to live my purpose. My time is best spent focusing on what I'm here to do, which is to increase consciousness and help people to be the best they can be and live out their legacy. That's my mission, and the gifts I've been given all lend themselves to that mission.

In the past, I've often found myself spending time researching a variety of very worthwhile causes, and getting into in-depth discussions (particularly on Facebook) with people about these causes. These are important topics that require awareness and robust debate, and I feel like I'm doing something worthwhile. However, my participation in them is not the best use of my time. Often these topics just became a distraction for me.

A much better way to aid these causes is to do what I do best, create sustainable wealth, and donate to the organisations dedicated to increasing awareness and fighting on the front line for those very worthy issues. That's their mission and it's what they're here to do. In the long term, when people are more conscious and aware due to the work I do, they are more likely to get on board with these causes too. Not because I brow-beat them into it, but because their consciousness has shifted to the point that they naturally see the other point of view.

I mentioned before about choosing your challenges, so they don't choose you. When you choose your challenges, you get to live life on your terms and your challenges will be rewarding and inspiring. When you don't set specific challenges that move you toward your goals and dreams, the Universe will set challenges for you, because they are an essential part of life. And the challenges the Universe chooses for you will be a lot less inspiring and rewarding than those you set for yourself.

Your soul yearns for growth and expansion and if you don't consciously fulfil that need for it, it will find it in other forms, which may not be so rewarding and pleasing to you.

So, if you're avoiding setting challenges and trying to just live an easy life, beware, because challenges are inevitable and you just never know what will be waiting around the corner for you.

16. Build Your Belief

The vast majority of people don't believe they can achieve their dreams, or that their dreams are even possible, let alone have any concept of the greatness they're truly capable of.

When you were born, you understood the magnificence of who you are, and the extraordinary things you're capable of achieving when you exercise and unleash your brilliance. As you evolved, your environment crushed this belief and you were conditioned to believe that you're average, and would probably never amount to much, so best to settle for mediocrity to avoid disappointment. This is one of the greatest travesties of the human race.

One of the most important components of achieving your vision is a belief that you're capable of achieving it. You will have doubts and reservations, but it's your job not to give them oxygen, and to take steps every day, doing what you know you're currently capable of. In this way, you will become the person you need to be in order to realise your goals.

The real question is, is your goal worthy of you? Does it reflect the grandest version of yourself? Does it inspire you and create a sense of excitement about where you're heading?

In society, we have the equation all backwards. There is a pervading belief that when we have what we want, we will be able to do the things we want and be the person we want to be. It is actually the complete reverse of this. You must become the person you need to be, in order to do the things you want to do, and have the lifestyle you want.

Abraham is the being, or group of beings, that imparts their wisdom through the channel Esther Hicks, referring to 'acting as if'. So if you want to be fit and healthy, you must act the way a fit and healthy person would act. Eat and exercise like a healthy person and generally adopt the behaviours a healthy person would. You need to 'be' a healthy person in your thoughts and actions in order to develop a healthy body.

If you want your relationships to be loving, respectful, kind, supportive, intimate, understanding, thoughtful, romantic and all those wonderful things women want in a relationship (men, you'll have to define your own definition of the perfect relationship), then you must be the person who attracts and nurtures that kind of relationship. In fact, you must be this for both yourself AND someone else in order to for it to be reflected back to you.

If you want to be a millionaire, you must be a millionaire in your mind first. So you feel and act like a millionaire, and I'm not referring to throwing money around as if you've already made millions. That's a recipe for disaster until you've mastered your mindset.

I'm talking about developing your million-dollar vision, creating a strategic action plan, staying focused and taking deliberate, daily action toward that vision. Being unstoppable is about doing whatever it takes, making the sacrifices,

18. Stack The Odds In Your Favour

overcoming your fears and doubts, taking calculated risks, investing in yourself and your team, being solution focused, surrounding yourself with the right people, and believing in your vision and your ability to achieve it.

A millionaire will always be a millionaire regardless of their financial status. They own the identity of a millionaire and act accordingly. When Donald Trump lost his multi-million dollar empire in the nineties, he was in a far worse financial position than most people in the world. But he never stopped being a millionaire. From being $900 million dollars in debt, Donald Trump created a billion dollar empire. He always believed in his ability to make it all back with interest, and he certainly proved that.

Build the belief in yourself by taking small steps every single day toward your vision. While you're building that belief, make sure you surround yourself with people who you can borrow that belief from when you're struggling with it. These people will be instrumental in getting you through those times when you feel like it's all too hard and beyond you.

17. Refuse To Conform

You're not here to please anyone else or make them happy. You're on this planet to be uniquely you. Being you is extremely liberating and much more powerful than trying to be someone you're not.

The vast majority of people are living out their lives as a shadow of their true selves, spending so much of their precious energy trying to be someone they're not, in an effort to fit in, not rock the boat and please the masses.

Big mistake. You're never going to please everyone, and you're not supposed to. That's the beauty of the diversity of personalities, belief systems, ways of seeing the world, cultural differences, differing opinions. It makes the world a very interesting place.

So drop your judgement of those who don't see the world the way you do. When you judge others, you judge yourself, and this causes a state of fear about being judged. It's a vicious circle. Instead, be respectful of other people's right to have a different opinion to you. Be curious about their point of view and how they came to their conclusions. Acknowledge them for their contribution to our interesting world of diverse thinking, and freedom to form their own opinions.

Dare to be different. Dare to challenge the status quo. Dare to be unique and controversial and ALL of you, not some shadow of yourself by conforming to cultural norms. Get to know yourself intimately, and enjoy letting others getting to know your true self as well.

You were born unique. You were born to be YOU. Not somebody else's contrived version of 'perfect'.

Be real. Be authentic. Be YOU. The world is waiting.

18. Master Your Mindset

This book is largely about mindset. Without the right mindset, you're never going to achieve your goals and dreams. In fact, you'll barely even get out of the starters gate.

Study the mindset of people who have gone before you. How do they think? What do they believe? What's their success blueprint? How can you adopt the same kind of blueprint?

18. Stack The Odds In Your Favour

Again, your mindset will be largely influenced by your environment, so make sure it's set up to support you to have a strong, powerful, success-focused attitude.

You must also be prepared to invest in yourself to develop the mindset that will take you 'to infinity and beyond'. This will include what you read, what you listen to, the workshops and courses you attend and the mentors and coaches you engage.

The only thing standing between the results you've already achieved, and the results you want to achieve, is the mindset you need to bridge the gap. If you want to be more successful, you must be willing to do whatever it takes and be unstoppable.

A millionaire isn't defined by the numbers in their bank account, but by the way they think, what they believe, and the actions they take. If a true millionaire loses all their money, they don't stop thinking like a millionaire. They return to their millionaire status in a relatively short period of time. The actions they take aren't compromises, but strategic steps toward returning to the status that matches their mindset.

For example, if a millionaire loses their financial status and must take a job to get by, they know it's just a temporary position and the income they receive will be leveraged as much as possible to return to being a millionaire as defined by their bank account.

When a person with a fit and healthy mindset encounters a health set-back, their focus is on strategies and actions required to return to being fit and healthy. In contrast, when a person who doesn't identify with being fit and healthy gets sick, they'll take whatever pain relief medication the doctor prescribes to ease their discomfort, but continue the same lifestyle behaviour that got them there in the first place.

Take the example of Joe Dispenza, a very fit and healthy man who, when he was in his twenties, was in a bicycle race and was run over by a car. His spine was crushed in several places and he was facing lifetime paralysis if he didn't have surgery to insert a rod into his back within the first couple of days. As an active individual and yoga instructor, this news was devastating for Joe. After multiple consultations and numerous opinions, all of which said virtually the same thing, Joe decided to take the risk and not have the surgery.

For several weeks he lay in a body cast and visualised his spine healing completely and perfectly, using the power of his subconscious mind to recreate his spine the same way it was initially created in human form in the womb. He literally engaged the organising intelligence of the Universe that created him in the first place to recreate his spine again.

It worked! Within 12 weeks Joe Dispenza returned to yoga, much to the amazement of the medical doctors and professionals who were ready to condemn him to a lifetime in a wheelchair or very limited mobility.

He was determined to do whatever it took to return to his former fit and healthy state, and he did. When you choose to adopt this kind of unstoppable mindset, you really can achieve anything you put your mind to.

19. Change State

A very popular and effective way to ensure your success is to use techniques to change your mental and emotional state.

When you're overwhelmed by a sense of despair because the shit just hit the fan, and you feel like your life is falling apart, do you think you'll improve the situation by staying in that state? Or would it be more productive to use a technique to alter that state and regain access to your ability to be creative, solution-focused and engage your genius?

Changing, or breaking state is a popular NLP term and there are a variety of ways to do this. For example, you could wear a thick rubber band on your wrist and every time you notice yourself thinking a negative thought, you snap the rubber band. Unless you're a masochist, this practice to change state will quickly have you paying close attention to your thoughts and thinking more positively.

Another example we have seen depicted often on television is when someone is hysterical and another person slaps them. The slap breaks their state of hysteria and gets them to calm down and focus. Now, I'm not recommending you go around slapping people as you'll probably end up in a lawsuit for assault, but as an example of breaking state, its effect is quite obvious.

You don't necessarily need physical pain to change state. I've mentioned Emotional Freedom Technique several times because I absolutely love it as a way to change state and release negative emotions and belief systems. It calms the nervous system, and brings a sense of calm, clarity and resourcefulness to all kinds of situations.

Whenever you feel out of control, overwhelmed, or in a state of anxiety or stress, another effective strategy is to simply stop, breathe deeply, centre yourself and carefully reflect on the situation without judgement.

You can also change state by changing your posture. Stand erect, head up looking at the world squarely and confidently, stand with your feet hip-width apart and your hands on your hips. This is referred to as the Wonder Woman pose and will give you more confidence and courage when you need it. And men, you can use it too! Just think of it as the Superman pose.

Taking positive action will also change state because you're being proactive about a situation rather than passively allowing it to get out of hand.

Increasing your conscious awareness is another powerful way for you to change state because you won't be as likely to get swept up in the emotion of the moment that robs you of your ability to respond effectively.

Other very effective ways to change state are:

- Dancing
- Listening to soothing or upbeat music
- Meditation
- Visualising the outcome you want
- A random act of kindness for someone else
- A hug or other heartfelt human touch
- Doing something you love such as gardening, cooking, playing sport
- Being with animals

18. Stack The Odds In Your Favour

- Laughing
- Singing

These are just a few of the simple and fun ways for you to change state so you are more effective at solving problems and navigating the challenges of life. When you give yourself permission to do these on a regular basis, you will naturally be more resourceful and resilient when challenges arise.

You are far more resourceful and have access to more brain faculties when you are cool, calm and collected. Using practices that can produce this state quickly and easily is highly beneficial to help you get better outcomes and master all areas of your life.

You can call on a peak performance state by becoming aware, refocusing your mind on a thought or memory that is empowering, aligning your posture and taking considered, decisive and positive action toward a solution or outcome you desire.

Imagine being able to stay calm and present when communicating with a loved one about an emotional situation, or keeping your wits about you when there is a crisis. The ultimate outcome is bound to be a lot more positive when you respond from a place of careful consideration and resourcefulness, than if you fly into a panic or rage and act from a place of emotional reactivity.

Adopt some practices that help you to change state quickly and at will, and you'll find life not only easier to navigate but much more rewarding. Your results will change dramatically too.

20. Be Confident

There was a study conducted at Wharton Business School where several thousand business professionals were asked to identify the main reason people made the decision whether or not to do business with them.

Do you think their decision was based on the:

- Amount of the fee?
- Credentials?
- Credibility?
- Reputation?
- Experience?
- State of the economy?

The answer was none of the above! The number one reason people brought from these professionals was the confidence and clarity with which they stated their fee.

Imagine you walk into a room ready to make a pitch to a new potential large client. In scenario one, you enter nervously, your body posture is stooped and shy, you stutter and falter through your presentation, you're uncertain when you reveal your price. What kind of response do you think you're going to get from the prospective client? If you don't have confidence in yourself, how on earth can the new client have confidence in you and the service or product you provide?

Now, in scenario two, you enter the room with confidence and your posture is erect and confident. Your presentation is clear, direct, polished and this time you've doubled your asking price, but you say it with certainty and conviction,

18. Stack The Odds In Your Favour

knowing you're offering exceptional value and that you can deliver exactly what the client wants. Do you think the client is more likely to buy from you in the second scenario, or the first, even though in the second one you have doubled your price?

Your posture and conviction is a game changer when it comes to engaging a new client or closing a sale. The purchaser is much more likely to invest in what you're offering when they feel they can have confidence in the person from whom they're buying.

So, when you enter a room for any reason or talk to a prospective client, stand, or sit, straight and tall as this will automatically make you feel more confident. Make sure you're well prepared for your presentation. Speak clearly and confidently. Know your stuff! Ask plenty of appropriate questions and listen intently so you know exactly how to frame your proposal to the client, and meet their specific needs with your offer. Outline the benefits of your offer clearly. Remember, these are not the specific features of your product or service, but the direct benefits to the client. People don't care what you do; they just want to know what's in it for them – the WIIFM factor. When they can clearly see and relate to how it will benefit them, they're far more likely to make the purchase.

21. Optimise Your Environments

In chapter twelve, I outlined the nine environments of success and how important they are to your success. Review each of the environments and outline ways you can optimise them to support your mindset, your growth, your vision and your ultimate success. Choose just one to start with and take simple steps to put you in the right state of mind to achieve your vision.

22. Invest In Yourself

Many business owners don't bat an eyelid at investing in store fit-outs, marketing campaigns, professionals such as lawyers and accountants, upgrading technology, but fail to make the number one most important investment they will ever make in the future of their business: themselves.

If you want better results than you're getting right now, you must invest in yourself. In order to become the person you need to be to achieve your goals and vision, you need to upgrade your mindset, learn to master new skills, absorb new information and adopt new behaviours.

The more you invest in yourself, the more you will achieve and the more quickly you will achieve it. Investments such as books, seminars, workshops, courses, coaches and mentors are an essential part of your business and your future if you want to reach new heights.

Always analyse the investment you're making carefully to make sure it has the potential to deliver what you need most to move forward. Everyone has experienced that sense of disappointment and frustration when something we've purchased or invested in hasn't delivered the return on investment we'd anticipated. Get over it, move on, and don't allow this to stop you from investing in yourself again. If it's happened to you on multiple occasions, perhaps it's time to look to the common denominator – YOU.

18. Stack The Odds In Your Favour

Have you played full out and given the programs or courses or coaching agreements everything you've got? Have you followed through with the program? Have you done the work? No one can do the work for you and your success is ultimately up to you. The investments in yourself are to give you the information, guidance, support and skills you need to get to where you want to be. BUT, in the end, you're fully responsible for implementing. This is where so many people mess up. Blaming someone or something else for your level of success is just a copout.

Many people want to purchase one program, one time and have it be the answer to all their prayers, but this is not the way it works. You must invest in a variety of skills and mindset based programs. As you adopt some of what you have learned from each, you'll become the person you need to be. It won't happen overnight, but as long as you keep moving forward and utilising what you've invested in, it will happen.

So don't waste time complaining that a course didn't deliver and get you the instant results you wanted. As long as you take one thing away with you, it was a worthy investment. Everything you learn will accumulate over time to help you to evolve mentally, emotionally and spiritually into the successful person you are destined to become.

Analyse what support, skills, guidance and information you need to accelerate your progress toward your goals and dreams, and then find courses or mentors to fill that need.

Will sales training benefit you? Do you need to know more about business? What about a system or strategy to streamline your client or customer acquisition process? Marketing is always a valuable skill to keep learning and expanding on, and there are plenty of courses and methodologies to help you improve your results. Personal development courses are a very valuable investment when you're specific about what you want out of them and choose the right ones.

There are a vast number of ways to invest in yourself to improve your results and help you to get closer to your goals. Make sure you spend at least 10% of your income monthly on investing in yourself and your future. You will receive that back many times over through your evolution and development. Once you've made the investment, you must take action on whatever you've learned. Otherwise, it's just been another WOFTAM – waste of freaking time and money!

23. Love Yourself Into Your Dreams

Dr. John Demartini says if you truly love someone then you will not want to deny them anything. If you truly love yourself, you won't deny yourself anything, and you will do whatever you need to in order to realise your vision for your future and have everything your heart desires. It will be non-negotiable and you'll open the way for you to succeed in all areas of your life.

In amongst this is frequency. It's scientifically recognised that everything in the Universe is energy. Energy vibrates, and everything that vibrates emits a particular frequency. According to the Law of Attraction like attracts like. The energy of love, unconditional love, is the highest frequency of all.

Abundance, peace, joy, freedom, acceptance, kindness, tolerance, contentment and forgiveness are embodied within the frequency of love. When you do the internal work to raise your vibration to the frequency of love, it makes perfect

18. Stack The Odds In Your Favour

sense that you will also be a vibrational match for abundance, freedom, joy and all the other desirable states of being.

Whilst this is not a prerequisite for being abundant and unleashing your greatness, it is the easy way to attract what you want into your life. You can work really long hours and drag yourself toward your goals, or you can do the internal work, match the frequency and magnetise yourself for what you want so it is drawn to you.

Let me tell you, I've done both, and I will choose the second option every time! Work on self-love as part of your quest to unleash your greatness, and realise your goals and dreams. It's so much more fun and you will increase your manifesting powers many times over!

24. You're Already Successful

Human beings have a natural tendency to focus on the negative. It's the way our brains are wired. We're always looking for danger, and so the first thing we pick up on is what's not working, or what could cause us harm. For this reason, no matter where we're at, most of us will tend to focus on what's not working and completely miss what is working.

The way you identify yourself will also play a big role in determining the results you achieve in life. If you identify yourself as a failure, your thoughts and habits are going to create scenarios that reinforce that identity. If you identify as a working-class employee, succeeding as an entrepreneur is going to conflict with that identity, which is going to make it harder to achieve your goals.

The truth is, you're already successful in many areas in your life, so it's time to start recognising those successes and acknowledging them so you identify yourself as successful. Start with getting out of bed this morning. Did you? If you did, you're already more successful than other people who didn't. Did you get yourself dressed? Have breakfast? Organise the kids? Drive the car? Get to work? Turn on the computer? Respond to emails?

Now expand your thinking to all the things you've achieved this month? This year? In your life? Write down and acknowledge as many things as you can think of, big and small, that you've successfully achieved to get you to where you are today. When you do this exercise correctly, you will have an extensive and impressive list of achievements.

The next step is to really congratulate yourself for having come so far in life. In spite of all the challenges you've faced, the setbacks you've experienced, the difficult experiences you've navigated, you're still here and you're still in the game. That in itself is an extraordinary achievement. Until now, you've probably failed to recognise and acknowledge how incredible this is. Instead, you've been beating yourself up for all the things you haven't done or achieved, and focusing on all the ways you've been failing. Recognise and acknowledge your successes now. Make this a daily ritual, particularly at the end of the day. It makes the day so much more rewarding.

25. An Attitude of Gratitude

Having a practice of gratitude is something that is heard often from almost every success publication or successful person. Appreciation appreciates. The more you are grateful for, the more you will have to be grateful for.

18. Stack The Odds In Your Favour

You get what you focus on. When you focus on what's missing or what you don't want, you're just going to get more of that. When you focus on what you're grateful for that you already have, you're going to receive more to be grateful for.

Grab a gratitude journal and every night write down five new things you are grateful for and review the list, along with your goals and vision, in the morning. The list doesn't have to be earth-shattering, just five simple things. By the end of the first week, you'll have a list of thirty-five things you're grateful for.

As you write your list, make sure you connect with the feeling of gratitude. Even if it's just a small flicker of a feeling at first, deliberately connect with and nurture that feeling. It will grow and become a habit over time. I now spend a lot of time during my day just in gratitude for my environment and all the amazing things I have in my life that give me so much joy. I rarely want for anything and more great stuff just keeps showing up as if by magic!

As you get better at gratitude, start being grateful for all your dreams materialising at some time in the future. When you display absolute faith that you've already achieved your dreams and received what your heart most desires by being grateful for them, the stronger your attraction and the more quickly you will pull them in. The state of wanting just produces more wanting as it's a symptom of lack. When you want something, you're saying you don't have it, so you produce more of the experiencing of not having it.

On the other hand, when you appreciate already having it in the future, the Universe responds and because you're in the space of allowing, not resistance, it comes into your reality much more quickly.

When you really master gratitude, you'll be able to be grateful for the blessings that come with the challenges in your life and you will see the perfection in everything. It's a wonderful space to exist in.

The practice of gratitude is incredibly powerful and will expand you spiritually, mentally and emotionally, and you'll become a master at manifesting what you want in life.

26. This Or Something Better

You're capable of creating anything you put your mind to. So when you create your vision and set your goals, why limit yourself to the possibilities that you have in mind?

As you write and review your goals and contemplate your vision board, always add, "This or something better" because this gives the Universe the licence to create something even more wonderful than what you had in mind. This practice opens up so many possibilities for you. You'll be amazed at what comes back to you just through this simple addition to your goals and dreams.

27. Expect Miracles

You get what you focus on, and you also get what you expect. If you expect bad things to happen to you, then that's what will happen, if you expect good things to happen, including miracles; you'll see more of those in your life.

Remarkably, when you expect miracles, not only will you see more of them turn up in your life, you'll also see all the miracles happening for you every day that you didn't see before. You'll even start to see miracles in the challenges you face because that's where you're choosing to put your attention.

Life is a miracle in thousands of ways. When you focus on miracles and expect them, you will begin to see the ones you already have in abundance, and you will also receive many more of them in your life.

28. Open Your Heart and Mind

I can honestly say from experience that there is no more rewarding way to experience life than with an open heart and mind. When your heart is open you get to experience fully the love and joy that exists in the Universe without resistance. You don't need anyone to provide this love or joyfulness for you. It's always there, within you and all around you, waiting for you to access it. When you open your heart to it all, fear and doubt melts away leaving you in a completely loving state.

Granted, maintaining this state permanently is still a challenge I'm working on, but I know it's there and I use several practices to access it more frequently. It's becoming increasingly more familiar to me every day.

Likewise, when you bring an open mind to every situation, you don't condemn or judge the situation. You're able to accept it for what it is, analyse it, and find the best way possible to navigate it, without all the hype and drama that so many of us love to bring to almost every circumstance we encounter.

An open mind gives you far greater access to solutions you're unable to think of when in an emotional state or have a rigid, closed frame of mind.

When you combine an open heart and an open mind, the world is literally yours to command. No situation is too challenging or able to defeat you. Practising opening your heart and mind through meditation and your sense of presence will help you to become unstoppable and be an absolute champion at whatever you turn your attention, gifts and talents to.

29. Give Yourself Permission

So many of us wait for someone else to give us permission to do what we want and go for our goals. If that sounds like you, STOP DOING THAT!

You don't need anyone else's approval or permission to take action toward your goals and do whatever it takes to achieve them. You're a strong, self-determining person who is in charge of your destiny. Own that and just do it!

There are many areas I suggest you look at in relation to giving yourself permission. Here are just a few. Read the statement and see if it resonates with you. If you feel resistance, like a contraction or heavy feeling, start using Emotional Freedom Technique to release the resistance.

    I give myself permission to succeed.

    I give myself permission to fail.

    I give myself permission to be all of me.

    I give myself permission to receive.

18. Stack The Odds In Your Favour

I give myself permission to have everything my heart desires.

I give myself permission to always be the best I can be.

I give myself permission to shine.

I give myself permission to achieve everything I put my mind to.

I give myself permission to make mistakes.

I give myself permission to have a big vision.

I give myself permission to go for it and never give up.

I give myself permission to be wrong.

I give myself permission to not have to know everything.

I give myself permission to feel the fear and do it anyway.

I give myself permission to enjoy life to the fullest.

I give myself permission to be free.

I give myself permission to do what I love.

I give myself permission to love myself and others freely.

I give myself permission to be open and vulnerable.

I give myself permission to be honest and speak my mind freely.

I give myself permission to be authentically me.

I give myself permission to take care of myself.

Think about yourself and your situation. If you could be, do and have anything you want, what would that be? How would giving yourself permission to be, have or do those things, change your life? This is a very liberating exercise if you choose to give yourself permission to do it!

30. Let Go and Let God

This is a popular saying, but have you ever stopped to think about what it really means?

So many of us are striving so hard and hanging on so tight to a belief that life is meant to be a struggle and if we don't push ourselves and work really hard we're not going to survive, let alone thrive. We've largely abandoned our belief in a higher power that is always there to support us, guide us and help us to achieve extraordinary things. No wonder we feel alone, unsupported and like our future is all on our shoulders.

Your attitude, mindset and beliefs are what determine your results. But what if you were to surrender your burden of responsibility to your higher power – to the Universe. This frees you up to do your job, which is to live and act from a place of passion, joy, love and faith while allowing the Universe to do the heavy lifting and take care of the details. Remember, your job is not the 'how', it's the 'what'. Hold onto your vision and take action trusting you're fully and completely supported in achieving your goals.

Letting go is also about letting go of attachment to outcomes, expectations, judgements and perceptions. When we set goals, we often become disappointed when things don't work out the way we want them to, which happens more often than we would like. Being in a state of emotional attachment and judgement about the outcomes we achieve, sets us up for disappointment. We lose motivation and our ability to stay in action, particularly when it happens over and over again, as it sometimes does.

18. Stack The Odds In Your Favour

When things don't turn out the way we'd hoped, rather than recognising and appreciating they've turned out exactly the way they were supposed to, we think something's gone wrong and condemn the eventual outcome. We beat ourselves up and blame ourselves, or, even worse, blame someone or something for screwing it up for us. This prevents us from being in flow with the process of realising our dreams.

We fail to recognise there's always a process that needs to happen, and we don't actually know what that is. We can't. We can only see a very minute part of the whole picture. But as we take action in faith, and allow things to unfold naturally, instead of trying to control everything, we open up space for miracles to unfold and everything to happen in the best way possible.

When you let go of your attachment to the outcome, you have a more pragmatic view of any situation. You're able to see it more clearly and from a place of awareness, you're able to adjust your action to take advantage of what has occurred to get the result you want. Or maybe even a better result than you anticipated.

Look for the blessing in every situation, and you'll be rewarded many times over for your ability to see beyond your circumstances to the perfection that always exists in everything.

All achievements come from going through one set of actions. After you decide what you want, then you must take action, analyse your results, adjust your approach and take more action. That's the simple formula every successful person who has ever lived has repeated over and over again until they achieve a satisfactory result. When you remove the emotional attachment from the equation and stop beating yourself up, you'll find this process a lot easier and infinitely more rewarding.

You'll also be a lot more creative, and more open to inspirational ideas on the best course of action to take next. When you're sitting in judgement and self-deprecation, you shut down your channels of inspiration and your access to the Universal wisdom that always supports you to achieve the best possible outcome for you in the moment.

Stop holding on so tight, thinking you have to do it all and get it right every time. Instead, trust, allow, let go and let God. Not only will your journey be a lot easier and more fun, you'll be amazed at how much more quickly and easily you achieve your outcomes when you get out of the way of the Divine process.

31. Fail Forward Fast

This is the catch cry of many large tech companies, such as Facebook, that work on implementing fast, breaking things, and fixing them as they go.

What would you do if you weren't afraid to fail? Go ahead and answer that question. Write the answer down, and then do it. No ifs, buts, maybes or excuses. Just find a way to do whatever it is and get it done.

When you give yourself permission to fail and let go of your attachment to your outcomes, you have the ability to throw yourself headlong into taking massive action toward your goals and dreams without fear. While planning your action with the intention of achieving the best possible outcome is always sensible, when you release yourself from having to get it right and make it okay to fail temporarily, nothing can stop you from moving forward.

32. Feel The Fear And Do It Anyway

It's really simple, but Nike's slogan, 'Just Do It' is a completely appropriate response to feeling challenged, out of your comfort zone, and in a state of fear when you're striving for new heights.

Whilst I always advocate using effective strategies for letting go of emotional boundaries and triggers, sometimes you've just got to embrace the fear and dive right in! In fact, doing this can be extremely exhilarating because it stimulates endorphins and gives us a natural high. People who love extreme sports tend to be addicted to the rush that pushing our natural boundaries can give us.

Living in a constant state of stress can also give us this rush, but this is not healthy long term. As well as the endorphins, this state causes the body to release a chemical called cortisol, which takes a terrible physical toll if endured for extended periods of time.

However, as a short-term tactic to overcome a particular hurdle, girding your loins, swallowing hard and just getting it over and done with is sometimes the best way to handle a situation that is making you uncomfortable. It also trains you to manage your nerves and utilise them to sharpen your senses.

For instance, I find when I perform that my nerves give me an edge and help me to come alive and give a better performance. Without that sense of excitement and nervousness, I might be flat and not at my best. As long as I manage my nerves and utilise that energy to my advantage, I enjoy the rush performing gives me.

So the next time you're feeling anxious about jumping out of your comfort zone, use the Emotional Freedom Technique to take the edge off whatever is causing you the fear, jump right into the experience and enjoy the rush! You'll find it can be quite liberating!

33. Practice Patience

This may sound contradictory in light of some of the previous points made, but whilst you're taking massive action and failing forward fast, you must also be patient and allow the journey toward your goals to unfold in the time frame that is Divinely allotted.

We live in a world that demands instant gratification. Like a petulant two-year-old, we know what we want and we have little concept of, or ability to wait to have what we want. If we do have to wait, it feels like a form of torture.

What's helped fuel this condition is the finance sector. Banks and finance companies issuing credit cards and interest-free finance, meaning we no longer have to save for what we want. These companies are not interested in whether or not we can pay back the money, in fact, they're happier if we're unable to pay it back because we pay interest on the borrowings and they make more profits. This has created a catastrophic situation for many of the current generation who are spending more than they're earning. It's so easy to get their hands on money that's not theirs, and they're encouraged to do so.

18. Stack The Odds In Your Favour

Consequently, we now have a situation where we are exceedingly impatient to get what we want and if it doesn't happen fast enough we become anxious, disappointed and frustrated. There's a sense of desperation and often people are freaking out internally thinking, "Why hasn't it happened yet?" "What's wrong with me?" "I should be there by now!" "It shouldn't have to be this hard!" "What am I doing wrong?"

These thoughts and emotions spill over into all areas of our life including our health, our finances, our careers, our relationships, and our businesses. *"Forget about enjoying the damn journey, just get me to the destination NOW!"*

Let's take the issue of weight because it's one that's more tangible and easier to relate to than money. When we're dissatisfied with our weight and we finally decide to actually do something about it, we join a gym, get a trainer, go to a dietician, or join a weight loss program. We work out hard and are disciplined for a few days, then look in the mirror expecting to see massive changes in our physiology. But instead of seeing Elle Macpherson starting back at us, we're greeted with virtually the same picture we saw before we started and instantly feel disappointed. We've worked so hard and nothing's changed. It's just not fair!

Having taken months or even years to put the weight on in the first place, we expect to see an instant reversal and the fat melting off right before our eyes. What we can't see is the changes happening beneath the surface. The fat deposits are starting to diminish and muscle starts to grow. The metabolism is adjusting and starting to quicken. Toxins are being released as we clean up our diet, drink more water and take supplements. Our hormones are changing and adjusting to the new healthier routine. The unseen changes that are happening are remarkable and quite staggering, but we don't understand or appreciate those because we can't see them. We just want our body back to what it was when we were a teenager, fast!

Disappointment is quickly followed by frustration and feelings of depression. We slip back into our old ways that got us overweight in the first place because it's all too hard and it's not working anyway. The fact is, it was working, but we didn't give it the time necessary to see the results.

It's the same with our overall health. We abuse our bodies for years, even decades, and we become sick (surprise, surprise). We go to the doctor and expect him to give us a pill to instantly make us all better again. A better way to respond to our body's inability to deal with our toxic habits and emotions would be to take a long-term approach to cleaning up our mind, body and spirit, but that could take years. The easier option, though not permanent, is the pill from the doctor.

Negative emotions and a sense of desperation set up resistance. Taking massive action and moving forward fast using the steps outlined in this book is the smart way to achieve your goals. At the same time, it's important to remember there is a divine timing to everything and some things will take longer than others.

Feeling desperation means you're chasing your desired outcomes with a sense of anxiety and neediness. Imagine if your goals were a lover, and you chased them with the same sense of neediness, anxiety and desperation. It's highly likely they'd run as fast as they could in the other direction

18. Stack The Odds In Your Favour

making sure they were out of your reach, wouldn't they? Your dreams are the same.

What if you had a sense of certainty, confidence and knowingness about achieving your goals? Imagine leaving an open invitation for your dreams to find you, instead of you chasing your dreams. Doing this creates a magnetic force, and your dreams gravitate toward you instead of staying perpetually out of reach.

I often see impatience in people with my coaching programs. Everyone wants results yesterday and many expect to see their goals transpire overnight. People who have done a lot of personal development work progress quite quickly because they've already released a lot of their resistance. Others might not have a lot of resistance or negative conditioning in the first place. Some will take longer to get results. The time it takes to reach goals is different for everyone, because we're all different and the variables, conditioning and transformation work we need to do are all different.

Impatience, and that feeling of desperation to have everything now, is a huge form of resistance and it causes blocks to achieving your goals. It comes from fear. Fear it won't happen for you. Fear of missing out. Fear something bad is going to happen if you don't get it now, or at least very soon.

How would it feel if you let go of the impatience and focused on your goal, knowing with absolute certainty, as long as you take deliberate, focused, consistent action every day, you'll get to your goal at the perfect time for you? Even thinking about it you can feel the resistance leaving you can't you? It feels different. It feels secure, peaceful, joyful, comfortable, doesn't it?

If you release the impatience and sense of desperation, you will become a conscious co-creator with the Universe, and a world of new possibilities will open up for you. Suddenly everything will move faster because there is no resistance and you'll call in your goals and dreams. They'll run toward you, instead of you running after them.

This is the mystery and mastery of life. Coming to a place of certainty and knowingness that you're safe, you're not ever going to miss out on anything, everything is perfect, and that by relaxing and partnering with the Universe, anything and everything are possible. Welcome to the world of conscious creation and how to live a life beyond your wildest dreams.

34. Breathe

This is similar to practicing patience but goes a lot deeper.

The other day I was sitting in my car in a car park by the highway watching the endless stream of cars racing past. It reminded me of how so many of us conduct our lives. All rushing to get somewhere. But where are we rushing to and for what?

The vast majority of people are unaware they're plugged into a paradigm which says the more you're doing the more successful you are. I often get messages and emails that start with something like, "I trust you've been busy", as if it's some sort of positive achievement. You know, I don't actually want or need to be super busy. I intend to be present, aligned, content and have time to move through life leisurely, with grace, enjoying every delicious moment, while achieving my mission here on earth.

18. Stack The Odds In Your Favour

My idea of success isn't being constantly in demand or harrowed by a busy schedule. It's being able to easily sustain my simple lifestyle doing what I love and making a difference in the lives of others, while having plenty of time to spend with my husband, my animals, enjoying the paradise I've chosen to live in, meditating, riding my horses, listening to good music, reading and living life on my terms.

Slow down. Breathe deeply. Be present. Pay attention. Stop rushing around being distracted by all the superfluous stuff you think you have to do and places you think you have to be. Most of what we do in life is actually irrelevant to what's really important and doesn't contribute to our long-term happiness or wellbeing. Be present to the needs of the moment and the incredible beauty and miracle of life. Be in awe of your existence, and as you are present, you will know exactly what you need to be doing in each moment to get closer to your goals, overcome obstacles and make a positive difference in the lives of others.

35. Systems Will Set You Free

The earth thrives when it follows its system, its plan, its blueprint for the life it sustains. The only thing that will cause this system to fail is some sort of disruption to its blueprint. This is why we call it the eco-system. Currently, humanity is the greatest disruptive force the planet has experienced in several millennia.

If you want to lose weight, you must consistently follow a system of healthy diet and exercise to achieve your goal weight. It's been proven over and over again.

To compete in a triathlon, you must train according to a system that would have been formulated, tried and tested by thousands of other triathletes before you.

To be successful in business, you must have a plan. Successful businesses all follow a system of some description.

Random, haphazard activity will only produce chaos, not results. No matter how hard you may try to disprove this, I encourage you to save yourself the heartache and just accept that you need a system to get from where you are to where you want to be.

Once you get over your resistance to following a system, you'll be amazed at just how much easier it is to achieve your goals and dreams by following a proven, step-by-step formula. It's almost like magic! Strangely enough, it's something the experts have been telling us for years.

There are plenty of different proven systems out there. Just pick one that resonates with you and follow it. You'll be grateful you did.

36. Be Open To Receive

This is such a logical point, but one that's often overlooked or just not considered. The subconscious mind is a clever little trickster. However hard you work on releasing your negative programming, achieving your goals will be virtually impossible if you're not open to receive.

Much of what gets in the way of being open to receive is worthiness and a sense of "I'm not good enough" or "I don't deserve it." Stop it right now. You were born worthy of the most wonderful life you could possibly imagine and nothing's changed. You are good enough and you do deserve it. Do whatever you can to realise this truth at the deepest level. Open your mind, body and soul to receiving all the things you have called in through your thoughts, and be prepared for a spectacular journey of epic proportions.

37. Take Responsibility

The moment you blame someone or something else outside of you for your results or your situation is the moment you lose your power. Sure, life happens. You can't control everything outside of your physical being. In fact, control is an illusion, though most of us seem to like to hold onto the hope that it's real and try to control everything!

What's important is that you recognise and exercise your control over how you respond when crap happens in your life. Your response is the only thing you do have control over, and it has the power to alter the course of your ultimate result from any situation.

As soon as you take responsibility for the situation by acknowledging your thoughts and actions that put you in that position, you have the power to determine how the rest of the story unfolds.

When you blame and complain, you become a victim, and a victim is powerless to change anything. When you take complete responsibility for where you're at in all stages of your life, you immediately become an empowered individual who can achieve great things and you're not at the mercy of life.

38. Accept Where You're At Right Now

What is, is. The situation you're in right now is because of the thoughts you had and the actions you took yesterday, and the day before that, and the day before that, and the day before that. Getting angry or frustrated or disappointed that you're not there yet, just adds negative energy. Regardless of whether it looks like it or not, the situation you find yourself in is perfect for where you're at right now and who you are to become.

The results you have can't be changed in the past, they must be changed in the future. Wasting time lamenting what has already been is a pointless waste of your precious energy. Not accepting where you're at right now will only set you up for more resistance and stop your progress.

It's really important you get real about where you're at, what your skill level is and what you're capable of achieving right now. Ironically, people overestimate what they can achieve in the short term and underestimate what they are capable of achieving in the long term.

Okay, so maybe you're not as far down the road as you would have liked. Maybe you haven't hit those big goals and realised those outrageous visions you have yet, but it is what it is. Stop beating yourself up and pushing against it. Accept where you're at right now and acknowledge how far you've come because I can guarantee you've actually come quite a long way from where you were one, three or ten years ago. Make a plan to start achieving your goals from where you're at right now. When you do this, you'll move forward more quickly, and with confidence, and you will achieve a lot more in the long term.

18. Stack The Odds In Your Favour

39. Do The Work

So many people spend so much of their time and energy looking for the quick fix, the magic pill. It's a symptom of our ADD existence and our impatience. The reality is, the hard way to achieve your goals and dreams is continuing to look for the quick fix. The easy way is to do the internal work to overcome the negative conditioning and beliefs stopping you from being all you can be.

Almost everyone has been conditioned to repress their uncomfortable emotions, fears and doubts, instead of processing them. When you repress your emotions they don't go anywhere. Instead, they build on themselves as we continue to push them down and try to pretend they're not there. Learning to acknowledge, accept and release our emotions as they arise increases our emotional IQ.

When we repress our emotions, we keep tripping over them and they continue to cause us discomfort in different areas of our lives. Even though an event only happened once, we may carry the associated sadness, frustration, anger, resentment, fear, grief, disappointment, guilt or shame our entire lives.

Emotions that become trapped in our energy body, keep surfacing saying, "I'm still here", guiding us to process and release them. We keep encountering situations that trigger these emotions over and over again. They're a part of our vibration and, almost without fail, each time we experience a new event triggering that emotion, we just repress even more emotion on top of the last one. This happens over and over until we're so full up with a negative emotion that our judgement and ability to function effectively is grossly impaired.

We sink into despair, depression or rage at the slightest stimuli, or for seemingly no reason at all.

The self-help industry is an enormous multi-billion dollar industry with many of its participants hungrily devouring books, attending seminars and spiritual retreats, maybe even doing some meditation, but ultimately getting nowhere fast. The results just don't change. The reason is that it's highly unlikely any book, seminar, workshop or retreat will significantly change your life unless you're prepared to back it up with the internal exploration and release work that must be continued when you return to your own natural environment.

In reality, if you do the work to deal with the emotions, fears, self-esteem issues that you've been tripping over much of your life, your way to success will be far easier and more rewarding than if you don't. If you choose not to do the work, as most people do, I can almost guarantee, you will end up living a life of mediocrity, disappointment, confusion, frustration and regret.

The thought of dealing with some of those emotions and belief systems can be downright scary. There's a reason you chose not to deal with them in the first place – they bloody hurt and caused you pain. So get a professional to help you, coach you, guide you and support you through them.

You'll be surprised when you actually take the time to do the work that those emotions you were so afraid of, and have been avoiding for so long, aren't so bad when you face them head on and use effective techniques, like Emotional Freedom Technique, to take the charge out of them.

40. Own Your Greatness

I cannot say enough how amazing, brilliant, extraordinary and exceptional you are. Most of us spend our lives denying our greatness and working hard at being average. THIS IS NOT WHO YOU ARE!

We hide our bright shining light so we don't stand out and make those around us feel uncomfortable or unworthy in our presence. We want to fit in and be liked by our peers; it's part of our human psychology. This is self-defeating and it doesn't help you, or others. When you give yourself permission to own your brilliance and demonstrate your greatness, you give others permission to do the same. It's up to you to be a reflection for people of who they truly are so they can realise their greatness too.

Let go of the lie that you're anything less than magnificent and extraordinary. Own your greatness. When you do, your whole world will open up and you will see opportunities and paths appear that you didn't see before. This is the only way to live your life and achieve extraordinary things. YOU ARE GREAT! Do whatever you have to in order to own that fact and do whatever you need to, to achieve your vision for your future.

41. Long Term Vision

What causes a lot of frustration and lacklustre results in the modern world is our need for instant gratification. A lot of people who decide to shoot for their dreams are not prepared for the long-term journey and become defeatist in a short period of time. When it doesn't work out in one month or even six months, they say, "I tried and it didn't work", or "It's too hard" or "I couldn't do it."

Great things can only be achieved through long-term commitment to your vision. Persistence, perseverance and resilience will be your best friends. Expecting everything to fall in your lap just because you're thinking positive thoughts will bring you undone.

Life is a constant invitation to step up and be more than you were yesterday and the day before that and the day before that. You must earn the right to step into and own the bigger version of you.

The level to which you're able to persevere and see your vision through to the end, no matter how long it takes, will either make you or break you.

42. Chunk Your Goals Down

To achieve a long-term vision you must take baby steps, one at a time. The bigger your goal, the smaller the steps you need to take. When you do this consistently, you'll find the momentum snowballs.

Every great achiever knows they must be able to see the big picture and then chunk it down into bite-size chunks they can accomplish progressively. This forward motion builds relatively quickly and before you know it, you'll have progressed from a walk to a sprint. This is the process of becoming the person you need to be in order to achieve great things.

Just keep at it, and make sure you chunk your vision down to smaller, short-term goals. Anything is possible when you break your goal down into manageable pieces and take consistent daily action.

43. Get A Coach

A good coach or a mentor will help you create a fast track to where you want to go. You have everything you need already to be an extraordinary success, and a good mentor will be able to guide you to make the mindset shift you need. I like to work with coaches who have an understanding of Emotional Freedom Technique, or another transformational process so once the blocking belief or fear has been identified, it can be shifted quickly with a minimum of effort.

You can try to do this all on your own, but I don't recommend it. It's the slow road to where you want to go, and it will be a lot more difficult to achieve your goals.

We all have blind spots and gaps in our knowledge and skills, and ability to see outside our current paradigms. A good coach is invaluable in helping to reframe situations and events so you're able to see different perspectives and new possibilities.

A coach will also help you to find clarity on your big vision, keep you accountable, pick you up when you're down, guide you when necessary, help you build belief in yourself, kick your butt when you need it and make sure you stay on track.

Engaging a coach or mentor is invaluable in your quest for greatness. Make sure you work with one who resonates with you and has the necessary skills to get you to where you want to be.

44. Adopt Daily Success Practices

Your daily actions will be key to whether or not you're successful, and how successful you'll be. Highly successful people are where they are because of their daily practices, not because they had one lucky shot one day and that's it for the rest of their lives.

More than 80% of the people who win the lottery return to their original position, or are even worse off within an average of two years. This is because they have a certain wealth consciousness that got them into the position they're in originally. Sudden wealth doesn't cause them to change their consciousness or habits and consequently they end up right back where they started, which is pretty tragic.

In order to shift your success consciousness, you need to adopt habits that tell your subconscious you're successful.

Below are some easy practices and rituals you can do on a daily basis to program your subconscious mind to have a success and wealth blueprint that will make you unstoppable.

- Vision board – focus on this daily.
- Script out what your life looks like when you achieve your vision – writing this out by hand is more powerful than typing it. Read it every day and connect with the feeling of having achieved your vision.
- Review your vision and goals daily and practice focusing on what you DO want instead of what you don't want.
- Exercise – just 20 minutes a day of exercise that raises your metabolic rate will help clear your mind and put you in a positive state. It also has a positive impact on your fitness and energy levels.
- Listen to positive music that increases your sense of well-being.
- Eat less sugar and processed foods and more fresh produce.

18. Stack The Odds In Your Favour

- Do more of what you love and less of what you don't.
- Have a 'to achieve' list for the day that you prepare in the morning or the night before and tick things off the list as you get them done.
- Positive Affirmations – any positive statement that's in alignment with who you need to be in the world to achieve your dreams.
- Stop saying "I can't" and replace it with "How can I?"
- Stop whinging and start telling people how amazing your life is, ALL the time.
- Intend to uplift people wherever you go.
- When people ask you how you are, or how your day was, reply with enthusiasm, "Amazeballs" or something equally as positive, uplifting and surprise the heck out of the person who asked you.
- Look for the good in others and praise and compliment people – when you criticise others, you're promoting a lack and failure consciousness.
- Meditate – the practice of meditation will help you to reconnect more deeply with who you truly are, be present, relax and put you in a positive frame of mind.
- Be present – when you are in the now, you don't get overwhelmed by your fears and anxieties and living from your past. Being present helps you take your power back, be solution focused and live life by design instead of by default.
- Read books on success and listen to audio tapes by success coaches – the more you immerse your mind

in successful principals, the more you'll become the person you need to be to achieve your goals.

- Personal development — do something every day to develop yourself personally and expand your consciousness and your mindset.
- Hang out with cool people who have a positive, 'can do' attitude.
- Adopt a positive 'can do' attitude.
- Challenge yourself and get out of your comfort zone — do something that scares you a little every day.
- Smile — even when you don't feel like it, making the effort to smile releases endorphins into the body and lifts your spirit.
- Keep money in your wallet — Always having a certain amount of money in your wallet tells your brain that you always have money.
- Treat money with respect:
  - Keep it neat in your wallet
  - Don't put receipts and bills in your wallet
  - Pay attention to what money you've got coming in and what you have going out
  - Get organised and have a plan to pay off debts
  - Speak about money with kindness as if it were your best friend
  - Have a plan for how you're going to invest and spend the income you desire
  - If you see five cents on the street, pick it up and give thanks for the abundance flowing through your life.

18. Stack The Odds In Your Favour

- Be generous – giving generously sends a message to the Universe that you know there's plenty more where that came from and you're open to receiving.

- Practice gratitude several times every day.

- Label your filtered water with positive words – In 1994, Dr. Masaru Emoto conducted experiments where he labelled samples of water collected from the same source and put them into separate containers. The containers were each labelled with positive words like love, gratitude and kindness, or negative words like hate, revenge and kill and then snap frozen. The water crystals with the positive words produced beautiful looking crystalline structures with beautiful symmetry and geometry, while the ones with the negative words looked ugly with no definitive shape or symmetry. The water took on the properties of the nature of the words. Label your filtered water containers with words like abundance, success, joy, kindness, inspiration, achievement, love, freedom, wealth, connection, or other words that define what you want to achieve and how you want to feel. Drink this water knowing you're infusing your cells with the blueprint you desire.

These are just some of the positive practices you can start doing daily to shift your consciousness and blueprint to identify with success and wealth, and change your results forever.

You must take positive action every day to become the person you need to be to achieve the goals you desire and unleash your greatness. Choosing a couple of these easy to adopt daily habits, and doing them until they become second nature, will make your success so much easier in the long term. Once you've mastered those ones, choose a couple more.

Many years ago, when my husband was in the army, he was posted to Sydney. About three times a week, we'd go for runs together early in the morning down to Coogee Beach and back home. When Spring came around people would start emerging from their Winter hibernation, having added two or three (or more) kilos to the weight they were already carrying. Intent on losing weight and getting fit for Summer, they would start flat out. Many of them were trying to run and it looked like pure torture. They were gasping for breath and really struggling. They didn't have a trainer to regulate a fitness program, keep them accountable or congratulate them on their progress. It was easy to tell which ones you would see two or three times and never see again, at least until next year.

I actually believe reality programs like The Biggest Loser help to fuel people's unreasonable and unrealistic attempts to transform their bodies quickly. A sustainable approach would be to go for a brisk, thirty-minute walk to get the heart rate up a little, increase the breathing rate, and enjoy the experience. The next step is to build on that gradually to a little interval training, and slowly lead into a run. This gradual approach creates long-term healthy habits. The individual is much more likely to continue to come day after day and eventually reach their health and fitness goals.

Instead of starting where they're at, people go all Rambo style straight out of the gate and this is a recipe for self-sabotage. The same goes for anything you're trying to achieve if you're just starting out on something new.

18. Stack The Odds In Your Favour

Just like weight training in a gym, toning and strengthening your physical muscles, your mind requires a gradual training program too. So start with a couple of activities at first, so you don't overload yourself or your system, and it doesn't feel like it's all too hard. Gradually build on that until you've changed your daily habits, and grown into the bigger person over time, and you will guarantee your long-term success.

If you improve your results by just one percent every day for 365 days, by the end of the year you will have improved your results by 365%! Actually, they will have increased more than that due to the compounding effect. The point is, you don't have to get everything done now. Trying to will likely cause you to crash and burn. By focusing on doing a little better every single day, great things can be accomplished in a relatively short period of time.

There's no time like the present. You can make your success difficult and drawn out, or you can choose a route that's simple, fast and gets you to where you want to be in the shortest possible time. I'm giving you the way to choose the second option.

It's not difficult to do, but you must do something if you want to change your life. This book can be just another one you pick up, spend some time reading and never actually makes a difference in your life. Or, you can choose right now to start to take small actions to achieving your big goals. This one thing will determine if you're the kind of person who will succeed, or not. It's your choice.

~ *Key Reflections* ~

You can unleash your greatness and achieve success, wealth and freedom the easy way or the hard way; it's your choice. There are many proven actions and strategies you can take to make this as easy as possible. I suggest you choose to stack the odds in your favour and gradually adopt the beliefs, thoughts, knowledge and skill wealthy and successful people have. This chapter contains a list of things you can start to take action on right now to start to turn your results right now. Write them out and make it your mission to live your life by them and you will grow to be ALL you can be, and achieve more than you ever imagined possible.

The Final Word

We've covered many strategies, techniques, practices and attitudes to help you to be successful, unleash your greatness and achieve more than you ever dreamed possible. I hope you've played along and participated in the exercises so you can adopt an easier path to realising your dreams. The only person who can determine your future is you.

Ultimately, however, achievement of material wealth and impossible goals will not provide lasting happiness.

Drop the illusion that you have to achieve anything to prove your worth and justify your existence on planet earth.

What matters most in life is that you're happy, content and in love with yourself and the many and varied experiences that make this existence rich, fun and satisfying, regardless of their nature.

Be true to yourself, do what brings you joy and bring joy to everything you do. You were born a divine, abundant, magical, powerful being. In the words of Abraham Hicks, "Your purpose is joy." Seek joy, be joy and your ultimate purpose will find you.

Everything in this book is valid for achieving better results in every part of your life. Unleashing your greatness and achieving your goals and dreams is an extremely rewarding and satisfying way to live life. We are creative beings on the leading edge of creation yearning to expand and experience new and wonderful things, discover what we're truly capable of and explore the richness and wonder this world has to offer.

But none of it is worth anything if it comes at the expense of your joy, peace and happiness.

Life can be hard if you choose to believe it is and judge the events that come your way as difficult and challenging. Or, life can be luscious, delicious, surprising and expansive. After all, you get what you focus on.

Whatever you do, make joy your focus and come from a place of love. This, above all else, will make your life the most wonderful experience.

Approaching all of life in this way will bring you back to you. It will help you to realise your ultimate truth and reconnect with the deepest understanding of who you truly are. When you reach this place, everything that has ever caused you grief, pain, anxiety and stress will pale into insignificance in the presence and awareness of the whole, limitless, exceptional, beautiful, powerful being that is You.

Together, we can change the world. And what the world desperately needs is more joy! Collectively, by deciding to be happy and joyful, we can transform the hearts and minds of those who don't know what we know or see what we see, and create heaven on earth.

Now there's a goal that's worthy of all of us.

To your greatness,

Marguerita Vorobioff

About The Author

Marguerita Vorobioff is an author, international speaker, mindset mentor, healer and light worker who is on a mission to raise conscious awareness in Divine Human Beings. Her goal is to inspire a movement to liberate humanity from self-imposed suffering and help create heaven on earth for all sovereign beings that occupy this wonderful planet.

She lives and plays on Tamborine Mountain in the picturesque Gold Coast Hinterland with her husband of 20 years, her three dogs and two horses.

Whilst working in Corporate Australia, Marguerita trained for 15 years to become an opera singer. Sustaining herself financially through mind numbing, unfulfilling employment whilst pursuing her love of singing, she finally came to the conclusion there had to be more to life.

Becoming a personal trainer was fulfilling, but only the beginning of a journey that caused her to explore the extraordinary power of the mind, as well as her reason for being.

Marguerita's study expanded to the body, mind, spirit connection and its effect on the human condition. Learning

Emotional Freedom Technique was a revelation, which was quickly followed by the surprising discovery she was born a Master Sound Healer.

Marguerita has explored the human mind, potential and spirituality for 15 years, and has come to a place of deep personal peace and contentment, living her dream life, while helping thousands of others around the world to improve the quality of their lives and realise their potential through her work.

Her website, www.PitBullMindset.com, focuses on helping people like you unleash your greatness, reconnect with your truth, and experience your infinite power and potential, so you can live life on your terms and create your own version of heaven on earth.

Resources

Marguerita has many resources and free and paid programs available to assist you to elevate your consciousness, adopt a strong success mindset and unleash your greatness so you can be ALL you can be, and achieve the success and wealth you desire and deserve.

<u>You can access these resources at the links below:</u>

Free Sound Healing To Unleash Your Greatness MP3
www.PitBullMindset.com/Sound-Healing-Greatness/

Free Money Story Mind Map
www.PitBullMindset.com/Money-Mind-Map/

Free 21 Days of Tapping Into Abundance Masterclass
www.PitBullMindset.com/Abundance-Tapping/

There are many other resources, tools and information available, at the PitBull website. To explore what else is available visit: www.PitBullMindset.com and take a look around.

Marguerita has an online TV show titled Liberate Humanity TV. To see episodes and join the movement, visit: www.Facebook.com/LiberateHumanityTV/

www.ingramcontent.com/pod-product-compliance
Lightning Source LLC
Chambersburg PA
CBHW050613300426
44112CB00012B/1481